Means
Spanish/
English
Construction
Dictionary

RSMeans
CMDGROUP

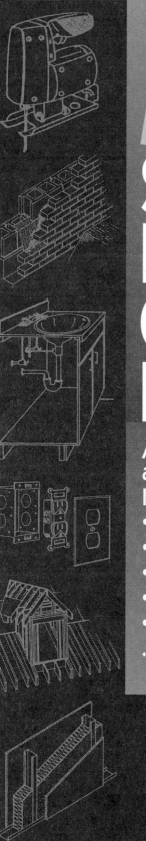

Means
Spanish/ English Construction Dictionary

An Essential Tool on the Job Site
and in the Office
Includes:
- The Most Common Construction Terms
- Useful On-the-Job Phrases
- Illustrated Building Systems
- Easy-to-Use Tools Section
- Practical Tables
... with Phonetic Pronunciation

Copyright 2000

R.S. Means Company, Inc.
Construction Publishers & Consultants
Construction Plaza
63 Smiths Lane
Kingston, MA 02364-0800
(781) 585-7880

The editor for this book was Danielle Georges. The managing editor was Mary Greene. The production manager was Michael Kokernak. The production coordinator was Marion Schofield. Composition was supervised by Paula Reale-Camelio. Robin Richardson assisted with proofreading and translation. The book and cover were designed by Norman R. Forgit.

Printed in the United States of America

10 9 8 7 6 5 4 3 2 1

Library of Congress Cataloging in Publication Data

ISBN 0-87629-578-2

Table of Contents

Preface

Today, Spanish is the primary language of more than 17 million people in the United States. According to the U.S. Census Bureau, within the next five years the Latino/Hispanic population will be the largest ethnic group in the United States. As more and more people in the work force speak Spanish, the need is growing for tools that facilitate communication between Spanish and English speakers.

Means customers have let us know in interactions by telephone, in seminars, and in consulting projects around the country, that there is a tremendous need for an easy-to-use dictionary with illustrations arranged in a way that is meaningful to the building construction industry.

Means' Spanish/English Construction Dictionary is a collaboration of R.S. Means Co., Inc., the International Conference of Building Officials (ICBO), and noted building code consultants, Rolf Jensen & Associates (RJA).

Featuring the most commonly used construction terms and phrases, along with phonetic pronunciations developed by ICBO, the dictionary includes more than 300 key terms related to building codes and fire protection. Unique to this dictionary is the series of systems illustrations that show not only the names, but the relationships of components in the most common building systems for all major trades. Additional drawings of tools and equipment are organized by construction specialty: carpentry, concrete, electrical, masonry, roofing, site work, and others.

The dictionary is based on extensive research performed in different areas of the construction industry. It will be useful to Spanish speakers learning English, and English speakers learning Spanish, helping to break down barriers that jeopardize safety, productivity, quality, and good working relationships. It is an essential tool for contractors, construction workers, architects, building officials, and inspectors for use in their everyday tasks—whether at the job site, in the office, or in training and apprenticeship programs. It also works toward unifying construction terminology in Latin America and the Latino/Hispanic sector of the United States.

We recognize that languages change and grow, and that dictionaries—which reflect languages—do the same. We therefore encourage your feedback. Please send your comments, along with any terms you would like to see included in future editions of the *Means Spanish/English Construction Dictionary* to us at: Reference Department, R.S. Means Company, Inc., 63 Smiths Lane, Kingston, MA 02364-0800.

Acknowledgments

Primary recognition must be given to the staff at ICBO, whose *Constructionary* is the basis of the *Means Spanish/English Construction Dictionary*. Terry Eddy, ICBO Human Resources Manager conceived of the idea for the *Constructionary*. Sergio Barrueto, Director of International Programs and Services; David Jamieson, Editor; Maria Aragon, Marketing Specialist; Suzane Nunes, Product Development Coordinator; and Alberto Herrera, Editor, are among those who developed the ICBO *Constructionary*. Contributors include Philip Ramos, Building Official from the City of Stanton, California; Mark Stevens, independent building contractor; Benjamin Rodriguez, Carpenters Union Representative; David Bautista, building products sales representative; and Miguel Lamas, building inspector from the City of Pomona, California.

The staff of Rolf Jensen & Associates contributed more than 300 terms pertinent to building codes and fire protection. Thanks are due to George Toth, Vice President of Marketing; Jaime Moncado, PE; and Berta Sabogal, a technical translator in Bogota, Columbia.

Special thanks are due to Francisco Polanco, President of R.M. Technologies, in Lawrence, Massachusetts, who provided valuable assistance with the illustration translations. (Some illustrations originally appeared in *Framing and Rough Carpentry* by Scot Simpson.)

The dictionary was reviewed in its entirety by Professor Raymond Issa and his team of graduate students—Zorina Montiel, Rodrigo Castro-Raventos, and Hector Valdez—at the University of Florida's M.E. Rinker, Sr. School of Building Construction.

Note: The pronunciation guides in both English and Spanish were developed based on simple communication principles rather than the international phonetic system used in many language dictionaries.

Pronunciation Guide

Accents (or stress) are indicated by uppercase letters. The stress on the Spanish word *remover* (to abate) is on the last syllable. The word therefore appears in the following way: *reh-moh-VEHR*.

Vowels

A-   -*AH* as in *father*
E-   -*EH* as in *mess*
I-   -*EE* as in *see*
O-   -*OH* as the first sound in *owe*
U-   -*OO* as in *boot*

Dipthongs

The most common dipthongs used here are:

io-   -*EEOH*
ie-   -*YEH* (the y sounds like *ee*)
ui-   -*WEE*
ua-   -*WAH*
ue-   -*WEH*

Consonants

Same as in English except:

D is voiced
T and *P* are soft
ny as in o*ni*on
R soft, *RR* rolled
CH always as in *ch*urch

A

Abate
Remover
(*reh-moh-VEHR*)
Anular
(*ah-noo-LAHR*)

Abatement
Remoción
(*reh-moh-SYON*)
Anulación
(*ah-noo-lah-SYON*)

Acceptance test
Prueba de aceptación
(*proo-EH-ba deh
ahk-sep-tah-SYON*)

Access
Acceso
(*ahk-SEH-soh*)

Access cover
Tapa de acceso
(*TAH-pa deh ahk-SEH-soh*)
Cubierta de acceso
(*koo-BYEHR-tah deh
ahk-SEH-soh*)

Acoustical tile
Panel acústico
(*pah-NEL ah-KOOS-tee-koh*)

Adapter fitting
Dispositivo adaptador
(*dees-poh-see-TEE-voh
ah-dahp-tah-DOHR*)

Addition
Ampliación
(*ahm-plee-ah-SYON*)
Expansión
(*ehk-spahn-SYON*)

Additives and Admixtures
Aditivos y mezclas
(*ah-dee-TEE-vos ee
mehs-klahs*)

Air compressor
Compresor de aire
(*kohm-preh-SOHR deh
AH-ee-reh*)

Aisle
Pasillo
(*pah-SEE-joh*)
Hilera
(*ee-LEH-rah*)

Air pump
Compresor de aire
(*kohm-preh-SOHR
deh ah-EE-reh*)

Alarm box
Pulsador de alarma
(*pool-sa-DOHR deh
a-LAHR-mah*)

Alley
Callejón
(*kah-jeh-HOHN*)

Alter
Modificar
(*moh-dee-fee-KAHR*)

Alteration
  Modificación
  (*moh-dee-fee-kah-SYON*)

Anchor
  Anclaje
  (*ahn-KLAH-heh*)

Anchor bolts
  Pernos de anclaje
  (*PEHR-nohs deh
  ahn-KLAH-heh*)
  Tornillos de anclaje
  (*tohr-NEE-johs deh
  ahn-KLAH-heh*)

Anchor rod
  Varilla de anclaje
  (*vah-REE-jah deh
  ahn-KLAH-heh*)

Annular grooved nail
  Clavo anular
  (*KLAH-voh ah-noo-LAR*)

Antisiphon
  Antisifonaje
  (*ahn-tee-see-foh-NAH-heh*)

Apartment house
  Edificio de departamentos
  (*eh-dee-FEE-syoh deh
  deh-par-tah-MEHN-tohs*)
  Apartamento residencial
  (*ah-par-tah-MEHN-toh
  reh-see-dehn-SYAL*)

Approved
  Aprobado
  (*ah-proh-BAH-doh*)

Apron
  Repisa
  (*reh-PEE-sah*)
  Delantal
  (*deh-lahn-TAHL*)
  Mandil
  (*mahn-DEEL*)

Architect
  Arquitecto
  (*ahr-kee-TEHK-toh*)

Area drain
  Desagüe de área
  (*deh-SAH-gweh deh
  AH-reh-ah*)
  Desagüe de patio
  (*deh-SAH-gweh deh
  PAH-tee-oh*)
  Resumidero
  (*reh-soo-mee-DEH-roh*)

Armover
  Brazo horizontal
  (*BRAH-so oh-ree-sohn-TAHL*)

Arson
  Incendio premeditado
  (*een-SEHN-dee-oh
  preh-meh-dee-TAH-doh*)

Asbestos cement shingle
Teja de cemento de asbestos
(*TEH-ha deh seh-MEHN-toh
deh ahs-BES-tohs*)
Tablilla de fibrocemento
(*tah-BLEE-jah deh
fee-broh-seh-MEHN-toh*)

Asphalt
Asfalto
(*ahs-FAHL-toh*)

Assembly
Conjunto
(*kohn-HOON-toh*)

Atrium
Atrio
(*AH-tree-oh*)

Attic
Tapanco
(*tah-PAHN-koh*)
Entrepiso
(*ehn-treh-PEE-soh*)

Audible signal
Señal acústica
(*seh-NYAL ah-KOOS-tee-kah*)

Authority having jurisdiction
Autoridad competente
(*oh-toh-ree-DAHD
kohm-peh-TEN-teh*)

Automatic
Automático
(*ah-oo-toh-MAH-tee-koh*)

Automatic closing device
Dispositivo de cierre
automático
(*dees-poh-see-TEE-voh
deh SYEH-rreh
ah-oo-toh-MAH-tee-koh*)

Automatic fire-extinguishing system
Sistema automático de
extinción de incendios
(*sees-TEH-mah
ah-oo-toh-MAH-tee-koh deh
ehk-steen-SYON deh
een-SEHN-dee-ohs*)

Automatic fire sprinkler system
Sistema de rociadores
automáticos
(*sees-TEH-mah deh
roh-see-ah-DOH-rehs
ah-oo-toh-MAH-tee-kohs*)

Awnings
Toldos
(*TOHL-dohs*)

B

Back hoe
Retroexcavadora
(*reh-troh-ex-kah-vah-DOH-rah*)
Excavadora
(*ex-kah-vah-DOH-rah*)

Back pressure
Presión de retorno
(*preh-SYON deh reh-TOHR-noh*)

Backfill
Relleno
(*reh-JEH-noh*)

Backflow
Contraflujo
(*kohn-trah-FLOO-hoh*)

Backflow preventer
Válvula de contraflujo
(*VAHL-voo-lah deh kohn-trah-FLOO-hoh*)

Backing
Soporte
(*soh-POHR-teh*)
Respaldo
(*rehs-PAHL-doh*)

Balcony
Balcón
(*bahl-KOHN*)

Ball cock
Válvula de flotador
(*VAHL-voo-lah deh floh-tah-DOHR*)
Flotador
(*floh-tah-DOHR*)
Llave de flotador
(*JAH-veh deh floh-tah-DOHR*)

Ball drip
Drenaje de bola
(*dreh-NAH-heh deh BOH-lah*)

Ball valve
Llave de flujo
(*JAH-veh deh FLOO-hoh*)

Ball weight
Contrapeso esférico
(*kohn-trah-PEH-soh es-FEH-ree-koh*)

Bar
Barra
(*BAH-rrah*)
Barretta
(*bah-RREH-tah*)

Bar joist
Viga de celosía
(*VEE-gah deh seh-LOH-syah*)

Barbed nail
Clavo afilado
(*KLAH-voh ah-fee-LAH-doh*)

B

Baseboard
Zócalo
(*SOH-kah-loh*)

Basement
Sótano
(*SOH-tah-noh*)

Bathroom
Cuarto de baño
(*KWAR-to deh BAH-nyoh*)
Sanitario
(*sah-nee-TAH-ryoh*)

Bathroom sink
Lavabo
(*lah-VAH-boh*)

Bathtub
Bañera
(*bah-NYEH-rah*)
Tina de baño
(*TEE-nah deh BAH-nyoh*)
Bañadera
(*bah-NYAH-deh-rah*)

Batten
Rastrillo
(*rahs-TREE-joh*)
Cubrejuntas
(*koo-breh-HOON-tahs*)
Listón travesaño
(*lees-TON
trah-veh-SAH-nyoh*)

Battery
Batería
(*bah-teh-REE-ah*)
Pila
(*PEE-lah*)

Beam
Viga
(*VEE-gah*)

Bedroom
Habitación
(*ah-bee-tah-SYON*)
Recámara
(*re-KAH-mah-rah*)
Dormitorio
(*dor-mee-TOH-ree-oh*)

Beech
Haya
(*AH-jah*)

Below-grade walls
Muros por debajo del nivel
de terreno
(*MOO-rohs pohr deh-BAH-ho
dehl nee-VEHL dehl
teh-RREH-noh*)

Bimetallic disc
Disco bimetálico
(*DEES-koh
bee-meh-TAL-ee-koh*)

Bleachers
Tribunas
(*tree-BOON-ahs*)
Gradas
(*GRAH-dahs*)

Blind nailed
Con clavos ocultos
(*kohn KLAH-vohs
oh-KOOL-tohs*)

Block, Blocking
Trabas
(*TRAH-bahs*)
Trabar
(*trah-BAHR*)
Bloque
(*BLOH-keh*)
Bloquear
(*bloh-KEAHR*)

Blow-off cap
Tapón que saltan con facilidad
(*tah-POHN keh sahl-TAHN
kohn fah-see-lee-DAHD*)

Board
Panel
(*PAH-nehl or pah-NEHL*)
Tabla
(*TAH-blah*)

Body drain plug
Tapón de drenaje del cuerpo
(*Tah-POHN deh
dreh-NAH-heh dehl
KWER-poh*)

Boiler
Caldera
(*kahl-DEH-rah*)
Boiler
(*boi-lehr*)

Boiler room
Cuarto de calderas
(*KWAR-toh deh
kahl-DEH-rahs*)

Bolt
Perno
(*PEHR-noh*)
Tornillo
(*tohr-NEE-joh*)

Bonding jumper
Borne de enlace
(*BOHR-neh deh ehn-LAH-seh*)
Terminal de enlace
(*tehr-mee-NAHL deh
ehn-LAH-seh*)

Box nail
Clavo para madera
(*KLAH-voh PAH-rah
mah-DEH-rah*)
Clavo de cabeza grande plana
(*KLAH-voh deh kah-BEH-sah
GRAHN-deh PLAH-nah*)

Brace
Tirante
(*tee-RAN-teh*)

Bracing
Arriostramiento
(*ah-rryohs-trah-MYEN-toh*)

Braced frame
Estructura arriostrada
(*ehs-trook-TOO-rah
ah-rryohs-TRAH-dah*)
Pórtico arriostrado
(*POHR-tee-koh
ah-rryohs-TRAH-doh*)

Bracket
Brazo
(*BRAH-soh*)

B

Branch
Ramal
(*rah-MAHL*)

Branch line
Ramal
(*rah-MAHL*)

Brass
Bronce
(*BROHN-seh*)
Latón
(*lah-TOHN*)

Braze
Soldar en fuerte
(*sohl-DAR ehn FWER-teh*)

Brazing alloy
Aleación para soldar
(*ah-leh-ah-SYON PAH-rah
sol-DAR*)

Brazing flux
Fundente para soldar
(*foon-DEHN-teh PAH-rah
sol-DAR*)

Brick
Ladrillo
(*lah-DREE-joh*)

Bridging
Puntales de refuerzo
(*poon-TAH-les deh
reh-FWEHR-soh*)

Brown coat
Revoque
(*reh-VOH-keh*)

Building
Edificación
(*eh-dee-fee-kah-SYON*)
Edificio
(*eh-dee-FEE-syoh*)

Building, high-rise
Rascacielos
(*rah-ska-SYEH-lohs*)

Building, multistory
Edificio de varias plantas
(*eh-dee-FEE-syoh deh
VAH-ryas PLAHN-tahs*)

Building, single story
Edificio de un piso
(*eh-dee-FEE-syoh deh
oon PEE-soh*)

Building department
Departamento de
construcción/edificación
(*deh-par-tah-MEN-toh
deh kohn-strook-SYON/
eh-dee-fee-kah-SYON*)
Departamento de obras de
edificación
(*deh-par-tah-MEN-toh
deh OH-brahs
deeh-dee-fee-kah-SYON*)
Departamento de obras
públicas/privadas
(*deh-par-tah-MEN-toh deh
OH-brahs POO-blee-kahs/
pree-VAH-dahs*)

Building drain
Desagüe de la edificación/del
edificio
(*deh-SAH-gweh deh lah
eh-dee-fee-kah-SYON/dehl
eh-dee-FEE-see-oh*)
Resumidero
(*reh-soo-me-DEH-roh*)

Building documentation
Documentación de
obra/ingeniería
(*doh-koo-mehn-tah-SYON deh
OH-brah/een-he-nyeh-
REE-ah*)

Building inspector
Inspector de obras
(*eens-pek-TOHR
deh OH-brahs*)
Inspector de construcción
(*eens-pek-TOHR
deh OH-brahs*)

Building official
Director de obras
(*dee-rek-TOHR
deh OH-brahs*)
Jefe de obras
(*HEH-feh deh OH-brahs*)
Autoridad competente
(*ah-oo-toh-ree-DAHD
kohm-peh-TEHN-teh*)

Building site
Terreno de obra
(*teh-RREH-noh deh OH-brah*)
Sitio de construcción
(*SEE-tee-oh deh
kohn-strook-SYON*)
Obra de construcción
(*OH-brah deh
kohn-strook-SYON*)

Built-up roofing
Cubierta de techo compuesta
(*koo-BYEHR-tah deh
TEH-choh kohm-PWEHS-tah*)

Bulk head
Mampara, barrera, muro de
contención
(*mahm-PAH-rah
ba-RREH-rah, MOO-roh
deh kohn-tehn-SYON*)

Bundle
Atado
(*ah-TAH-doh*)
Bulto
(*BOOL-toh*)

Bypass
Derivación
(*deh-ree-vah-SYON*)

C

Cabinet
Gabinete
(gah-bee-NEH-teh)

Cabinetmaker
Ebanista
(eh-bah-NEES-tah)

Cable tray
Bandeja portacables
*(bahn-DEH-hah
pohr-tah-KAH-blehs)*

Caissons
Cajones de aire comprimido
*(kah-HOH-nehs deh ah-ee-reh
kohm-pree-MEE-doh)*

Canopy
Toldo
(TOHL-doh)
Cubierta
(koo-BYER-tah)

Cantilever
Voladizo
(volah-DEE-soh)

Cap
Caperuza
(kah-peh-ROO-sah)

Carbon dioxide
Dioxido de carbono
*(dee-OHK-see deh
car-BOH-noh)*

Carpenter
Carpintero
(kahr-peen-TEH-roh)

Cartridge fuse
Fusible de cartucho
*(foo-SEE-bleh deh
kahr-TOO-choh)*

Casing nail
Clavo de cabeza perdida
*(KLAH-voh deh kah-BEH-sah
pehr-DEE-dah)*

Cast stone
Piedra moldeada
*(PYEH-drah
mohl-deh-AH-dah)*
Piedra de sillar
(PYEH-drah deh see-JAHR)

Caulking
Masillado
(mah-see-JAH-doh)
Masillar
(mah-see-JAHR)

Cavity wall
Muro hueco
(moo-roh WEH-koh)

C-Clamp
abrazadera en C
*(ah-brah-sah-DEH-rah ehn
SEH)*

Ceiling
Cielorraso
(SYEH-loh-RRAH-soh)

Ceramic floor
Piso cerámico
(PEE-soh seh-RAH-mee-koh)

C

Ceramic tile
Baldosas cerámicas
*(bahl-DOH-sahs
seh-RAH-mee-kahs)*

Certificate of occupancy
Certificado de uso
*(sehr-tee-fee-KAH-doh deh
OO-soh)*

Chain
Cadena
(kah-deh-nah)

Chalk line
Linea de marcar
*(LEE-neh-ah deh
mahr-KAHR)*
Tendel
(tehn-DEHL)
Linea de gis
(LEE-neh-ah de HEES)

Chase
Canaletas
(kah-nah-LEH-tahs)
Muesca
(moo-EHS-kah)

Check valve
Válvula de contraflujo
*(VAHL-voo-lah deh
kohn-trah-FLOO-hoh)*

Chimney
Chimenea
(chee-meh-NEH-ah)

Chimney chase
Acanaladura de chimenea
*(ah-kah-nah-lah-DOO-rah
deh chee-meh-NEH-ah)*

Chimney, factory-built
Chimenea prefabricada
*(chee-meh-NEH-ah
preh-fah-bree-KAH-dah)*

Chimney liner
Revestimiento de chimenea
*(reh-vehs-tee-MYEHN-toh deh
chee-meh-NEH-ah)*

Chute
Ducto
(DOOK-toh)

Chute, linen
Ducto de lencería
*(DOOK-toh deh
lehn-seh-REE-ah)*

Chute, rubbish
Ducto de basura
(DOOK-toh deh bah-soo-rah)

Circuit
Circuito
(seer-KWEE-toh)

Circuit breaker
Apagador
(ah-pah-gah-DOR)
Interruptor automático
*(een-teh-rroop-TOHR
ah-oo-toh-MAH-tee-koh)*
Interruptor de circuito
*(een-teh-rroop-TOHR
de seer-KWEE-toh)*

Circuit breaker panel
Cuadro de cortacircuito
*(KWAH-droh dehl
kor-tah-seer-KWEE-toh)*
Tablero de cortacircuito
*(tah-BLEH-roh deh
kor-tah-seer-KWEE-toh)*

Cistern
Aljibe
(*ahl-HE-beh*)
Cisterna
(*sees-TEHR-nah*)

Clamp
Soporte
(*soh-POHR-teh*)

Clamp, center load
Abrazadera de carga central
(*ah-brah-sah-DEH-rah deh
KAHR-gah sehn-TRAHL*)

Clamp, large flange
Abrazadera grande con brida
(*ah-brah-sah-DEH-rah
GRAHN-deh kohn BREE-dah*)

Clamp, T beam
Abrazadera para viga doble T
(*ah-brah-sah-DEH-rah
pah-rah VEE-gah DOH-bleh
TEH*)

**Clamp, universal top and bottom
beam**
Abrazadera universal de viga
superior e inferior
(*ah-brah-sah-DEH-rah
oo-nee-vehr-SAHL
deh VEE-gah
soo-peh-RYOR ee een
feh-RYOR*)

Clapper
Clapeta
(*klah-PEH-tah*)

Clapper-type drip
Purga tipo clapeta
(*POOHR-gah TEE-poh
klah-PEH-tah*)

Clay
Arcilla
(*ar-SEE-jah*)
Barro
(*BAH-rroh*)

Clean agent
Agente limpio
(*ah-HEN-teh LEEM-pyoh*)

Cleanout
Registro
(*reh-HEES-troh*)

Cleanout (chimney)
Abertura de limpieza
(*ah-behr-TOO-rah deh
leem-PYEH-zah*)

Closed loop pipe
Tubería en bucle cerrado
(*too-beh-REE-ah ehn
BOO-kleh seh-RAH-doh*)

Coal
Hulla
(*OO-jah*)
Carbón
(*kahr-BOHN*)

Coarse
Grueso
(*GRWEH-soh*)
Áspero
(*AHS-peh-roh*)

C

Code
Código
(KOH-dee-goh)

Code official
Autoridad competente
*(ah-oo-toh-ree-DAHD
kohm-peh-TEHN-teh)*
Director/Jefe de obras
*(dee-rek-TOHR/HEH-feh
deh OH-brahs)*
Oficial de códigos
*(oh-fee-SYAHL deh
KOH-dee-gohs)*

Collar joint
Junta de collar
(HOON-tah deh koh-JAHR)

Column
Columna
(koh-LOOM-nah)

Combination fixture
Artefacto de combinación
*(ar-teh-FAK-toh deh
kohm-been-ah-SYON)*
Mueble de combinación
*(MWEH-bleh deh
kohm-bee-nah-SYON)*

Combustible liquid
Líquido combustible
*(LEE-kee-doh
kohm-boos-TEE-bleh)*

Compensating vents
Respiradero de compensación
*(rreh-spee-rah-DEH-roh deh
kohm-pehn-sah-SYON)*

Compression coupling
Acoplamiento de compresión
*(ah-koh-plah-MYEHN-toh
deh kohm-preh-SYON)*
Empalme de compresión
*(ehm-PAHL-meh deh
kohm-preh-SYON)*
Manguito
(mahn-GY-toh)
Manchón de manguito
*(mahn-CHON deh
mahn-GY-toh)*

Concealed spaces
Espacios ocultos
*(ehs-PAH-syohs
oh-KOOL-tohs)*
Cavidades ocultas
*(kah-vee-DAH-dehs
oh-KOOL-tahs)*

Concrete
Hormigón
(ohr-mee-GOHN)
Concreto
(kohn-KREH-toh)

Concrete cover
Cubierta de hormigón/
concreto
*(koo-BYEHR-tah
deh ohr-mee-GOHN/
kohn-KREH-toh)*

Condominium
Condominio residencial
*(kohn-doh-MEE-nee-oh
reh-see-dehn-SYAL)*

Conductor
Conductor
(kohn-dook-TOHR)

Conductor wire
Alambre conductor
(ah-LAHM-breh
kohn-dook-TOHR)

Conduit
Conducto
(kohn-DOOK-toh)
Tubería
(too-beh-REE-ah)

Congregate residence
Residencia comunitaria
(reh-see-DEHN-see-ah
koh-moo-nee-TAH-ree-ah)

Connection
Conexión
(koh-nek-SYON)
Unión
(oon-YOHN)

Connector
Conector
(koh-nek-TOHR)

Construction Health and Safety
Higiene y seguridad en la
construcción
(ee-hee-EH-neh ee seh
goo-ree-DAHD ehn lah
kohn-strook-SYON)

Construction joint
Junta de construcción
(HOON-tah deh
kohn-strook-SYON)

Construction schedule (CPM)
Cronograma de construcción
(kroh-noh-GRAH-mah
deh kohn-strook-SYON)
Plan de avance de obra
(PLAHN deh ah-VAHN-seh
deh OH-brah)

Contamination
Contaminación
(kohn-tah-mee-nah-SYON)

Contraction joint
Junta de contracción
(HOON-tah deh
kohn-trak-SYON)

Contractor
Constructor
(kohn-strook-TOHR)
Contratista
(kohn-trah-TEE-stah)

Coping
Albardilla
(ahl-bar-DEE-jah)
Mojinete
(mo-hee-NEH-teh)
Cumbrera
(koom-BREH-rah)
Caballete
(kah-bah-JEH-teh)

Copper, hard drawn
Cobre estirado en frío
(KOH-breh
ehs-tee-RAH-doh ehn
FREE-oh)

C

Copper, sheet
Lámina de cobre
(LAH-mee-nah deh
KOH-breh)

Copper, wrought
Cobre forjado
(KOH-breh fohr-HAH-doh)

Cornerite
Guardaesquinas
(gwar-dah-ehs-KEE-nahs)

Cornices
Cornisas
(kor-NEE-sahs)

Corrosion-resistant
Anticorrosivo
(ahn-tee-koh-rroh-SEE-voh)
Resistente a la corrosión
(reh-sees-TEHN-teh ah lah
koh-rroh-SYON)

Corrosive
Corrosivo
(koh-rroh-SEE-voh)

Coupling
Acoplamiento
(ah-koh-plah-MYEHN-toh)
Copla
(KOH-plah)
Manguito
(man-GY-toh)

Coupling beams
Vigas de acoplamiento
(VEE-gahs deh
ah-koh-plah-MYEHN-toh)

Court
Patio interno
(PAH-tee-oh een-TEHR-noh)

Cover, Covering
Recubrimiento
(reh-koo-bree-MYEHN-toh)
Tapadera
(tah-pah-DEH-rah)
Revestimiento
(reh-veh-stee-MYEHN-toh)
Cubierta
(koo-BYEHR-tah)

Cracked walls
Muros rajados
(moo-rohs rah-HA-dohs)
Paredes rajadas
(pah-REH-dehs rah-HA-dahs)

Cracks
Rajadas
(rah-HA-dahs)
Grietas
(GRYEH-tahs)
Partidas
(pahr-TEE-dahs)

Crawl space
Espacio angosto
(ehs-PAH-syoh
ahn-GOHS-toh)
Sótano de poca altura
(SOH-tah-noh deh POH-kah
ahl-TOO-rah)

Cross connection
Conexión cruzada
(koh-nek-SYON
kroo-SAH-dah)

Cross connection
Interconexión
(*een-tehr-koh-nek-SYON*)

Cross main
Tubería principal transversal
(*too-beh-REE-ah
preen-see-PAL
trahns-vehr-SAHL*)

Cross-grain
Fibra transversal
(*FEE-brah trans-vehr-SAL*)
Contragrano
(*kohn-trah-GRAH-noh*)

Crown
Corona (grapas)
(*koh-ROH-nah (GRAH-pahs)*)

Culvert
Alcantarilla
(*al-kan-tah-REE-jah*)
Desagüe
(*deh-SAH-gweh*)

Curb
Guarnición
(*gwahr-nee-SYON*)
Cordón
(*kohr-DON*)
Flanco
(*FLAHN-koh*)
Bordillo
(*bohr-DEE-joh*)

Curtain wall
Pared tipo cortina
(*pah-RHED TEE-poh
kohr-TEE-nah*)

Cut-off valve
Válvula de cierre
(*VAHL-voo-lah
deh SYEH-rreh*)

D

Damper
Regulador
(reh-goo-lah-DOHR)

Damper, fire
Regulador cortafuego
*(reh-goo-lah-DOHR
kohr-ta-FWEH-goh)*

Damper, smoke
Regulador estanco al humo
*(reh-goo-lah-DOHR
eh-STAHN-koh ahl OO-moh)*

Dead end
Terminal
(tehr-mee-NAHL)
Extremos cerrados
*(ehk-STREH-mohs
seh-RRAH-dohs)*
Sin salida
(seen sah-LEE-dah)

Dead-end corridor
Corredor ciego
(koh-reh-DOHR SYE-goh)

Dead load
Carga muerta
(KAHR-gah MWEHR-tah)
Carga permanente
*(KAHR-gah
pehr-mah-NEHN-teh)*

Deck, Decking
Cubierta
(koo-BYEHR-tah)

Deflector
Deflector
(Deh-flehk-TOHR)

Deluge system
Sistema de diluvio
o inundación total
*(sees-TEH-mah deh
dee-LOO-vyoh oh
ee-noon-dah-SYON toh-TAL)*

Design drawings
Planos
(PLAH-nohs)

Designer
Diseñador
(dee-seh-nyah-DOHR)

Detached building
Edificación separada
*(eh-dee-fee-kah-SYON
seh-pah-RAH-dah)*

Detector, air sampling
Detector por muestreo de aire
*(deh-tehk-TOHR pohr
MWES-treh-oh deh
ah-EE-reh)*

Detector, photoelectric
Detector fotoeléctrico
*(deh-tehk-TOHR
foh-toh-eh-LEHK-tree-koh)*

Detector, gas
Detector de gas
(deh-tehk-TOHR deh gahs)

D

Detector, heat
Detector de calor
(*deh-tehk-TOHR deh
kah-LOHR*)

Detector, ionization
Detector iónico
(*deh-tehk-TOHR
YOH-nee-koh*)

Detector, lineal beam
Detector de haz de luz
(*deh-tehk-TOHR deh hahs
deh loos*)

**Detector, multisensor
multicriteria**
Detector de múltiples
sensores y criterios
(*deh-tehk-TOHR
deh MOOL-tee-plehs
sehn-SOH-rehs ee
kree-TEHR-ryos*)

Detector, rate of rise heat
Detector de calor
termovelocimetro
(*deh-tehk-TOHR deh
kah-LOHR TEHR-moh-vehl-
oh-see-meh-troh*)

Detector, smoke
Detector de humo
(*deh-tehk-TOHR deh oo-moh*)

Detector, UV/IR
Detector ultravioleta/
infrarrojo
(*deh-tehk-TOHR
ool-trah- vyoh-LEH-tah/
een-frah-ROH-hoh*)

Diagonal bracing
Arriostramiento diagonal
(*ah-rryohs-trah-MYEHN-toh
dyah-goh-NAHL*)

Dig
Excavar
(*ex-kah-VAHR*)

Disability
Discapacidad
(*dees-kah-pah-see-DAHD*)

Discharge pipe
Tubo de descarga
(*TOO-boh deh
dehs-KAHR-gah*)

Discontinuous beams
Vigas discontinuas
(*VEE-gahs
dees-kohn-TEE-nwahs*)

Dispense
Trasvasar
(*trahs-vah-SAHR*)

Dispersal area, safe
Área segura de dispersión
(*AH-reh-ah seh-GOO-rah
deh dees-pehr-SYON*)

Displacement
Corrimiento
(*koh-rree-MYEHN-toh*)
Desplazamiento
(*dehs-plah-sah-MYEHN-toh*)

Door
Puerta
(*PWER-tah*)

Door assemblies
Sistemas de puertas
(*sees-TEH-mahs deh
PWEHR-tahs*)

Door sill
Umbral
(*oom-BRAL*)

Doorbell
Timbre
(*TEEM-breh*)

Doorway
Claro de puerta
(*KLAH-roh deh PWEHR-tah*)
Entrada
(*ehn-TRAH-dah*)
Portal
(*pohr-TAHL*)

Dormer
Buharda
(*boo-AHR-dah*)

Dormitory
Residencias para estudiantes
(*reh-see-DEN-see-ahs
PAH-rah
ehs-too-DYAHN-tehs*)
Dormitorio estudiantil
(*dor-mee-TOH-ree-oh
ehs-too-dyahn-TEEL*)

Double interlock
Doble enclavamiento
(*DOH-bleh
ehn-klah-vah-MYEHN-toh*)

Double plate
Solera doble
(*soh-LEH-rah DOH-bleh*)

Double pole breaker
Interruptor automático
bipolar
(*een-teh-rroop-TOHR
ah-oo-toh-MAH-tee-koh
bee-poh-LAHR*)

Doubled
Adosado
(*ah-doh-SAH-doh*)

Doubler plates
Placas
(*PLAH-kahs*)
Placas de refuerzo
(*PLAH-kahs deh
reh-FWEHR-soh*)

Drain seat
Asiento de drenaje
(*ah-SYEN-toh deh
dreh-NAH-heh*)

Draft stop
Cierre de tiro
(*SYEH-rreh deh TEE-roh*)
Barrera contra corriente
de aire
(*ba-RREH-rah kohn-trah
koh-RRYEHN-teh
deh ah-ee-reh*)

Draftsman
Dibujante
(*dee-boo-HAHN-teh*)

Drain, Drainage
Desagüe
(*deh-SAH-gweh*)
Drenaje
(*dreh-NAH-heh*)

D

Dressing room
Vestidor
(vehs-tee-DOHR)

Drilling
Perforación
(pehr-foh-rah-SYON)

Drip cup
Copa de drenaje
(KOH-pah deh
dreh-NAH-heh)

Drip valve
Válvula de drenaje
(VAHL-voo-lah deh
dreh-NAH-heh)

Driven
Impulsado
(eem-pool-SAH-doh)

Dry chemical powder
Polvo químico seco
(POHL-voh KEE-mee-koh
SEH-koh)

Dry wall
Muro en seco
(MOO-roh ehn SEH-koh)
Tablero de yeso
(tah-bleh-roh deh YEH-soh)

Dryer
Secadora
(seh-kah-DOH-rah)

Dual system
Sistema doble
(sees-TEH-mah DOH-bleh)

Duct
Conducto
(kohn-DOOK-toh)

Dumbwaiter
Montacargas
(mohn-tah-KAHR-gahs)
Montaplatos
(mohn-tah-PLAH-tohs)

Dwelling
Vivienda
(vee-VYEHN-dah)
Residencia
(reh-see-DEHN-syah)
Habitación
(ah-bee-tah-SYON)

Dwelling unit
Unidad de vivienda
(oo-nee-DAHD deh
vee-VYEHN-dah)
Unidad habitacional
(oo-nee-DAHD
ah-bee-tah-syo-NAL)

E

Earth work
Terraplén
(teh-rrah-PLEN)

Earthquake load
Carga sísmica
(KAHR-gah SEES-mee-kah)

Eave
Alero
(ah-LEH-roh)

Edge (on edge)
Canto (de canto a canto)
*(KAHN-toh (deh KAHN-toh
ah KAHN-toh))*
Borde
(BOHR-deh)

Egress
Salida
(sah-LEE-dah)

Elbow
Codo
(KOH-doh)

Electrical fixture
Artefactos eléctricos
*(ar-teh-FAK-tohs
eh-LEHK-tree-kohs)*

Electrical outlet
Enchufe
(ehn-CHOO-feh)
Tomacorriente
(toh-mah-koh-RRYEHN-teh)

Electrician
Electricista
(eh-lehk-tree-SEES-tah)

Electricity
Electricidad
(eh-lehk-tree-see-DAHD)

Elevator
Ascensor
(ah-sehn-SOHR)
Elevador
(eh-leh-vah-DOHR)

Elevator car
Coche de ascensor
*(KOH-cheh deh
ah-sehn-SOHR)*

Elevator hoistway
Hueco del elevador
*(WEH-koh dehl
eh-leh-vah-DOHR)*

Embankment
Terraplén
(teh-rrah-PLEN)

Embedded
Empotrados
(ehm-poh-TRAH-dohs)
Incrustado
(een-kroos-TAH-doh)
Arraigado
(ah-rrah-ee-GAH-doh)

Embedment
Empotradura
(ehm-poh-trah-DOO-rah)

Enclose
Encerrar
(*ehn-seh-RRAHR*)

Enclosed
Encerrado
(*ehn-seh-RRAH-doh*)

Enclosure
Cerramiento
(*seh-rrah-MYEHN-toh*)

Encompass
Incluir
(*een-kloo-EER*)

Enforce
Hacer cumplir
(*ah-SEHR koom-PLEER*)

Engineer
Ingeniero
(*een-heh-NYEH-roh*)

Emergency light
Luz de emergencia
(*loos deh
eh-mehr-hen-SEE-ah*)

Emergency lighting
Iluminación de emergencia
(*ee-loo-mee-nah-SYON deh
eh-mehr-hen-SEE-ah*)

Emergency relief venting
Desfogue de alivio de
emergencia
(*dehs-foh-heh deh
ah-LEE-vyoh deh
eh-mehr-hen-SEE-ah*)

Enclosure
Cerramiento, recinto
(*seh-rrah-MYEHN-toh,
reh-SEEHN-toh*)

Engine driven
Generador a motor
(*heh-neh-rah-DOHR ah
moh-TOHR*)

Equipment grounding
Puesta a tierra de equipos
(*PWEHS-tah ah tee-EH-rah
deh eh-KEE-pohs*)

Escalator
Escalera mecánica
(*ehs-kah-LEH-rah
meh-KAH-nee-kah*)

Escutcheon
Escudo de techo
(*ehs-KOO-doh deh TEH-koh*)

Essential facilities
Instalaciones esenciales
(*eens-tah-lah-SYOH-nehs
eh-sehn-SYAH-lehs*)
Edificaciones esenciales
(*eh-dee-fee-kah-SYOH-nehs
eh-sehn-SYAH-lehs*)

Exhaust
Escape
(*ehs-KAH-peh*)
Extracción
(*ehk-strak-SYON*)

Exhaust fan
Ventilador de extracción
(*vehn-tee-lah-DOHR
deh-ehk-strak-SYON*)

Exhauster
Válvula de retención del
flotador
(*VAHL-voo-lah deh
reh-tehn-SYON dehl
floh-tah-DOHR*)

Exit
Salida
(*sah-LEE-dah*)

Exit door
Puerta de evacuación, salida
(*PWER-tah deh
eh-vah-koo-ah-SYON,
sah-LEE-dah*)

Exit sign
Señal de evacuación
(*seh-NYAL deh
eh-vah-koo-ah-SYON*)

Exit stair
Escalera de evacuación
(*ehs-kah-LEH-rah deh
eh-vah-koo-ah-SYON*)

Exit width
Ancho de la salida
(*AHN-koh deh lah
sah-LEE-dah*)

Expansion bolt
Perno de expansión
(*PEHR-noh deh
ehk-spahn-SYON*)
Tornillo de expansión
(*tohr-NEE-joh deh
ehk-spahn-SYON*)

Expansion joint
Junta de dilatación/expansión
(*HOON-tah deh
dee-lah-tah-SYON/
ehk-spahn-SYON*)

Explosion
Explosión
(*ehks-ploh-SYON*)

Extension cord
Cable de extensión
(*KAH-bleh deh
ehk-stehn-SYON*)

Exterior wall
Muro/Pared exterior
(*MOO-roh/pa-REHD
ehk-steh-RYOHR*)

Exterior/interior surface
Superficie exterior/interior
(*soo-per-FEE-see-eh
ehk-steh-RYOHR/
een-teh-RYOHR*)

Eye nut
Tuerca de ojete
(*TWER-kah deh oh-heh-teh*)

Eye rod
Hembrilla
(*ehm-BREE-jah*)

F

Façade
Alzado
(*al-ZAH-doh*)
Fachada
(*fah-CHAH-dah*)

Face grain
Veta superficial
(*VEH-tah
soo-pehr-fee-SYAHL*)

Face shield
Careta
(*kah-REH-tah*)

Facing brick
Ladrillos para frentes
(*lah-DREE-johs PAH-rah
FREHN-tehs*)

Factory-built fireplace
Chimenea prefabricada
(*chee-meh-NEH-ah
preh-fah-bree-KAH-dah*)
Hogar prefabricado
(*oh-GAR
preh-fah-bree-KAH-doh*)

Fan
Ventilador
(*vehn-tee-lah-DOHR*)
Abanico
(*ah-bah-NEE-koh*)

Fasteners
Anclajes
(*ahn-KLAH-hehs*)

Faucet
Llave
(*JAH-veh*)
Grifo
(*GREE-foh*)

Feed main
Tubería de distribución
principal
(*too-beh-REE-ah
deh dees-tree-boo-SYON
preen-see-PAL*)

Feeder
Línea de alimentación
(*LEE-nya deh
ah-lee-mehn-ta-SYON*)

Feeder cable
Cable de alimentación
(*KAH-bleh de
ah-lee-mehn-tah-SYON*)

Felt
Fieltro
(*FYEHL-troh*)

Fence
Cerca
(*SEHR-ka*)
Barda
(*BAR-dah*)
Mediera
(*meh-DYEH-rah*)

Fiberboard
Tablero de fibra
(*tah-BLEH-roh deh FEE-
brah*)

F

Filled
Rellenado
(reh-jeh-NAH-doh)

Fillcup
Copa de llenado
(KOH-pah deh jeh-NAH-doh)

Finish
Acabado
(ah-kah-BAH-doh)
Terminado
(tehr-mee-NAH-doh)

Finishing nail
Clavo sin cabeza
(KLAH-voh seen
kah-BEH-sah)

Fire
Incendio
(een-SEHN-dee-oh)

Fire alarm
Alarma de incendios
(a-LAHR-ma deh
een-SEHN-dee-oh)

Fire alarm adressable system
Sistema direccional de alarma
de incendios
(sees-TEH-mah
dee-rehk-syon-AHL
deh a-LAHR-ma deh
een-SEHN-dee-oh)

Fire alarm system
Sistema de alarma contra
incendios
(sees-TEH-mah deh
ah-LAR-mah kohn-trah
een-SEHN-dee-ohs)

Fire brigade
Brigada de incendios
(bree-GAH-dah deh
een-SEHN-dee-ohs)

Fire chief
Jefe de bomberos
(HEH-feh deh
bohm-BEH-rohs)

Fire Code
Código de Incendios
(KOH-dee-goh deh
een-SEHN-dee-ohs)

Fire department
Cuerpo/Departamento
debomberos
(KWER-poh/
deh-par-tah-MEHN-toh
deh bohm-BEH-rohs)

Fire department access
Acceso para bomberos
(ahk-SEH-soh PAH-rah
bohm-BEH-rohs)

Fire department connection
Toma de impulsión
(TOH-mah deh
eem-pool-SYON)
Conexión para bomberos
(koh-nek-SYON PAH-ra
bohm-BEH-rohs)

Fire department siamese connection
Toma de bomberos siamesa
(TOH-mah deh
bohm-BEH-rohs
syah-MEH-sah)

Fire engine
Carro de bomberos
*(KAH-roh deh
bohm-BEH-rohs)*

Fire escape
Escalera de incendios
*(ehs-kah-LEH-rah deh
een-SEHN-dee-ohs)*

Fire extinguisher
Extinguidor
(ehk-steen-ghee-DOHR)
Extintor
(ehk-steen-TOHR)
Matafuegos
(mah-tah-FWEH-gohs)

Fire notification
Notificación de incendios
*(noh-tee-fee-kah-SYON
deh een-SEHN-dee-ohs)*

Fireblock
Bloque antifuego
*(BLOH-keh
ahn-tee-FWEH-goh)*

Firebox
Fogón
(foh-GOHN)

Firebrick
Ladrillo de fuego
*(lah-DREE-joh deh
FWEH-goh)*

Fireplace
Chimenea
(chee-meh-NEH-ah)
Hogar
(oh-GAHR)

Fire prevention
Prevención de incendios
*(preh-vehn-SYON deh
een-SEHN-dee-ohs)*

Fire protection
Protección contra incendios
*(proh-tehk-SYON KOHN-trah
een-SEHN-dee-ohs)*

Fire pump
Bomba contra incendios
*(BOHM-bah KOHN-trah
een-SEHN-dee-ohs)*

Fire pump, centrifugal
Bomba contra incendios
centrífuga
*(BOHM-bah KOHN-trah
een-SEHN-dee-ohs
sehn-tree-FOO-gah)*

Fire pump, controller
Controlador de la bomba
contra incendios
*(kon-troh-la-DOHR deh la
BOHM-bah deh KOHN-trah
een-SEHN-dee-ohs)*

Fire pump, split-case
Bomba contra incendios
de carcasa partida
*(BOHM-bah KOHN-trah
een-SEHN-dee-ohs deh
kahr-KAH-sah pahr-TEE-dah)*

Fire rated (time)
Resistente al fuego
(en tiempo)
*(reh-sees-TEHN-teh
ahl FWEH-go (ehn
tee-EHM-poh))*

Fire rated assembly
Muro cortafuego
*(MOO-roh
kohr-tah-FWEH-go)*

Fire resistance
Resistente al fuego
*(reh-sees-TEHN-teh
ahl FWEH-go)*

Fire retardant
Retardante al fuego
*(reh-tahr-DEHN-teh
ahl FWEH-go)*

Fire safety
Seguridad contra incendios
*(seh-goo-ree-DAHD
KOHN-trah
een-SEHN-dee-ohs)*

Fire station
Estación de bomberos
*(eh-stah-SYON deh
bohm-BEH-rohs)*

Fire, high challenge
Fuego de gran intensidad
*(FWEH-go deh grahn
een-tehn-see-DAHD)*

Fire, shielded
Fuego con obstáculos
*(FWEH-go kohn
ohb-STAH-koo-lohs)*

Fireball
Bola de fuego
(BOH-lah deh FWEH-go)

Fireproof
Incombustible
(een-kohm-boos-TEE-blehs)

First floor/story
Primer piso
(pree-MER PEE-soh)

Fish tape
Cinta pescadora
*(SEEN-tah
pehs-kah-DOH-rah)*

Fitting
Accesorio
(ahk-seh-SOH-ree-oh)
Conexión
(koh-nek-SYON)

Fixture
Artefactoh
(ar-teh-FAHK-toh)
Accesorioh
(ahk-seh-SOH-ree-oh)

Fixture, bathroom
Artefacto-sanitario
*(ar-teh-FAHK-toh
sah-nee-TAH-ree-oh)*

Fixture trap
Trampa hidráulica
*(TRAM-pah
ee-DRAH-oo-lee-kah)*
Sifón
(see-FOHN)
Trampa de artefacto
*(TRAM-pah deh
ar-teh-FAHK-toh)*

Flammable liquid
Líquido inflamable
*(LEE-kee-doh
een-flah-MAH-bleh)*

Flange
Brida
(BREE-dah)

Flanged
Embridada
(*ehm-bree-DAH-dah*)

Flash fire
Fuego rápido y generalizado
(*FWEH-go RRAH-pee-doh ee
heh-neh-rah-LEE-sah-doh*)

Flashing
Cubrejuntas
(*koo-breh-HOON-tahs*)
Tapajuntas
(*tah-pah-HOON-tahs*)
Plancha de escurrimiento
(*PLAHN-cha deh
ehs-koo-rree-MYEHN-toh*)
Vierteaguas
(*vee-er-teh-AH-gwahs*)
Botaguas
(*boh-TAH-gwahs*)

Flashlight
Linterna
(*leen-TEHR-nah*)
Lámpara
(*LAHM-pah-rah*)

Flashover
Incendio generalizado
(*een-SEHN-dee-oh
heh-neh-rah-LEE-sah-doh*)

Flex conduit
Conducto portacables flexible
(*kohn-DOOK-toh
pohr-tah-KAH-blehs
flek-SEE-bleh*)

Flood drain
Grifo de purga
(*GREE-foh deh POOR-gah*)

Floodlight
Iluminación industrial
(*ee-loo-mee-nah-SYON
een-doos-tree-AHL*)
Foco industrial
(*FOH-koh een-doos-tree-AHL*)

Floor
Piso
(*PEE-soh*)

Floor deck
Plataforma
(*plah-tah-FOHR-mah*)

Floor tile (small slab)
Loseta
(*loh-SEH-tah*)

Flooring
Revestimientos para pisos
(*reh-vehs-tee-MYEHN-tohs
PAH-rah PEE-sohs*)
Material para pisos
(*mah-teh-RYAHL PAH-rah
PEE-sohs*)

Flow
Caudal
(*ka-oo-DAHL*)

Flue
Conductos de humo
(*kohn-DOOK-tohs deh
OO-moh*)

Fluorescent
Fluorescente
(*floo-oh-reh-SEHN-teh*)

Foam maker
Camara de espuma
(*kah-MAH-rah deh
ehs-POO-mahs*)

F

Foam monitor
Cañón de espuma
(*kah-NYON deh*
ehs-POO-mah)

Foam proportioner
Proporcionador de espuma
(*proh-pohr-syon-ah-DOHR*
deheh-POO-mah)

Foam, aqueous film forming (AFFF)
Espuma de formación de capa
acuosa
(*ehs-POO-mah deh*
forh-mah-SYON deh KAH-
pah)

Foam, fluoroprotein
Espuma fluoroproteínica
(*ehs-POO-mah*
floh-roh-proh-teh-EE-nee-
kah)

Foam, low expansion
Espuma de baja expansión
(*ehs-POO-mah deh BAH-hah*
ehk-spahn-SYON)

Footboard
Tabla de piso
(*TAH-blah deh PEE-soh*)

Foot candles
Bujía pie (medida de
iluminación)
(*boo-HEE-ah pyeh*
(*meh-dee-dah deh*
ee-loo-mee-nah-SYON))

Footing
Zapata
(*sah-PAH-tah*)
Zarpa
(*SAR-pah*)
Cimiento
(*see-MYEHN-toh*)

Foreman
Capataz
(*kah-pah-TAHS*)
Sobrestante
(*soh-breh-STAHN-teh*)
Supervisor
(*soo-pehr-vee-SOHR*)

Fork
Horquilla
(*ohr-KEE-jah*)

Forms (concrete)
Encofrados
(*ehn-koh-FRAH-dohs*)

Formwork
Encofrado
(*ehn-koh-FRAH-doh*)

Foundation
Fundación
(*foon-dah-SYON*)
Cimentación
(*see-men-tah-SYON*)

Foundation sill plate
Placa de solera de fundación
(*PLAH-kah deh soh-LEH-rah*
deh foon-dah-SYON)

Foundation walls
Muros de fundación
(*MOO-rohs deh
foon-dah-SYON*)

Frame
Marco
(*MAR-koh*)
Estructura
(*ehs-trook-TOO-rah*)
Pórtico
(*POHR-tee-koh*)
Bastidor
(*bahs-tee-DOHR*)
Armazón
(*ar-mah-SOHN*)

Frame, door/window
Marco de puerta/ventana
(*MAR-koh deh PWER-tah/
vehn-TAH-nah*)

Framed
Armado
(*ar-MAH-doh*)

Framework
Armazón
(*ar-mah-SOHN*)

Framing
Estructura
(*ehs-trook-TOO-rah*)

Fumes
Gases
(*GAH-sehs*)

Furred out, Furring
Enrasado
(*ehn-rah-SAH-doh*)

Fuse
Fusible
(*foo-SEE-bleh*)

Fuse box
Caja de fusibles
(*KAH-hah deh foo-SEE-blehs*)

Fusible link
Elemento termosensible
(*eh-leh-MEHN-toh
tehr-moh-sehn-SEE-bleh*)

G

Gable
Hastial
(*ahs-TYAHL*)

Gable construction
Construcción a dos aguas
(*kohns-trook-SYON ah dohs
AH-gwahs*)

Gable roof
Techo a dos aguas
(*TEH-cho ah dos AH-gwahs*)

Gable rake
Cornisa inclinada
(*kor-NEE-sah
een-klee-NAH-dah*)

Gage/Gauge (thickness)
Calibre
(*kah-LEE-breh*)

Gage
Manómetro
(*mah-NOH-meh-troh*)

Gallons per minute (GPM)
Galones por minuto
(*gah-LOH-nehs pohr
mee-NOO-toh*)

Garage
Garaje
(*gah-RAH-heh*)
Cochera
(*koh-CHEH-rah*)

Garbage disposal
Triturador de basura/
desperdicios
(*tree-too-rah-DOHR
deh bah-SOO-rah/
dehs-pehr-DEE-see-ohs*)

Gasket
Arandela
(*ar-ahn-DEH-lah*)
Empaque
(*ehm-PAH-keh*)
Junta
(*HOON-tah*)

Gas main
Conducto/cañería principal
de gas
(*kohn-DOOK-toh/
kah-nyeh-REE-ah
preen-see-PAL deh GAHS*)

Gate valve
Llave de paso
(*JAH-veh deh PAH-soh*)

Gauge/Gage (instrument)
Manómetro
(*mah-NOH-meh-troh*)
Indicador
(*een-dee-kah-DOHR*)

Generator
Generador
(*heh-neh-rah-DOHR*)

G

Girder
Viga maestra
(*VEE-gah mah-EHS-trah*)
Viga principal
(*VEE-gah preen-see-PAL*)
Viga
(*VEE-gah*)
Jácena
(*HAH-seh-nah*)

Glazed, Glazing
Vidriado
(*vee-dree-AH-doh*)
Encristalado
(*ehn-krees-tah-LAH-doh*)

Glue
Pegamento
(*peh-gah-MEHN-toh*)

Grab bars
Barras de apoyo
(*BAH-rrahs deh ah-POH-joh*)
Barra de soporte
(*BAH-rrahs deh
soh-POHR-teh*)
Agarraderas
(*ah-gah-rrah-DEH-rahs*)

Grade
Nivel de terreno
(*nee-VEHL deh
teh-RREH-noh*)

Grade (ground elevation)
Rasante
(*rah-SAHN-teh*)

Grade beam
Viga de fundación
(*VEE-gah deh
foon-dah-SYON*)

Graded lumber
Madera elaborada
(*mah-DEH-rah
eh-lah-boh-RAH-dah*)
Madera clasificada
(*mah-DEH-rah
klah-see-fee-KAH-dah*)

Grading
Nivelación de terreno
(*nee-veh-lah-SYON
deh teh-RREH-noh*)

Grandstands
Tribunas
(*tree-BOON-ahs*)
Gradas
(*GRAH-dahs*)

Gravel
Grava
(*GRAH-vah*)
Cascajo
(*kahs-KAH-hoh*)
Ripio
(*REE-pee-oh*)

Grease interceptor
Interceptor de grasas
(*een-tehr-sehp-TOHR
deh GRAH-sahs*)

Grease trap
Colector de grasas
(*koh-lehk-TOHR
deh GRAH-sahs*)

Grille
Rejilla
(*reh-HEE-jah*)
Reja
(*REH-hah*)

Gridded piping
Tubería en forma de parrilla
(*too-beh-REE-jah ehn
FOHR-mah deh pah-REE-jah*)

Grip
Agarre
(*ah-GAH-rreh*)

Grommet
Arandela
(*ar-ahn-DEH-lah*)
Ojal
(*oh-HAHL*)

Groove
Ranura
(*rah-NOO-rah*)

Gross area
Área total
(*AH-reh-ah toh-TAHL*)
Área bruta
(*AH-reh-ah BROO-tah*)

Ground bond
Cable de enlace
(*KAH-bleh de ehn-LAH-seh*)

Ground connection
Conexión a tierre
(*koh-nek-SYON
ah TYEH-rrah*)

Ground fault
Falla a tierra
(*FAH-jah ah TYEH-rrah*)

Ground fault circuit
Interruptor fusible de
seguridad a tierra
(*een-teh-rroop-TOHR
foo-SEE-bleh deh
seh-goo-ree-DAHD
ah TYEH-rrah*)

Ground level
Planta baja
(*PLAHN-tah BAH-hah*)

Ground/neutral bus bar
Bandeja neutra/a tierra
(*bahn-DEH-hah
NEH-oo-trah/ah TYEH-rrah*)

Ground wire
Cable a tierra
(*KAH-bleh ah TYEH-rrah*)

Grout
Lechada de cemento
(*leh-CHAH-dah deh
seh-MEHN-toh*)
Mortero de cemento
(*mohr-TEH-roh deh
seh-MEHN-toh*)

Guard
Jaula rociador
(*HOW-lah roh-syah-DOHR*)

Guardrail
Baranda
(*bah-RAHN-dah*)

G

Guest
Huésped
(*WEHS-pehd*)

Guest room
Cuarto de huéspedes
(*KWAR-toh deh*
WEHS-peh-dehs)

Guide rail
Riel de guía
(*RYEHL deh GY-ah*)

Gusset plate
Placa de unión
(*PLAH-kah deh oon-YOHN*)
Placa de cartela
(*PLAH-kah deh*
kahr-TEH-lah)

Gutter
Gotera
(*goh-TEH-rah*)
Canal
(*kah-NAHL*)
Canaleta
(*kah-nah-LEH-tah*)

Gutter partition
Tabiques
(*tah-BEE-kehs*)

Gypsum
Yeso
(*YEH-soh*)

Gypsum board
Panel de yeso
(*pah-NEHL deh YEH-soh*)
Tablero de yeso
(*tah-BLEH-roh deh YEH-soh*)
Plancha de yeso
(*PLAHN-chah deh YEH-soh*)
Plafón de yeso
(*plah-FOHN deh YEH-soh*)

Gypsum lath
Listón yesero
(*lees-TOHN yeh-SEH-roh*)

Gypsum plaster
Revoque de yeso
(*reh-VOH-keh deh YEH-soh*)

Gypsum wallboard
Panel de yeso
(*pah-NEHL deh YEH-soh*)
Plancha de yeso
(*PLAHN-cha deh YEH-soh*)

H

Hallway
Pasillo
(*pah-SEE-joh*)

Halogenated agent
Agente halogenado
(*A-HEN-teh
ha-loh-hen-NAH-doh*)

Hand hose
Manguera manual
(*mahn-GEH-rah
mahn-oo-AHL*)

Handicapped
Discapacitado
(*dees-kah-pah-see-TAH-doh*)
Minusválido
(*mee-noos-VAH-lee-doh*)

Handle
Manipular
(*mah-nee-poo-LAHR*)
Manija
(*mah-NEE-hah*)
Mango
(*MAHN-goh*)
Brazo
(*BRAH-soh*)
Agarradera
(*ah-gah-rrah-DEH-rahs*)

Handling
Manipulación
(*mah-nee-poo-lah-SYON*)

Handrail
Pasamanos
(*pah-sah-MAH-nohs*)

Handset
Teléfono transmisor receptor
(*te-LEH-foh-noh
trahn-mee-SOHR
reh-sehp-TOHR*)

Hanger, adjustable swivel
Colgante de bucle ajustable
y oscilante
(*kohl-GAHN-teh deh
BOO-kleh ah-hoos-TAH-bleh
ee oh-see-LAHN-teh*)

Hanger, clevis type
Colgante de horquilla
(*kohl-GAHN-teh deh
ohr-KEE-jah*)

Hanger, malleable swivel
Colgante giratorio y elástico
(*kohl-gahn-teh
hee-rah-TOH-ree-oh
ee eh-LAHS-tee-koh*)

Hanger, side beam adjustable
Colgante ajustable para vigas
laterales
(*kohl-GAHN-teh
ah-hoos-TAH-bleh pah-rah
VEE-gahs lah-teh-RAH-les*)

Hangers
Ganchos
(*GAHN-chohs*)
Colgaderos
(*kohl-gah-DEH-rohs*)

Hangings
Cortinajes
(*kor-tee-NAH-hehs*)
Colgaderos
(*kohl-gah-DEH-rohs*)

Hardboard
Tablero duro
(*tah-BLEH-roh DOO-roh*)

Hard hat
Casco de seguridad
(*KAHS-koh deh
seh-goo-ree-DAHD*)

Hatch
Compuerta
(*kohm-PWEHR-tah*)

Haunches
Cartelas
(*kahr-TEH-lahs*)

Hazard
Peligro
(*peh-LEE-groh*)

Hazardous
Peligroso
(*peh-lee-GROH-soh*)
Nocivo
(*noh-SEE-voh*)
Dañino
(*dah-NYEE-noh*)

Hazardous material
Material peligroso
(*mah-teh-RYAL
peh-lee-GROH-soh*)

Head (door frame)
Dintel (de la puerta)
(*deen-TEHL (deh lah
PWEHR-tah)*)

Head joint
Junta vertical
(*HOON-tah vehr-tee-KAHL*)

Header
Cabezal
(*kah-beh-SAL*)
Dintel
(*deen-TEHL*)
Colector
(*koh-lehk-TOHR*)

Headquarters
Oficina principal
(*oh-fee-SEE-nah
preen-see-PAL*)

Heat release rate
Tasa de liberación de calor
(*TAH-sah deh
lee-beh-rah-SYON
deh kah-LOHR*)

Heater
Calefactor
(*kahl-eh-fak-TOHR*)
Estufa
(*ehs-TOO-fah*)
Calentador
(*kahl-ehn-tah-DOHR*)

Heating
Calefacción
(*kahl-eh-fak-SYON*)

Helmet
Casco
(*KAHS-koh*)

High challenge fire
Fuego de gran intensidad
(*FWEH-go deh
grahn een-tehn-see-DAHD*)

High-piled storage
Almacenamiento apilado
(*ahl-mah-sehn-ah-MYEHN-
toh ah-pee-LAH-doh*)
Almacenamiento en pilas altas
(*ahl-mah-seh-nah-MYEHN-
toh ehn PEE-lahs AHL-tahs*)

High rack storage
Almacenamiento en
estanterías
(*ahl-mah-sehn-ah-MYEHN-
toh ehn
ehs-tahn-teh-REE-ahs*)

High rise building
Edificio de gran altura
(*eh-dee-FEE-syoh deh grahn
ahl-TOO-rah*)

Highly toxic material
Material altamente tóxico
(*mah-teh-RYAHL
AHL-tah-mehn-teh
TOHK-see-koh*)

Hinge
Bisagra
(*bee-SAH-grah*)

Hip
Lima
(*LEE-mah*)
Lima hoya
(*LEE-mah OH-yah*)
Lima tesa
(*LEE-mah TEH-sah*)

Hip roof
Techo a cuatro aguas
(*TEH-cho ah KWAH-tro
AH-gwas*)

Hip tile
Teja para limas
(*TEH-hah
PAH-rah LEE-mahs*)

Hod
Cuezo
(*KWEH-soh*)

Hold-down anchor
Ancla de retención
(*AHN-klah deh
reh-tehn-SYON*)

Hole
Hoyo
(*OH-yoh*)
Agujero
(*ah-goo-HEH-roh*)
Boquete
(*boh-KEH-teh*)

Hood (chimney/kitchen)
Campana (chimenea/cocina)
(*kahm-PAH-nah
(chee-meh-NEH-ah/
koh-SEE-nah)*)

Hoop
Lazo
(*LAH-soh*)

H

Horizontal bracing system
> Sistema de arriostramiento
> horizontal
> *(see-STEH-mah deh*
> *ah-rryoh-strah-MYEHN-toh*
> *oh-ree-sohn-TAHL)*

Horizontal pipe
> Tubo horizontal
> *(TOO-boh oh-ree-sohn-TAHL)*

Horn
> Corneta
> *(kohr-NEH-tah)*

Hose bibb valves
> Válvulas para grifos
> de mangueras
> *(VAHL-voo-lahs PAH-rah*
> *GREE-fohs deh*
> *mahn-GEH-rahs)*

Hose
> Manguera
> *(mahn-GEH-rah)*

Hose threads·
> Rosca de manguera
> *(ROHS-kah deh*
> *mahn-GEH-rah)*

Hot bus bar
> Bandeja de carga
> *(bahn-DEH-hah*
> *deh KAHR-gah)*
> Barra ómnibus de carga
> *(BAH-rra OHM-nee-boos*
> *deh KAHR-gah)*

Hot water
> Agua caliente
> *(AH-gwah kah-LYEHN-teh)*

House trap
> Trampa doméstica
> *(TRAHM-pah*
> *doh-MEHS-tee-kah)*

HVAC
> Calefacción, ventilacion y aire
> acondicionado
> *(kah-leh-fahk-SYON,*
> *vehn-tee-lah-SYON*
> *ee AH-ee-reh*
> *ah-kohn-dee-syoh-NAH-doh)*

Hydrant botts
> Salida de un hidrante
> *(sah-LEE-dah deh*
> *oon ee-DRAHN-teh)*

Hydrant wrench
> Herramienta para hidrantes
> *(eh-rah-MYEN-tah pah-rah*
> *ee-DRAHN-tehs)*

Hydrant, dry
> Hidrante seco
> *(ee-DRAHN-teh SEH-koh)*

Hydrant, wall
> Hidrante de pared
> *(ee-DRAHN-teh deh*
> *pah-RHED)*

Hydrant, wet
> Hidrante húmedo
> *(ee-DRAHN-teh OO-meh-doh)*

Hydraulic calculation
> Cálculo hidráulico
> *(KAHL-koo-loh*
> *ee-DRA-oo-lee-koh)*

Incline
Declive
(deh-KLEE-veh)
Inclinación
(een-klee-nah-SYON)
Ladera
(lah-DEH-rah)
Pendiente
(pehn-DYEHN-teh)
Inclinar
(een-klee-NAHR)
Ladear
(lah-deh-AHR)

Initiating device
Dispositivo activador
*(dees-po-see-TEE-voh
ahk-tee-vah-DOHR)*

Inlet
Orificio de entrada
*(oh-ree-FEE-syoh deh
ehn-TRAH-dah)*

Inspector
Inspector
(eens-pek-TOHR)
Supervisor
(soo-pehr-vee-SOHR)

Inspector test assembly
Unidad de inspección
*(oo-nee-DAHD de
een-spehk-SYON)*

Inspector's test gage
Manómetro de inspección
*(mah-NOH-meh-troh
deh een-spehk-SYON)*

Insulating
Aislante
(ah-ees-LAHN-teh)

Insulation
Aislamiento
(ah-ees-lah-MYEHN-toh)
Aislante
(ah-ees-LAHN-teh)

Interior finish
Terminado interior
*(tehr-mee-NAH-doh
een-teh-RYOR)*

Interior room
Cuarto interior
(KWAR-toh een-teh-RYOR)

Interlay
Contrachapar
(koh-trah-chah-PAHR)

I

Interlayment
Capa intermedia
*(KAH-pah
een-tehr-MEH-dee-ah)*

Interlocking
Enclavamiento
(ehn-klah-vah-MYEHN-toh)

Interlocking roofing tiles
Tejas entrelazadas para techo
*(TEH-hahs
ehn-treh-lah-SAH-dahs
PAH-rah TEH-choh)*

Intertied
Entrelazados
(ehn-treh-lah-SAH-dohs)

Intervening rooms
Cuartos intermedios
*(KWAR-tohs
een-tehr-MEH-dee-ohs)*

Isolation joint
Junta de aislamiento
*(HOON-tah deh
ah-ees-lah-MYEHN-toh)*

J

Jacking force
Fuerza de estiramiento
(*FWEHR-sah deh*
ehs-tee-rah-MYEHN-toh)

Jamb (door frame)
Jamba
(*HAHM-bah*)
Quicial
(*kee-SYAHL*)

Jobsite
Lugar de la obra/en la obra
(*loo-GAR deh lah OH-brah/*
ehn lah OH-brah)
Sitio de construcción
(*SEE-tee-oh deh*
kohn-strook-SYON)

Joint
Unión
(*oon-YOHN*)
Junta
(*HOON-tah*)

Joint compound
Pasta de muro
(*PAHS tah deh MOO-roh*)

Joist
Vigueta
(*vee-GEH-tah*)
Viga
(*VEE-gah*)

Joist, end
Vigueta esquinera
(*vee-GEH-tah es-kee-NEH-*
rah)

Joist, floor
Vigueta del piso
(*vee-GEH-tah del PEE-soh*)

Joist hanger
Estribo para vigueta
(*ehs-TREE-boh*
PAH-rah vee-GEH-tah)

Junction
Empalme
(*ehm-PAHL-meh*)
Unión
(*oon-YOHN*)

Junction box
Caja de conexiones de
empalme
(*KAH-hah deh*
koh-nek-SYOH-nehs
deh ehm-PAHL-meh)

K

Kettle
Caldera
(*kahl-DEH-rah*)

Key
Llave
(*JAH-veh*)

Keystone
Clave
(*KLAH-veh*)

King post
Poste principal
(*POHS-teh preen-see-PAL*)
Columna
(*koh-LOOM-nah*)

Kiosk
Quiosco
(*KYOHS-koh*)

Kitchen oven
Horno de cocina
(*OHR-noh deh koh-SEE-nah*)

Kitchen hood
Campana de cocina
(*kahm-PAH-nah deh
koh-SEE-nah*)

Kitchen stove
Estufa de cocina
(*ehs-TOO-fah deh
koh-SEE-nah*)

Kitchen sink
Fregadero de cocina
(*freh-gah-DEH-roh deh
koh-SEE-nah*)

Knockout
Agujero ciego
(*ah-goo-HEH-roh SYEH-goh*)

Kraft paper
Papel Kraft
(*pah-PEHL krahft*)

L

Ladder
Escalera
(*ehs-kah-LEH-rah*)

Landing (stair)
Descanso de escaleras
(*dehs-KAHN-soh deh
ehs-kah-LEH-rahs*)

Lap siding
Revestimiento de tablas con
traslape/solape
(*reh-vehs-tee-MYEHN-toh
deh TAH-blahs kohn
trahs-LAH-peh/soh-LAH-peh*)

Lap splice
Traslape
(*trahs-LAH-peh*)

Lapping
Traslapo
(*trahs-LAH-poh*)

Latch
Cerrojo
(*seh-RROH-hoh*)
Trinquete
(*treen-KEH-teh*)

Latch lever
Palanca de trinquete
(*pah-LAHN-kah deh
treen-KEH-teh*)

Latched clapper type
Tipo clapeta con trinquete
(*TEE-poh klah-PEH-tah kohn
treen-KEH-teh*)

Latching device
Dispositivo de traba
(*dees-poh-see-TEE-voh deh
TRAH-bah*)

Lateral (pipe)
Ramal lateral
(*rahm-AHL lah-teh-RAHL*)

Lath
Listón
(*lees-TOHN*)
Malla de enlucir
(*MAH-jah deh ehn-loo-SEER*)
Tiras de yeso
(*TEE-rahs deh YEH-soh*)
Tira
(*TEE-rah*)

Lawn
Césped
(*SEHS-pehd*)
Pasto
(*PAHS-toh*)

Lay out
Croquis
(*KROH-kees*)
Diseño
(*dee-SEH-nyo*)

L

Leader (pipe)
Tubo de bajada
(*TOO-boh deh bah-HAH-dah*)

Lead-free
Sin plomo
(*seen PLOH-moh*)

Lead-free solder and flux
Soldadura y fundente sin
plomo
(*sohl-dah-DOO-rah ee
foon-DEHN-teh seen
PLOH-moh*)

Ledger
Travesaño
(*tra-veh-SAH-nyo*)
Solera
(*soh-LEH-rah*)

Lever
Palanca
(*pah-LAHN-kah*)

Life safety
Seguridad humana
(*seh-goo-ree-DAHD
oo-MAH-nah*)

Lift
Levantamiento
(*leh-vahn-tah-MYEHN-toh*)
Alzada
(*ahl-SAH-dah*)
Lote
(*LOH-teh*)
Hormigonada
(*ohr-mee-goh-NAH-dah*)
Colada
(*koh-LAH-dah*)

Lightbulbs
Focos
(*FOH-kohs*)
Bombillas
(*bohm-BEE-jahs*)

Light fixture
Artefacto de iluminación
(*ar-teh-FAK-toh
deh ee-loo-mee-nah-SYON*)

Limbs
Miembros
(*MYEHM-brohs*)
Extremidades
(*ehk-streh-mee-DAH-dehs*)

Lime putty
Mastique de cal
(*mah-STEE-keh deh kahl*)

Limestone
Caliza
(*kah-LEE-sah*)

Line and grade
Trazar y nivelar
(*trah-SAR ee nee-veh-LAR*)

Lining
Recubrimiento
(*reh-koo-bree-MYEHN-toh*)
Revestimiento
(*reh-vehs-tee-MYEHN-toh*)

Link, Linkage
Enlace
(*ehn-LAH-seh*)
Tirante
(*tee-RAHN-teh*)
Conexión
(*koh-nek-SYON*)

Link eye holes
Huecos del eslabón
(*WEH-kohs del
ehs-lah-BOHN*)

Lintel
Dintel
(*deen-TEHL*)

Live load
Cargas vivas
(*KAHR-gahs VEE-vahs*)
Carga variable
(*KAHR-gah vah-ree-AH-bleh*)

Load combination
Combinación de cargas
(*kohm-bee-nah-SYON
deh KAHR-gahs*)

Load-bearing joist
Viga de carga
(*VEE-gah deh KAHR-gah*)

Loaded area
Área cargada
(*AH-reh-ah kahr-GAH-dah*)
Área sometida a carga
(*AH-reh-ah soh-meh-TEE-dah
ah KAHR-gah*)

Lobby
Lobby
(*LOH-bee*)
Vestíbulo
(*vehs-TEE-boo-loh*)

Local vent stack
Tubo vertical de ventilación
(*TOO-boh vehr-tee-KAHL deh
vehn-tee-lah-SYON*)

Lock
Candado
(*kan-DAH-doh*)
Cerradura
(*seh-rrah-DOO-rah*)
Cerrojo
(*seh-RROH-hoh*)

Lock bolts
Pernos de seguridad
(*PEHR-nohs deh
seh-goo-ree-DAHD*)

Lock nut
Tuerca de seguridad o fijación
(*TWER-kah deh
seh-goo-ree-DAHD
oh fee-hah-SYON*)

Locking receptacle
Tomas con traba
(*TOH-mahs kohn TRAH-bah*)

L

Lodging house
Hospedaje
(*ohs-peh-DAH-heh*)

Loop
Lazadas
(*lah-SAH-dahs*)
Anillo, bucle
(*ah-nee-joh, BOO-kleh*)

Looped piping
Tubería en forma de bucle
(*too-beh-REE-ah ehn
FORH-mah deh BOO-kleh*)

Lot
Terreno
(*teh-RREH-noh*)
Lote
(*LOH-teh*)

Louver
Celosía
(*seh-loh-SEE-ah*)

Lumber
Madera de construcción
(*mah-DEH-rah deh
kohns-trook-SYON*)
Madera elaborada
(*mah-DEH-rah
eh-lah-boh-RAH-dah*)

M

Mail box
Buzón
(boo-SOHN)

Main
Principal
(preen-see-PAHL)
Matriz
(mah-TREES)

Main breaker
Interruptor automático
principal
*(een-teh-rroop-TOHR
ah-oo-toh-MAH-tee-koh
preen-see-PAHL)*

Main power cable
Cable principal
(KAH-bleh preen-see-PAHL)

Main vent
Respiradero matriz
*(rehs-pee-rah-DEH-roh
mah-TREES)*

Mall
Centro comercial
*(SEHN-troh
koh-mehr-SYAHL)*

Manager
Gerente
(heh-REHN-teh)

Manhole
Pozo de confluencia
*(POH-soh deh
kohn-FLWEHN-syah)*
Boca de inspección
*(BOH-kah deh
eens-pehk-SYON)*
Boca de acceso
(BOH-kah deh ahk-SEH-soh)
Pozo de entrada
*(POH-soh deh
ehn-TRAH-dah)*

Mansard roof
Mansarda
(mahn-SAHR-dah)

Mansion
Mansión
(mahn-SYON)
Residencia
(reh-see-DEHN-syah)

Manual fire alarm box
Caja manual de alarma
de incendios
*(KAH-hah mahn-oo-AHL
deh a-LAHR-ma deh
een-SEHN-dee-ohs)*

M

Manual pull station
Pulsador manual de alarma
(*pool-sah-DOHR
mahn-oo-AHL deh
a-LAHR-ma*)
Alarma de incendio manual
(*ah-LAHR-mah deh
een-SEHN-dee-oh
mah-NWAHL*)

Marquee
Marquesina
(*mar-keh-SEE-nah*)

Mason
Albañil
(*ahl-bah-NYEEL*)

Masonry
Mampostería
(*mahm-pohs-teh-REE-ah*)
Albañilería
(*ahl-bah-nyee-leh-REE-ah*)

Mastic
Mastique
(*mahs-TEE-keh*)

Means of egress
Medios de salida
(*MEH-dee-ohs deh
sah-LEE-dah*)
Vías de evacuación
(*VEE-ahs deh
eh-vah-koo-ah-SYON*)

Measuring tape
Cinta de medir
(*SEEN-tah deh meh-DEER*)

Mechanical anchorage
Anclaje mecánico
(*ahn-KLAH-heh
meh-KAH-nee-koh*)

Metal deck
Plataforma metálica
(*plah-tah-FOR-mah
meh-TAH-lee-kah*)

Metal flagpole
Mástil metálico
(*MAHS-teel
meh-TAH-lee-koh*)

Metal roof covering
Cubierta metálica para techos
(*koo-BYEHR-tah
meh-TAH-lee-kah
PAH-rah TEH-chohs*)

Metal scribe
Trazador de metal
(*trah-sah-DOHR
deh meh-TAHL*)

Meter
Medidor
(*meh-dee-DOHR*)

Mixing valve
Llave de mezcla
(*JAH-veh deh MEHS-clah*)

Moist curing
> Curado con humedad
> *(koo-RAH-doh kohn
> oo-meh-DAHD)*

Molding
> Moldura
> *(mohl-DOO-rah)*

Monitor nozzle
> Monitor de agua
> *(moh-nee-TOHR
> deh AH-gwah)*

Mortar
> Mortero
> *(mohr-TEH-roh)*
> Argamasa
> *(ar-gah-MAH-sah)*
> Mezcla
> *(MEHS-klah)*

Mortise
> Ranura
> *(rah-NOO-rah)*

Motor driven
> Movido por motor
> *(moh-VEE-doh pohr
> moh-TOHR)*

Mullion (door)
> Larguero central
> *(lar-GEH-roh sehn-TRAHL)*

Multiple gabled roofs
> Techos a aguas múltiples
> *(TEH-chohs ah AH-gwahs
> MOOL-tee-plehs)*

N

Nailing, face
Con clavos sumidos
(*kohn KLAH-vohs
soo-MEE-dohs*)

Nailing strip
Listón para clavar
(*lee-STOHN PAH-rah
klah-VAHR*)

Nails
Clavos
(*KLAH-vohs*)

Neutral service wire
Cable principal neutro
(*KAH-bleh preen-see-PAHL
neh-OO-troh*)

Neutral wire
Cable neutro
(*KAH-bleh neh-OO-troh*)

Nip and caps
Manguito y tapa
(*mahn-GEE-toh ee TAH-pah*

Nipple
Manguito, niple
(*mahn-KEE-toh, NEE-pleh*)

Nonwoven
No tejido
(*noh teh-HEE-doh*)

Nosings
Vuelos
(*VWEH-lohs*)

Nozzle
Boquilla
(*boh-KEE-jah*)

Nozzle, water fog
Boquilla de neblina
(*boh-KEE-jah deh
neh-BLEE-nah*)

Nuisance
Perjuicio
(*pehr-hoo-EE-syoh*)

Nursing homes
Asilos de ancianos
(*ah-SEE-lohs deh
ahn-see-AH-nohs*)
Ancianatos
(*ahn-see-ah-NAH-tohs*)
Casas de convalecencia
(*KAH-sahs deh
kohn-vah-leh-SEHN-see-ah*)

Nut
Tuerca
(*TWEHR-kah*)

O

Occupancy
Destino
(*deh-STEE-noh*)
Tenencia
(*tehn-EHN-see-ah*)
Actividades
(*ahk-tee-vee-DAH-dehs*)
Clasificación
(*klah-see-fee-kah-SYON*)
Función
(*foon-SYON*)
Ocupación
(*oh-koo-pah-SYON*)
Zona
(*soh-NAH*)
Capacidad
(*kah-pah-see-DAHD*)

Occupant load
Número de ocupantes
(*NOO-meh-roh deh
oh-koo-PAHN-tehs*)

Offset
Desplazamiento
(*dehs-plah-sah-MYEHN-toh*)
Pieza en "S"
(*PYEH-sah ehn "EH-seh"*)
Pieza de inflexión
(*PYEH-sah deh
een-flek-SYON*)
Desvío
(*dehs-VEE-oh*)
Compensar
(*kohm-pehn-SAR*)

Offset bars
Barras desviadas
(*BAH-rrahs dehs-VYAH-dahs*)

On center
De centro a centro
(*deh SEHN-troh
ah SEHN-troh*)

Open air
Aire libre
(*AH-ee-reh LEE-breh*)

O

Opening
Abertura
(ah-behr-TOO-rah)

Outlet
Boca
(BOH-kah)

Outlet box
Caja de enchufe
(KAH-hah deh
ehn-CHOO-feh)
Caja de tomacorriente
(KAH-hah deh
toh-mah-koh-RRYEHN-teh)

Output signal
Señal de salida
(seh-NYAL deh sah-LEE-dah)

Outside air intake plenum
Pleno de aire con entrada
externa de aire
(pleh-noh de ah-EE-reh
kohn ehn-TRAH-dah
ehks-TEHR-nah deh
ah-EE-reh)

Overhang
Voladizo
(voh-lah-DEE-soh)
Vuelo
(VWEH-loh)
Alero
(ah-LEH-roh)

Overhaul
Reparación
(reh-par-ah-SYON)
Reparo
(reh-PAH-roh)

Overhead
Suspendido
(soos-pehn-DEE-doh)

Overlap
Traslape
(trahs-LAH-peh)
Sobresolape
(soh-breh-soh-LAH-peh)
Superposición
(soo-pehr-poh-see-SYON)

Override
Cancelar
(kahn-seh-LAR)
Anular
(ah-noo-LAR)

Overstrength
Sobreresistencia
(soh-breh-reh-sees-TEHN-
see-ah)

Overturning
Volcamiento
(vohl-kah-MYEHN-toh)
Vuelco
(VWEHL-koh)
Volteo
(vohl-TEH-oh)

Oxidizers
Oxidantes
(ohk-see-DAHN-tehs)

P

Pallet
> Estante
> *(ehs-TAHN-teh)*
> Tarima
> *(tah-REE-mah)*
> Plataforma de carga
> *(plah-tah-FOHR-mah
> deh KAHR-gah)*

Paint
> Pintura
> *(peen-TOO-rah)*

Painter
> Pintor
> *(peen-TOHR)*

Panel edge clips
> Pinzas de canto de panel
> *(peen-sahs deh KAHN-toh
> deh pah-NEHL)*

Panel sheathing
> Revestimiento de tableros
> *(reh-veh-stee-MYEHN-toh
> deh tah-BLEH-rohs)*

Panel zone
> Franja de tableros
> *(FRAHN-hah deh
> tah-BLEH-rohs)*

Paneling
> Empanelado
> *(ehm-pah-neh-LAH-doh)*

Panic bar
> Barra de emergencia
> *(BAH-rrah deh
> eh-mehr-HEN-see-ah)*

Panic hardware
> Herrajes antipánico
> *(eh-RRAH-hehs
> ahn-tee-PAH-nee-koh)*
> Cerrajería o herrajes de
> emergencia
> *(seh-rrah-heh-REE-ah
> oh eh-RRAH-hehs deh
> eh-mehr-HEN-see-ah)*

Paper dispensers
> Dispensadores de papel
> *(dees-pehn-sah-DOH-rehs
> deh pah-PEHL)*

Parapet wall
> Muro de parapeto
> *(MOO-roh deh
> pah-rah-PEH-toh)*

Particleboard
> Madera aglomerada
> *(mah-DEH-rah
> ah-gloh-meh-RAH-dah)*

Partition
> Tabique
> *(tah-BEE-keh)*
> Separación
> *(seh-pah-rah-SYON)*
> División
> *(dee-vee-SYON)*

P

Partition, folding
Tabique plegable
(tah-BEE-keh pleh-GAH-bleh)

Partition, movable
Tabique movible
(tah-BEE-keh moh-VEE-bleh)

Partition, portable
Tabique portátil
(tah-BEE-keh pohr-TAH-teel)

Passageway
Pasillo
(pah-SEE-joh)

Passageway (chimney)
Conducto de humo
*(kohn-DOOK-toh
deh OO-moh)*

Pavement
Pavimento
(pah-vee-MEHN-toh)

Pedestrian walkway
Camino peatonal
*(kah-MEE-noh
peh-ah-toh-NAHL)*

Penthouse
Cuarto de azotea
*(KWAR-toh deh
ah-soh-TEH-ah)*

Performance
Desempeño
(deh-sehm-PEH-nyoh)
Rendimiento
(rehn-dee-MYEHN-toh)
Comportamiento
(kohm-pohr-tah-MYEHN-toh)

Performance based design
Diseño basado en criterios de
desempeño
*(dee-SEH-nyoh bah-SAH-doh
ehn kree-TEHR-ryos deh
deh-sehm-PEH-nyoh)*

Performance criteria
Criterio de funcionamiento
*(kree-TEHR-ryoh deh
foonk-syon-ah-MYEHN-toh)*

Perlite
Perlita
(pehr-LEE-tah)

Permit
Permiso (de construcción)
*(pehr-MEE-soh (deh
kohns-trook-SYON))*

Piles
Pilotes
(pee-LOH-tehs)

Pipe, Piping
Cañería
(kah-nyeh-REE-ah)
Caño
(KAH-nyoh)
Tubería
(too-beh-REE-ah)
Tubo
(TOO-boh)

Pipe clamps
Anclajes para tubería
*(ahn-KLAH-hes pah-rah
too-beh-REE-ah)*

Pipe fitting
Accesorio de tubería
*(ahk-seh-soh-ryoh deh
too-beh-REE-ah)*

Pipe hanger
Colgante para tubería
(*kohl-GAHN-teh pah-rah
too-beh-REE-ah*)

Pipe schedule
Tabla de tubería
(*TAH-blah deh
too-beh-REE-ah*)

Pipe test
Tubo de prueba
(*TOO-boh deh proo-EH-bah*)

Pipe thread connection
Conexión roscada
(*koh-nek-SYON
rohs-KAH-dah*)

Pipe, overflow
Tubería de sobrellenado
(*too-beh-REE-ah deh
soh-breh-jeh-NAH-doh*)

Piping layout
Tendido de tubería
(*tehn-DEE-doh deh
too-beh-REE-ah*)

Pitch
Pendiente
(*pehn-DYEN-teh*)

Pitot tube
Tubo "Pitot"
(*TOO-boh pee-toht*)

Plan review/reviewer
Revisión/Revisor de planos
(*reh-vee-SYON/reh-vee-SOHR
deh PLAH-nohs*)

Plank
Tablón
(*tah-BLON*)

Planking
Entablonado
(*ehn-tah-bloh-NAH-doh*)
Tablones
(*tah-BLOH-nehs*)

Plaster
Azotado
(*ah-soh-TAH-doh*)
Jaharro
(*hah-AH-rroh*)
Enjarre
(*ehn-HAH-rreh*)
Enlucido
(*ehn-loo-SEE-doh*)
Yeso
(*YEH-soh*)

Plaster backing
Soporte para forjados
(*soh-POHR-teh PAH-rah
fohr-HAH-dohs*)

Plastering
Revoque
(*reh-VOH-keh*)
Enlucido
(*ehn-loo-SEE-doh*)
Repello
(*reh-PEH-joh*)
Forjados
(*fohr-HAH-dohs*)

Plastic foam
Espuma de plástico
(*ehs-POO-mah deh
PLAH-stee-koh*)

Plastic insulator
Aislante plástico
(*ah-ee-SLAHN-teh
PLAH-stee-koh*)

P

Plate girder
Viga de alma llena
(*VEE-gah deh
AHL-mah JEH-nah*)

Plenum
Pleno
(*PLEH-noh*)
Cámara de distribución
de aire
(*KAH-mah-rah deh
dee-stree-boo-SYON deh
AH-ee-reh*)

Plug
Clavija
(*klah-VEE-hah*)
Enchufe
(*ehn-CHOO-feh*)

Plug fuse
Fusible de rosca
(*foo-SEE-bleh deh ROHS-kah*)
Tapón fusible
(*tah-POHN foo-SEE-bleh*)

Plumber
Plomero
(*ploh-MEH-roh*)

Plumbing
Instalaciones hidráulicas y
sanitarias
(*een-stahl-ah-SYON-ehs
ee-DRAH-oo-lee-kahs ee
sahn-ee-TAH-ree-ahs*)
Plomería
(*ploh-meh-REE-ah*)

Plumbing appliance
Mueble sanitario
(*MWEH-bleh
sah-nee-TAH-ree-oh*)

Plumbing fixture
Artefacto sanitario
(*ar-teh-FAK-toh
sah-nee-TAR-ee-oh*)

Plunger
Destapacaños
(*dehs-tah-pah-KAH-nyos*)
Sopapa
(*soh-PAH-pah*)
Desatascador
(*deh-sah-tah-skah-DHOR*)

Ply
Capa
(*KAH-pah*)

Plywood
Madera prensada
(*mah-DEH-rah
prehn-SAH-dah*)
Tableros de madera prensada
(*tah-BLEH-rohs deh
mah-DEH-rah
prehn-SAH-dah*)

Poles, Posts
Postes
(*POHS-tehs*)

Ponding
Estancamiento de agua
(*ehs-tahn-kah-MYEHN-toh
deh AH-gwah*)

Portable
Portátil
(*pohr-TAH-teel*)

Pounds per square inch (PSI)
Libras por pulgadas cuadradas
(LEE-brahs pohr
pool-GAH-dahs
kwah-DRAH-dahs)

Pour coat
Capa de colada
(KAH-pah deh koh-LAH-dah)
Capa de vaciado
(KAH-pah deh
vah-SYAH-doh)

Powder driven
Accionado por pólvora
(ahk-SYO-nah-doh pohr
POHL-voh-rah)

Power doors
Puertas mecánicas
(PWEHR-tahs
meh-KAH-nee-kahs)

Power strip
Zapatilla eléctrica
(sah-pah-TEE-jah
eh-LEHK-tree-kah)

Power supply
Fuente de alimentación
(FWEHN-teh deh
ah-lee-mehn-ta-SYON)

Preaction system
Sistema de preacción, acción
previa
(sees-TEH-mah deh
preh-ah-SYON, ah-SYON
PREH-vee-ah)

Premises
Local
(loh-KAHL)
Sitio
(SEE-tee-oh)

Press box
Palco de prensa
(PAHL-koh deh PREHN-sah)

Pressure
Presión
(preh-SYON)

Pressure operated switch
Dispositivo de presión
(dees-po-see-TEE-voh
deh preh-SYON)

Prestressed concrete
Hormigón preesforzado
(ohr-mee-GOHN
preh-ehs-fohr-SAH-doh)
Hormigón precargado
(ohr-mee-GOHN
preh-kahr-GAH-doh)
Hormigón precomprimido
(ohr-mee-GOHN
preh-kohm-pree-MEE-doh)
Hormigón prefatigado
(ohr-mee-GOHN
preh-fah-tee-GAH-doh)

Primed
Imprimado
(eem-pree-MAH-doh)

Primer
Imprimador
(eem-pree-mah-DOHR)

Priming chamber
Cámara de cebado
(KAH-mah-rah deh
seh-BAH-doh)

P

Private
Privado
(*pree-VAH-doh*)

Professional engineer
Ingeniero licenciado
(*een-heh-NYEH-roh
lee-sehn-SYAH-doh*)

Property
Propiedad
(*proh-pyeh-DAHD*)
Parcela
(*par-SEH-lah*)

Property line
Línea de propiedad
(*LEE-neh-ah deh
proh-pyeh-DAHD*)
Lindero
(*leen-DEH-roh*)

Proportion
Proporción
(*proh-pohr-SYON*)
Proporcionalidad
(*proh-pohr-syoh-nah-
lee-DAHD*)
Dimensionar
(*dee-mehn-syoh-NAHR*)
Determinar las dimensiones
(*deh-tehr-mee-NAHR lahs
dee-meh-SYOH-nehs*)

Proportioned
Dimensionado
(*dee-mehn-syoh-NAH-doh*)

Provision/Proviso
Disposición
(*dee-spoh-see-SYON*)
Estipulación
(*ehs-tee-poo-lah-SYON*)

Public main
Red de abastecimiento público
(*rhed deh
ah-bahs-teh-see-MYEHN-toh
POO-blee-koh*)

Public safety
Seguridad pública
(*seh-goo-ree-DAHD
POO-blee-kah*)
Protección al público
(*proh-tehk-SYON ahl
POO-blee-koh*)

Public way
Vía pública
(*VEE-ah POO-blee-kah*)

Public welfare
Bienestar público
(*byehn-ehs-TAHR
POO-blee-koh*)

Pull station
Pulsador de alarma
(*pool-sah-DOHR deh
a-LAHR-mah*)

Pump
Bomba
(*BOHM-bah*)

Push-rod
Varilla de empuje
(*vah-REE-jah deh
ehm-poo-heh*)

Putty coat
Enlucido
(*ehn-loo-SEE-doh*)

Q

Queen post
Columna
(koh-LOOM-nah)

Quicklime
Cal viva
(KAHL vee-vah)

Quoin
Piedra angular
(PYEH-drah ahn-goo-LAHR)
Cuña
(KOO-nyah)

Quota
Cuota
(kwoh-tah)

R

Rabbet
> Muesca
> *(MWEHS-kah)*
> Ranura
> *(rah-NOO-rah)*

Raceways
> Conducto eléctrico
> *(kohn-DOOK-toh
> eh-LEHK-tree-koh)*

Rack
> Cremallera
> *(krehm-ah-JEH-rah)*
> Tarima
> *(tah-REE-mah)*

Rack storage
> Almacenamiento en estantes
> *(ahl-mah-sehn-ah-MYEHN-
> toh ehn eh-STAHN-tehs)*

Rafter
> Cabrio
> *(KAH-bree-oh)*
> Cabio
> *(KAH-bee-oh)*

Rail
> Cremallera
> *(krehm-ah-JEH-rah)*
> Baranda
> *(bah-RAHN-dah)*
> Barandilla
> *(bah-rahn-DEE-jah)*

Railing
> Baranda
> *(bah-RAHN-dah)*
> Barra
> *(BAH-rrah)*
> Carril
> *(kah-RREEL)*

Range poweroutlet
> Tomacorriente/Enchufe para
> estufa
> *(toh-mah-koh-RRYEHN-teh/
> ehn-CHOO-feh PAH-rah
> ehs-TOO-fah)*

Ratchet
> Trinquete
> *(treen-KEH-teh)*

Rate
> Relación
> *(reh-lah-SYON)*
> Proporción
> *(proh-pohr-SYON)*
> Razón
> *(rah-SOHN)*
> Caudal
> *(kah-oo-DAHL)*

Rate of heat release
> Emisión de calor
> *(eh-mee-SYON
> deh kah-LOHR)*

Rate of rise
> Velocidad de incremento
> *(veh-loh-see-DAHD
> deh een-kreh-MEHN-toh)*

R

Rating
Clasificación
(klah-see-fee-kah-SYON)

Ratio
Relación
(reh-lah-SYON)
Cociente
(koh-SYEHN-teh)
Razón
(rrah-SON)
Coeficiente
(koh-eh-fee-SYEHN-teh)

Rebar
Barra de refuerzo
*(BAH-rrah de
reh-FWEHR-soh)*
Varilla
(vah-REE-jah)

Recessed
Empotrado
(ehm-poh-TRAH-doh)

Redwood
Madera de secoya
*(mah-DEH-rah
deh seh-KOH-yah)*

Reformatory
Reformatorio
(reh-fohr-mah-TOH-ree-oh)

Refuge area
Área de refugio
*(AH-reh-ah deh
reh-FOO-hee-oh)*

Region
Región
(reh-hee-ONH)
Tramo
(TRAH-moh)

Register (baseboard/ceiling/wall)
Rejilla (de piso/techo/pared)
*(reh-HEE-jah (deh PEE-soh/
TEH-cho/pa-REHD))*

Reglet
Regleta
(reh-GLEH-tah)

Regulator
Regulador
(reh-goo-lah-DOHR)

Reinforced masonry
Mampostería reforzada
*(mahm-pohs-teh-REE-ah
reh-fohr-SAH-dah)*

Reinforcement
Refuerzo
(reh-FWEHR-soh)
Armadura
(ar-mah-DOO-rah)

Rekindle
Reanimar fuego
(rreh-ah-nee-mahr FWEH-go)

Release
Descarga
(dehs-KAHR-gah)
Liberación
(lee-beh-rah-SYON)
Desenganchador
(deh-sehn-gahn-chah-DOHR)
Desenganchar
(deh-sehn-gahn-CHAR)
Disparador
(dees-pah-rah-DOHR)

Reliability
Fiabilidad
(fyah-bee-lee-DAHD)

Relief valve
Válvula de alivio
(*VAHL-voo-lah deh
ah-LEE-vee-oh*)
Llave de alivio
(*JAH-veh deh ah-LEE-vee-oh*)

Removal
Eliminación
(*eh-lee-mee-nah-SYON*)
Remoción
(*reh-moh-SYON*)

Repair
Reparación
(*reh-par-ah-SYON*)

Reports
Informes
(*een-FOR-mehs*)
Reportes
(*reh-POHR-tehs*)

Reservoir
Depósito
(*dehs-POH-see-toh*)

Reset
Volver a graduar
(*vohl-VEHR ah grah-DWAHR*)

Reshores
Puntales de refuerzo
(*poon-TAH-lehs deh
reh-FWEHR-soh*)

Response Time Index (RTI)
Indice de tiempo de respuesta
(ITR)
(*een-DEE-cheh deh
tee EHM-poh deh
rehs-PWES-tah*)

Residence
Residencia
(*reh-see-DEHN-syah*)

Restraints
Sujetadores
(*soo-heh-tah-DOH-rehs*)
Fijadores
(*fee-hah-DOH-rehs*)

Restroom
Baño
(*BAH-nyoh*)
Sanitario
(*sah-nee-TAH-ree-oh*)

Retrofitting
Retroajuste
(*reh-troh-ah-HOOS-teh*)

Return bend vent pipe
Tubo de ventilación con codo
doble
(*TOO-boh deh
vehn-tee-lah-SYON kohn
KOH-doh DOH-bleh*)

Return lip
Remate de borde
(*reh-MAH-teh deh BOR-deh*)

Revolving door
Puerta giratoria
(*PWEHR-tah
hee-rah-TOH-ree-ah*)

Rib
Costilla
(*koh-STEE-jah*)

R

Ridge
Cresta
(KREH-stah)
Cumbrera
(koom-BREH-rah)

Ridge board
Tabla de cumbrera
*(TAH-blah deh
koom-BREH-rah)*

Ridge tile
Tejas para cumbrera
*(TEH-hahs PAH-rah
koom-BREH-rah)*

Riffled
Ranurado
(rah-noo-RAH-doh)
Acanalada
(ah-kahn-ah-LAH-dah)

Rim
Borde
(BOR-deh)

Ring shank nail
Clavos con fuste corrugado
*(KLAH-vohs kohn
FOO-steh koh-rroo-GAH-doh)*

Ringed shanks
Varillas en aro
(vah-REE-jahs ehn AR-oh)

Riser (pipe)
Tubo vertical
(TOO-boh vehr-tee-KAHL)
Tubería ascendente
*(too-beh-REE-ah
ah-sehn-DEHN-teh)*

Riser (stair)
Contrahuella
(kohn-trah-WEH-jah)

Riser nipple
Niple montante
(NEE-pleh mon-TAHN-teh)

Rivet
Remache
(reh-MAH-cheh)

Rod-coupling
Acoplamiento para barras
varillas
*(ah-koh-plah-MYEHN-toh
pah-rah BAH-rahs
(vah-REE-jahs))*

Rock
Roca
(ROH-kah)
Piedra
(PYEH-drah)

Roof
Techo
(TEH-choh)

Roof covering
Revestimiento de techo
*(reh-veh-stee-MYEHN-toh
deh TEH-choh)*
Cubierta de azotea
*(koo-BYEHR-tah
deh ah-soh-TEH-ah)*
Cubierta de techo
*(koo-BYEHR-tah
deh TEH-choh)*

Roof deck
Cubierta de techo
*(koo-BYEHR-tah deh
TEH-choh)*

Roof drain
Desagüe de techo
*(deh-SAH-gweh
deh TEH-choh)*

Roof, flat
Techo plano
(TEH-choh PLAH-noh)

Roof sheating
Entarimado de tejado
*(ehn-tah-ree-MAH-doh
deh teh-HAH-doh)*

Roof, sloped
Techo en pendiente
*(TEH-choh ehn
pehn-DYEHN-teh)*

Roof tile
Teja
(TEH-ha)

Roofing
Techado
(teh-CHAH-doh)

Roofing square
Cuadro de cubierta de techo
*(KWAH-droh deh
koo-bee-EHR-tah
deh TEH-choh)*

Room
Cuarto
(KWAR-toh)
Sala
(SAH-lah)
Habitación
(ah-bee-tah-SYON)

Room, assembly
Sala
(SAH-lah)
Salón
(sah-LOHN)
Cuarto de asambleas
*(KWAR-toh deh
ah-sahm-BLEH-ahs)*

Rough-in
Instalación en obra
Negra/gruesa
*(een-stah-lah-SYON
ehn OH-brah NEH-grah/
GROO-eh-sah)*

Row
Fila
(FEE-lah)

Rubbish
Basura
(bah-SOO-rah)

Rubble
Escombro
(ehs-KOM-broh)

Runners
Largueros
(lar-GWUEH-rohs)

S

Safety glazing
Vidriado de seguridad
(*vee-dree-AH-do deh
seh-goo-ree-DAHD*)

Safety
Seguridad industrial
(*seh-goo-ree-DAHD
een-doos-TREE-ahl*)

Sand
Arena
(*ah-REH-nah*)

Sandstone
Areniscas
(*ah-reh-NEES-kahs*)
Piedra arenisca
(*PYEH-drah
ah-reh-NEES-kah*)

Sanitation
Higiene
(*ee-hee-EH-neh*)

Sawn timber
Maderos aserrados
(*mah-DEH-rohs
ah-seh-RRAH-dohs*)

Sawtooth
Diente de sierra
(*DYEHN-teh deh SYEH-rrah*)

Scaffold
Andamio
(*ahn-DAH-myoh*)

Scaffolding
Andamiaje
(*ahn-dah-MYAH-heh*)

Schedule
Horario
(*oh-RAH-ree-oh*)

Scope
Alcance
(*ahl-KAHN-seh*)

Scouring
Rozamiento
(*roh-sah-MYEHN-toh*)

Screw
Tornillo
(*tohr-NEE-joh*)
Tornillo pasante
(*tohr-NEE-joh pa-SAHN-teh*)

Screw connector
Conector con tornillo
(*koh-nehk-TOHR kohn
tohr-NEE-joh*)

Screwed fitting
Acoplamiento roscado
(*ah-koh-plah-MYEHN-toh
roh-SKAH-doh*)

Sealants
Selladores
(*seh-jah-DOH-rehs*)

Seasoned wood
Madera estacionada
(*mah-DEH-rah
ehs-tah-syoh-NAH-dah*)

S

Security
Seguridad física
(*seh-goo-ree-DAHD*
FEE-see-kah)

Self-closing
Autocierre
(*ah-oo-toh-SYEH-rreh*)

Self-closing device
Dispositivo autocerrante
(*dee-spoh-see-TEE-voh*
ah-oo-toh-seh-RRAHN-teh)
Dispositivo de cierre
mecanizado
(*dee-spoh-see-TEE-voh*
deh SYEH-rreh
meh-KAH-nee-zah-doh)

Self-closing faucet
Grifo de cierre automático
(*GREE-foh deh SYEH-rreh*
ah-oo-toh-MAH-tee-koh)

Self-drilling screws
Tornillos autoperforantes
(*tohr-NEE-johs ah-oo-toh-*
pehr-foh-RAHN-tehs)

Self-ignition
Auto-ignición
(*ah-oo-toh-ee-gnee-SYON*)

Self-luminous
Autoluminoso
(*ah-oo-toh-loo-mee-NOH-soh*)

Self-tapping screws
Tornillos autorroscantes
(*tohr-NEE-johs*
ah-oo-toh-rrohs-KAHN-tehs)

Sensitizer
Sensibilizador
(*sehn-see-bee-lee-sah-DOHR*)

Set out
Resaltar
(*reh-sahl-TAHR*)

Setback
Retiro
(*reh-TEE-roh*)

Sewage
Aguas negras
(*AH-gwahs NEH-grahs*)
Cloacas
(*KLOAH-kahs*)

Sewage ejector
Eyector de aguas negras
(*eh-jehk-TOHR deh*
AH-gwahs NEH-grahs)

Sewer
Cloaca
(*KLOAH-kah*)
Alcantarilla
(*ahl-kahn-tah-REE-jah*)

Shaft
Recinto
(*reh-SEEN-toh*)

Shake, wood
Teja de madera
(*TEH-hah deh mah-DEH-rah*)
Ripia
(*REE-pee-ah*)

Shear wall
Muro cortante
(*MOO-roh kor-TAHN-teh*)
Muro de corte
(*MOO-roh deh KOR-teh*)
Muro sismorresistente
(*MOO-roh sees-moh-rreh-
sees-TEHN-teh*)

Sheathing
Entablado
(*ehn-tah-BLAH-doh*)

Sheathing edges
Bordes del entablado
(*BOHR-dehs dehl
ehn-tah-BLAH-doh*)

Sheet
Pliego
(*PLYEH-goh*)
Chapa
(*CHAH-pah*)
Plancha
(*PLAHN-chah*)
Lámina
(*LAH-mee-nah*)
Tablestacado
(*tah-bleh-stah-KAH-doh*)

Sheet metal
Lámina/Chapa metálica
(*LAH-mee-nah/CHAH-pah
meh-TAH-lee-kah*)
Laminado
(*lah-mee-NAH-doh*)

Sheeting
Laminado
(*lah-mee-NAH-doh*)
Lámina
(*LAH-mee-nah*)

Shelf
Repisa
(*reh-PEE-sah*)

Shell
Cáscara
(*KAHS-kah-rah*)
Cubierta
(*koo-BYEHR-tah*)

Shingle
Teja
(*TEH-jah*)
Tejamanil
(*teh-hah-mah-NEEL*)

Shingle, asphalt
Teja de asfalto
(*TEH-ha deh as-FHAL-to*)

Shingle, wood
Ripia
(*REE-pee-ah*)

Shiplap
Traslape
(*trah-SLAH-peh*)
Rebajo a media madera
(*reh-BAH-hoh ah MEH-dyah
mah-DEH-rah*)

Shop
Taller
(*tah-JEHR*)

Shored/Unshored construction
Construcción apuntalada/no
apuntalada
(*kohn-strook-SYON
ah-poon-tah-LAH-dah/noh
ah-poon-tah-LAH-dah*)

77

S

Shotcrete
Hormigón proyectado
(*ohr-mee-GOHN
proh-jehk-TAH-doh*)
Gunita
(*goo-NEE-tah*)

Shotcrete structures
Estructura de hormigón
proyectado
(*ehs-trook-TOO-rah
deh ohr-mee-GOHN
proh-jehk-TAH-doh*)
Estructuras de gunita
(*ehs-trook-TOO-rahs
deh goo-NEE-tah*)

Show window
Vitrina
(*vee-TREE-nah*)

Showcase
Armario de exhibición
(*ar-MAH-ree-oh deh
ehk-see-bee-SYON*)

Shower door
Mampara de ducha
(*mahm-PAH-rah deh
DOO-chah*)

Shower stall
Ducha
(*DOO-chah*)
Regadera
(*reh-gah-DEH-rah*)
Cuarto de regadera
(*KWAR-toh deh
reh-gah-DEH-rah*)

Showerhead
Regadera
(*reh-gah-DEH-rah*)

Shrinkage
Contracción
(*kohn-trahk-SYON*)
Encogimiento
(*ehn-koh-hee-MYEN-toh*)
Reducción
(*reh-dook-SYON*)

Shut off
Cerrar
(*seh-RAHR*)

Shutoff valves
Válvulas de cierre
(*VAHL-voo-lahs deh
SYEH-rreh*)

Side-hinged door
Puerta con bisagras laterales
(*PWEHR-tah kohn
bee-SAH-grahs
lah-teh-RAH-lehs*)

Sidewalk
Acera
(*ah-SEH-rah*)
Vereda
(*veh-REH-dah*)
Banqueta
(*bahn-keh-tah*)

Sill
Soporte
(*soh-POHR-teh*)

Sill cock
Grifo de manguera
(*GREE-foh deh
mahn-GUEH-rah*)

Sill plate
Solera inferior
(soh-LEH-rah een-feh-RYOR)

Single-family dwelling
Vivienda unifamiliar
(vee-VYEN-dah
oo-nee-fah-mee-LYAR)

Single pole breaker
Interruptor automático
unipolar
(een-teh-rroop-TOHR
ah-oo-toh-MAH-tee-koh
oo-nee-poh-LAHR)

Sink
Lavabo
(lah-VAH-boh)

Sink, kitchen
Fregadero
(freh-gah-DEH-roh)
Pileta de cocina
(pee-LEH-tah deh
koh-SEE-na)
Tarja de cocina
(TAR-hah deh koh-SEE-na)

Site
Sitio
(SEE-tee-oh)

Skylight
Tragaluz
(trah-gah-LOOS)
Claraboya
(klar-ah-BOH-yah)

Skyscraper
Rascacielos
(rahs-kah-SYEH-lohs)

Slab
Losa
(LOH-sah)

Slags
Escorias
(ehs-KOH-ree-ahs)

Slate shingle
Teja de pizarra
(TEH-hah deh pee-SAH-rrah)

Sleeper
Traviesa
(trah-VYEH-sah)
Durmiente
(door-MYEHN-teh)

Sleeve
Camisa
(kah-MEE-sah)
Manga
(MAHN-gah)

Sliding doors/windows
Puertas/ventanasdeslizantes/
corredizas
(PWEHR-tahs/vehn-TAH-nahs
deh-slee-SAHN-tehs/koh-rreh-
DEE-sahs)

Slope
Pendiente
(pehn-DYEHN-teh)
Talud
(tah-LOOD)
Declive
(deh-KLEE-veh)

Slump
Asentamiento
(ah-sehn-tah-MYEHN-toh)

S

Smoke
Humo
(OO-moh)

Smoke barrier
Barrera antihumo
(bah-RREH-rah
ahn-tee-OO-moh)

Smoke curtain
Cortina antihumo
(kor-TEE-nah
ahn-tee-OO-moh)

Smoke density
Densidad de humo
(dehn-see-DAHD
deh OO-moh)

Smoke detector
Sensor de humo
(sehn-SOHR deh OO-moh)
Detector de humo
(deh-tehk-TOHR
deh OO-moh)

Smoke exhaust
Extracción de humo
(ehks-trak-SYON
deh OO-moh)

Smoke exhaust system
Sistema de extracción de
humo
(see-STEH-mah
deh ehk-strak-SYON
deh OO-moh)

Smoke layer
Capa de humo
(kah-pah deh OO-moh)

Smoke tight
Impermeables al humo
(eem-pehr-meh-AH-blehs
ahl OO-moh)

Smoke-control zone
Zona de control de humo
(SOH-nah deh kohn-TROL
deh OO-moh)

Smoke-detection system
Sistema de detección de humo
(see-STEH-mah deh
deh-tehk-SYON deh OO-moh)

Snap disc
Disco de acción rápida
(DEES-koh deh ahk-SYON
RAH-pee-dahs)
Disco de disparo
(DEES-koh deh dees-PAH-roh)

Snap disc module
Disco de disparo
(DEES-koh deh dees-PAH-roh)

Snap switches
Interruptores de resorte
(een-teh-roop-TOH-rehs deh
reh-SOHR-teh)

Soffit
Sofito
(soh-FEE-toh)

Soft story
Piso blando
(PEE-soh BLAHN-doh)
Piso flexible
(PEE-soh flek-SEE-bleh)

Soil pipe
Tubo bajante de aguas negras
(*TOO-boh bah-HAHN-teh deh
AH-gwahs NEH-grahs*)

Soil stack
Bajante sanitaria
(*bah-HAHN-teh
sah-nee-TAH-ree-ah*)

Solder link
Enlace fusible
(*ehn-LAH-seh foo-SEE-bleh*)

Sole plate
Placa de base
(*PLAH-kah deh BAH-seh*)

Solenoid valve
Válvula solenoide
(*VAHL-voo-lah
soh-leh-NOY-deh*)

Spacing
Separación, distanciamiento
(*seh-pah-rah-SYON,
dees-tahn-syah-MYEHN-toh*)

Spalling
Astilladuras
(*ah-stee-jah-DOO-rahs*)

Span
Luz
(*loos*)
Vano
(*VAH-noh*)
Claro
(*KLAH-roh*)

Spandrel
Jácena exterior
(*HAH-seh-nah
ehk-steh-RYOHR*)
Tímpano
(*TEEM-pah-noh*)
Enjuta
(*ehn-HOO-tah*)
Muro de relleno
(*MOO-roh deh reh-JEH-noh*)

Spark arrester
Trampa para chispas
(*TRAHM-pah PAH-rah
CHEES-pahs*)

Speaker
Parlante
(*pahr-LAHN-teh*)

Special hazards
Peligros especiales
(*peh-LEE-grohs
eh-speh-SYAH-lehs*)

Spigot
Llave
(*JAH-veh*)
Grifo
(*GREE-foh*)
Canilla
(*kah-NEE-jah*)
Espiga
(*ehs-PEE-gah*)

Spike
Clavo especial para madera
(*KLAH-voh eh-speh-SYAHL
PAH-rah mah-DEH-rah*)

Spiked
Clavado
(KLAH-vah-doh)

Spiral stairs
Escaleras de caracol
(ehs-kah-LEH-rahs deh kah-rah-KOHL)

Spirals
Espirales
(eh-spee-RAH-lehs)

Spire
Aguja
(ah-GOO-hah)

Splice
Empalme
(ehm-PAHL-meh)
Traslape
(trah-SLAH-peh)
Junta
(HOON-tah)
Unión
(oon-YOHN)

Splice plates
Planchas de empalme
(PLAHN-chas deh ehm-PAHL-meh)

Splined
Acanalado
(ah-kah-nah-LAH-doh)

Spot mopped
Adherido en secciones
(ah-deh-REE-doh ehn sehk-SYOH-nehs)

Spring
Resorte
(reh-SOHR-teh)

Sprinkler
Rociador
(roh-see-ah-DOHR)

Sprinkler head
Boquilla de rociador
(boh-KEE-jah deh roh-see-ah-DOHR)
Cabeza del rociador
(kah-BEH-sah dehl roh-syah-DOHR)

Sprinkler systems (automatic)
Sistemas de rociadores (automáticos)
(see-STEH-mahs deh roh-SYAH-dohrehs (ah-oo-toh-MAH-tee-kohs))

Sprinkler riser
Tubería ascendente a los rociadores
(too-beh-REE-ah roh-syah-DOHR-ehs)

Sprinkler, bulb
Rociador de ampolla
(roh-syah-DOHR deh ahm-POH-jah)

Sprinkler, concealed
Rociador oculto
(roh-syah-DOHR)

Sprinkler, cover plate assembly
Tapa de rociador en forma de disco
(tah-PAH deh roh-syah-DOHR ehn for-MAH deh DEES-koh)

Sprinkler, dry pendent
Rociador colgante de tubería
seca
(*roh-syah-DOHR*
kohl-GAHN-teh deh
too-beh-REE-ah SEH-kah)

**Sprinkler, early suppression fast
response (ESFR)**
Rociador de supresión
temprana y respuesta rápida
(*roh-syah-DOHR deh*
soo-preh-SYON
tehm-PRAH-nah
ee rehs-PWES-tah
RRAH-pee-dah)

Sprinkler, extended coverage
Rociador de cobertura
extendida
(*roh-syah-DOHR deh*
koh-behr-TOO-rah
eks-tehn-DEE-dah)

Sprinkler, fast response
Rociador de respuesta rápida
(*roh-syah-DOHR*
deh reh-PWES-tah
RRAH-pee-dah)

Sprinkler, flush type
Rociador de techo para
empotrar
(*roh-sya-DOHR deh*
TEH-choh par-rah
ehm-poh-TRARH)
Rociador empotrado
(*roh-syah-DOHR*
ehm-poh-TRAH-doh)

Sprinkler, frangible bulb style
Rociador tipo ampolla frágil
(*roh-syah-DOHR TEE-poh*
ahm-POH-jah FRAH-heel)

Sprinkler, in-rack
Rociador en estanterías
(*roh-syah-DOHR ehn*
ehs-tahn-teh-REE-ahs)

Sprinkler, intermediate level
Rociador de nivel intermedio,
de pantalla
(*roh-syah-DOHR deh nee-*
VEHL een-tehr-MEH-dyo, deh
pahn-TAH-jah)

Sprinkler, large drop
Rociador de gota gorda
(*roh-syah-DOHR deh HO-tah*
HOR-dah)

Sprinkler, listed
Rociador automático
aprobado y certificado
(*roh-syah-DOHR ah-oo-toh-*
MAH-tee-koh ah-proh-BAH-
do ee sehr-tee-fee-KAH-do)

Sprinkler, on-off
Rociador de apertura y cierre
automático
(*roh-syah-DOHR deh*
ah-pehr-too-rah ee SYEH-rreh
ah-oo-toh-MAH-tee-koh)

Sprinkler, open
Rociador abierto sin elemento
activo
(*roh-syah-DOHR*
ah-BYER-toh seen
eh-leh-MEHN-toh
AHK-tee-voh)

Sprinkler, pendent
Rociador colgante
(*roh-syah-DOHR kohl-GAHN-teh*)

Sprinkler, quick response
Rociador de respuesta ultra rápida
(*roh-syah-DOHR deh rehs-PWES-tah OOL-trah RAH-pee-doh*)

Sprinkler, recessed
Rociador empotrado
(*roh-syah-DOHR ehm-poh-TRAH-doh*)

Sprinkler, sidewall
Rociador de pared
(*roh-syah-DOHR deh pah-RHED*)

Sprinkler, standard
Rociador normalizado
(*roh-syah-DOHR nohr-mah-lee-SAH-doh*)

Sprinkler, standard spray
Rociador de rocío normalizado
(*roh-syah-DOHR deh roh-SYOH nohr-mah-lee-SAH-doh*)

Sprinkler, upright
Rociador montante
(*roh-syah-DOHR mohn-TAHN-teh*)

Square drive
Herramienta cuadrada
(*eh-rah-MYEN-tah KWA-drah-dah*)

Stack
Tubería vertical/bajante
(*too-beh-REE-ah vehr-tee-KAHL/bah-HAHN-teh*)
Tubo vertical de evacuación
(*TOO-boh vehr-tee-KAHL deh eh-vah-kwah-SYON*)

Stack vent
Respiradero de bajante
(*reh-spee-rah-DEH-roh deh bah-HAHN-teh*)
Tubería bajante de respiradero
(*too-beh-REE-ah bah-HAHN-teh deh reh-spee-rah-DEH-roh*)

Stainless steel
Acero inoxidable
(*ah-SEH-roh ee-nok-see-DAH-bleh*)

Stair, landing
Rellano
(*rreh-JAH-noh*)

Stair, rise
Contrahuella
(*kohn-trah-WEH-jah*)

Stair, tread
Huella
(*WEH-jah*)

Stairs
Escaleras
(*ehs-kah-LEH-rahs*)

Stairway
Escalera
(ehs-kah-LEH-rah)

Stairway, enclosed
Recinto de escaleras
*(reh-SEEN-toh deh
ehs-kah-LEH-rahs)*

Stairwells
Recinto de escaleras
*(reh-SEEN-toh deh
ehs-kah-LEH-rahs)*

Standpipe
Columna hidrante
*(koh-LOOM-nah
ee-DRAHN-teh)*
Tubería vertical
*(too-beh-REE-ah
vehr-tee-KAHL)*
Columna de agua
*(koh-LOOM-nah deh
AH-gwah)*

Standpipe hose conexion
Toma fija de agua para
manguera
*(TOH-mah fee-HA
deh AH-gwah pah-rah
mahn-GEH-rah)*

Standpipe system
Sistema de columna hidrante
*(sees-TEH-mah deh
koh-LOOM-nah
hee-DRAHN-teh)*

Stands (reviewing)
Estrados
(eh-STRAH-dohs)
Tribunas
(tree-BOO-nah)
Gradas
(GRAH-dahs)

Steam
Vapor
(vah-POHR)

Steel
Acero
(ah-SEH-roh)

Steel framing
Estructura en/de acero
*(eh-strook-TOO-rah ehn/
deh ah-SEH-roh)*

Steel studs
Montantes de acero
*(mohn-TAHN-tehs
deh ah-SEH-roh)*

Steeple
Campanario
(kahm-pah-NAH-ree-oh)

Steps
Escalones
(ehs-kah-LOH-nehs)
Peldaños
(pehl-DAH-nyohs)

Sterilizer
Esterilizador
(eh-steh-ree-lee-sah-DOHR)

S

Stiffener
Pieza de refuerzo
*(PYEH-sah deh
reh-foo-EHR-soh)*
Refuerzo
(reh-foo-EHR-soh)
Atiesador
(ah-tee-eh-sah-DOH-rehs)

Stiffness
Rigidez
(ree-he-DEHS)

Stirrups
Estribos
(eh-STREE-bohs)

Stone
Piedra
(PYEH-drah)
Roca
(ROH-kah)

Stops (door frame)
Topes
(TOH-pehs)

Storage room
Cuarto de almacenamiento
*(KWAR-toh deh ahl-mah-seh-
nah-MYEHN-toh)*
Bodega
(boh-DEH-gah)
Depósito
(deh-POH-see-toh)

Store
Tienda
(TYEHN-dah)

Storm drain
Alcantarilla
(ahl-kahn-tar-EE-jah)

Story
Piso
(PEE-soh)

Strap
Fleje
(FLEH-heh)
Cincho
(SEEN-choh)

Strapping
Flejes
(FLEH-hehs)

Strainer
Filtro
(FEEHL-troh)

Street main
Conexión urbana
*(koh-nek-SYON
oohr-BAH-nah)*

Stress
Esfuerzo
(ehs-foo-EHR-soh)

Strip
Listón
(lee-STON)

Stripping
Tiras metálicas
*(TEE-rahs
meh-TAH-lee-kahs)*

Structure
Estructura
(eh-strook-TOO-rah)

Strobe light
Luz estroboscópica
*(loos eh-stroh-boh-SKOH-
pee-kah)*

Strut
Varilla de sujeción
(*vah-REE-jah deh
soo-heh-SYON*)
Puntal
(*poon-TAHL*)

Stucco
Revoque
(*reh-VOH-keh*)
Enlucido
(*ehn-loo-SEE-doh*)
Estuco
(*ehs-TOO-koh*)

Stud
Montante
(*mohn-TAHN-teh*)
Parante
(*par-AHN-teh*)
Barrote
(*ba-RROH-teh*)

Stud anchors
Barras de anclaje
(*BAH-rrahs deh
ahn-KLAH-heh*)

Stud bearing wall
Muro portante con montante
(*MOO-roh pohr-TAHN-teh
kohn mohn-TAHN-teh*)

Stud walls
Muros con montantes
(*MOO-rohs kohn
mohn-TAHN-tehs*)
Paredes de barrotes
(*pah-REH-dehs deh
bah-RROH-tehs*).

Stud finder
Buscador de montantes
(*boos-kah-DOHR deh
mohn-TAHN-tehs*)

Subfloor
Contrapiso
(*kohn-trah-PEE-soh*)
Bajopiso
(*bah-ho-PEE-soh*)
Subpiso
(*soob-PEE-soh*)

Subroof
Base de techo
(*BAH-seh deh TEH-choh*)

Substandard
Inferior a lo normal
(*een feh-RYOR ah loh
nohr-MAHL*)

Substrate
Substrato
(*soob-STRAH-toh*)

Suite (hotel)
Suite
(*soo-EE-teh*)

Sump
Sumidero
(*soo-mee-DEH-roh*)

Sump pump
Bomba de sumidero
(*BOHM-bah deh
soo-mee-DEH-roh*)

Sump vent
Respiradero de sumidero
(*reh-spee-rah-DEH-roh deh
soo-mee-DEH-roh*)

Superintendent
Superintendente
(*soo-pehr-een-tehn-DEHN-teh*)

Supervisor
Supervisor
(*soo-pehr-vee-SOHR*)
Inspector
(*eens-pek-TOHR*)

Supervisory switch
Interruptor de supervisión
(*een-TEH-roop-tohr deh soo-pehr-vee-SYON*)

Supply piping
Tubería de alimentación
(*too-beh-REE-ah deh ah-lee-mehn-tah-SYON*)

Support
Apoyo
(*ah-POH-joh*)
Soporte
(*soh-POHR-teh*)

Support (v)
Resistir
(*reh-see-STEER*)
Sostener
(*sohs-teh-NEHR*)
Soportar
(*soh-pohr-TAR*)

Suppressor
Amortiguador
(*ah-mohr-tee-gwah-DOHR*)

Suspended ceiling
Falso plafón
(*fahl-soh plah-FOHN*)
Cielorraso suspendido
(*syeh-loh-RRAH-soh soos-pehn-DEE-doh*)

Swelling
Expansión
(*ehk-spahn-SYON*)
Hinchazón
(*heen-chah-SOHN*)

Swimming pool
Piscina (de natación)
(*pee-SEE-nah (deh nah-tah-SYON)*)
Alberca
(*ahl-BEHR-kah*)

Swinging door
Puerta pivotante
(*PWEHR-tah pee-voh-TAHN-teh*)

Switch
Interruptor
(*een-teh-rroop-TOHR*)
Apagador
(*ah-pah-gah-DOHR*)

Switch plate
Placa del interruptor
(*PLAH-kah deh een-teh-rroop-TOHR*)

T

Tag
Etiqueta
(*eh-tee-KEH-tah*)

Tag closed cup tester
Prueba de copa cerrada
(*proo-EH-ba deh KOH-pah
seh-RAH-doh*)

Tank, conic roof
Tanque de techo cónico
(*TAHN-keh deh TEH-choh
KOH-nee-koh*)

Tank, floating roof
Tanque de techo suspendido
(*TAHN-keh deh TEH-koh
soos-pen-DEE-doh*)

Tank, gravity
Deposito por gravedad
(*deh-POH-see-toh pohr
grah-veh-DAHD*)

Tank, pressure
Depósito a presión
(*deh-POH-see-toh ah
preh-SYON*)

Tank, underground
Depósito enterrado
(*deh-POH-see-toh
ehn-teh-RAH-doh*)

Taping compound
Pasta de muro
(*PAHS tah deh MOO-roh*)

Tar
Alquitrán
(*ahl-kee-TRAHN*)
Brea
(*BREH-ah*)
Chapopote
(*chah-poh-POH-teh*)

Tar paper
Papel de brea
(*pah-PEHL de BREH-ah*)

Tarp
Lona
(*LOH-nah*)

TEE
T, injerto
(*T, een-HEHR-toh*)

Technician
Técnico
(*TEHK-nee-koh*)

Temperature rating
Clasificación por temperatura
(*kla-see-fee-kah-SYON pohr
tehm-peh-rah-TOO-rah*)

Templates
Plantillas
(*plahn-TEE-jahs*)

Temporary
Provisional
(*proh-vee-syoh-NAHL*)

T

Tenant
Inquilino
(*een-kee-LEE-noh*)

Tendons
Tendones
(*tehn-DOH-nehs*)
Tensores
(*tehn-SOH-rehs*)

Tension
Tensión
(*tehn-SYON*)

Terminal
Terminal
(*tehr-mee-NAL*)

Termite
Termita
(*tehr-MEE-tah*)

Test
Ensayo
(*ehn-SAH-joh*)
Prueba
(*PRWEH-bah*)
Someter a ensayo/prueba
(*soh-meh-TEHR
ahehn-SAH-joh/PRWEH-bah*)

Test apparatus
Aparato de ensayo
(*ah-par-AH-toh deh
ehn-SAH-joh*)
Aparato de prueba
(*ah-par-AH-toh deh
PRWEH-bah*)

Texture
Textura
(*tehks-TOO-rah*)

Thawing
Descongelación
(*dehs-kohn-heh-lah-SYON*)

Thermal lag
Retardo térmico
(*reh-TAHR-doh tehr-mee-koh*)

Thermocouple
Termopar
(*tehr-moh-PAHR*)

Thermosensitive device
Dispositivo termosensible
(*dees-po-see-TEE-voh
tehr-moh-sehn-SEE-bleh*)

Thread
Hilo
(*EE-loh*)

Threshold
Umbral
(*oom-BRAHL*)

Thrust blocks
Puntal de empuje
(*poon-TAHL deh
ehm-POO-heh*)

Tie
Amarra
(*ah-MAH-rrah*)
Ligadura
(*lee-gah-DOO-rah*)
Tirante
(*tee-RAHN-teh*)

Tier
Hilera
(*ee-LEH-rah*)

Tile
Teja
(*TEH-hah*)

Tile, floor
Baldosas
(*bahl-DOH-sahs*)

Tile, masonry
Ladrillo cerámico
(*lah-dree-joh
seh-RAH-mee-koh*)

Time relay
Relé temporizador
(*reh-LEH
tehm-poh-ree-sah-DOHR*)

Timber
Maderos
(*mah-DEH-rohs*)
Madera de construcción
(*mah-DEH-rah deh
kohn-strook-SYON*)

Tin
Lata
(*LAH-tah*)
Chapa
(*CHAH-pah*)
Estaño
(*ehs-TAH-nyoh*)

Toeboard
Tabla de pie
(*TAH-blah deh PYEH*)

Toenail
Clavo oblicuo
(*KLAH-voh oh-BLEE-koo-oh*)

Toilet
Inodoro
(*ee-noh-DOH-roh*)
Sanitario
(*sah-nee-TAH-ree-oh*)
Excusado
(*ehk-skoo-SAH-doh*)
Retrete
(*reh-TREH-teh*)

Toggle effect
Efecto de golpe de ariete
(*eh-FEHK-toh deh HOHL-peh
deh ah-ree-EH-teh*)

Tongue and groove
Machihembrado
(*mah-chee-ehm-BRAH-doh*)

Tools
Herramientas
(*eh-rrah-MYEHN-tahs*)

Torch
Antorcha
(*ahn-TOHR-chah*)

Tracer
Alambre testigo
(*ah-LAHM-breh teh-stee-goh*)
Alambre rastreador
(*ah-LAHM-breh
rah-streh-ah-dohr*)

Trade-off
Concesión
(*kohn-seh-SYON*)

T

Trap
Sifón
(see-FOHN)
Trampa hidráulica
*(TRAHM-pah
hee-DRAH-oo-lee-kah)*

Trap seal
Sello de trampa hidráulica
*(SEH-joh deh TRAHM-pah
hee-DRAH-oo-lee-kah)*

Trapped drain pipe
Tubería de drenaje entrapada
*(too-beh-REE-ah deh
dreh-NAH-heh
ehn-trah-PAH-dah)*

Travel distance
Distancia de desplazamiento/
recorrido
*(dees-TAHN-syah deh
dehs-plah-sah-MYEN-toh/
rreh-koh-RREE-doh)*

Travel distance
Distancia a recorrer
*(dees-TAHN-syah ah
reh-koh-REHR)*

Tread (stair)
Huella
(WEH-jah)
Peldaño
(pehl-DAH-nyoh)

Treated wood
Madera tratada
*(mah-DEH-rah
trah-TAH-dah)*

Trench
Zanja
(SAHN-hah)

Trim
Molduras
(mohl-DOO-rahs)
Juego de accesorios
*(WEH-goh deh
ahk-seh-SOH-ryos)*

Trimmings
Accesorios
(ahk-seh-SOH-ryos)

Trip panel
Tablero de activación
*(tahb-LEH-roh deh
ahk-tee-vah-SYON)*

Trip point
Punto de actuación,
activación
*(POON-toh deh
ahk-too-ah-SYON,
ahk-tee-vah-SYON)*

Tripping device
Dispositivo de activación
*(dees-po-see-TEE-voh deh
ahk-tee-vah-SYON)*

Tripping valve
Válvula de disparo
*(VAHL-voo-lah deh
dees-PAH-roh)*

Trouble shooting
Localización de averías
*(lo-ka-lee-sah-SYON deh
ah-veh-REE-ahs)*

Truss
 Cercha
 (SEHR-chah)
 Reticulado
 (reh-tee-koo-LAH-doh)
 Armadura
 (ar-mah-DOO-rah)
 Cabreada
 (kah-breh-AH-dah)
 Caballete
 (kah-bah-JEH-teh)

Tubing
 Cañería
 (kah-nyeh-REE-ah)
 Tubería
 (too-beh-REE-ah)

Tufted
 De bucles
 (deh BOO-klehs)

Turned-down footings
 Zapatas invertidas
 (sah-PAH-tahs
 een-vehr-TEE-dahs)

Two-family dwelling
 Vivienda bifamiliar
 (vee-VYEN-dah
 bee-fah-mee-LYAR)

U

U-hook
Gancho en U
(*GAHN-choh ehn OO*)

Unbalanced fill
Relleno sin consolidar
(*reh-JEH-noh seen kohn-soh-lee-DAR*)

Unbalanced loads
Cargas no balanceadas
(*KAHR-gahs noh bah-lahn-seh-AH-dahs*)

Uncased concrete piles
Pilotes sin encamisar/sin camisa
(*pee-LOH-tehs seen ehn-KAH-mee-SAR/seen kah-MEE-sah*)

Undercut
Resquicio
(*rehs-KEE-syoh*)

Underground
Subterráneo
(*soob-teh-RRAH-neh-oh*)

Underlap
Subsolape
(*soob-soh-LAH-peh*)

Underlayment
Capa base
(*KAH-pah BAH-seh*)
Capa de soporte
(*KAH-pah deh soh-POHR-teh*)
Capa bituminosa debajo del piso de madera
(*KAH-pah bee-too-mee-NOH-sah deh-BAH-joh dehl PEE-soh deh mah-DEH-rah*)
Substrato
(*soob-STRAH-toh*)
Bajopiso
(*bah-joh-PEE-soh*)

Uniform Building Code
Código Uniforme de la Edificación
(*KOH-dee-goh oo-nee-FOHR-meh deh lah eh-dee-fee-kah-SYON*)

Uniform Fire Code
Código Uniforme de Protección contra Incendios
(*KOH-dee-goh oo-nee-FOHR-meh deh proh-tehk-SYON KOHN-trah een-SEHN-dee-ohs*)

U

Uniform Mechanical Code
Código Uniforme de
Instalaciones Mecánicas
(*KOH-dee-goh
oo-nee-FOHR-meh deh
een-stah-lah-SYOH-nehs
meh-KAH-nee-kahs*)

Uniform Plumbing Code
Código Uniforme para
Instalaciones Hidráulicas y
Sanitarias
(*KOH-dee-goh
oo-nee-FOHR-meh PAH-rah
een-stah-lah-SYOH-nehs
ee-DRAH-oo-lee-kahs ee
sah-nee-TAH-ree-ahs*)

Union
Unión
(*oon-YOHN*)
Junta
(*HOON-tah*)

Unlimited area
Área ilimitada
(*AH-reh-ah
ee-lee-mee-TAH-dah*)

Unsafe buildings
Edificaciones inseguras
(*eh-dee-fee-kah-SYOH-nehs
een-seh-GOO-rahs*)

Unstable ground
Terreno inestable
(*teh-RREH-noh
ee-neh-STAH-bleh*)

Uplift (wind)
Remonte
(*reh-MOHN-teh*)
Levantamiento (por viento)
(*leh-vahn-tah-MYEHN-toh
(pohr VYEHN-toh)*)

Urinal
Urinario
(*oo-ree-NAH-ree-oh*)
Urinal
(*oo-ree-NAHL*)
Mingitorio
(*meen-hee-TOH-ree-oh*)

Use
Uso
(*OO-soh*)
Utilizar
(*oo-tee-lee-SAR*)

Utility
Utilidad
(*oo-tee-lee-DAHD*)
Uso general
(*OO-soh heh-neh-RAHL*)

Utility (public service)
Servicios públicos
(*sehr-VEE-syohs
POOH-blee-kohs*)

V

Vacuum
Vacío
(vah-SEE-oh)
Aspiradora
(ahs-pee-rah-DOH-rah)

Vacuum breaker
Interruptor de vacío
*(een-teh-rroop-TOHR deh
vah-SEE-oh)*

Vale, post indicator (PIV)
Válvula de poste indicador
*(VAHL-voo-lah
deh POHS-teh
een-dee-kah-DOHR)*

Valuation
Valuación
(vah-luah-SYON)

Value
Valor
(vah-LOHR)

Valve, angle
Válvula de paso angular
*(VAHL-voo-lah deh
PAH-so ahn-goo-LAR)*

Valve, ball drip
Válvula de purga del deflector
*(VAHL-voo-lah deh
POOHR-gah dehl
deh-flehk-TOHR)*

Valve, bleeder
Válvula de purga
*(VAHL-voo-lah
deh POOR-gah)*

Valve, blow-off
Válvula de escape
*(VAHL-voo-lah
deh eh-SKA-peh*

Valve, butterfly
Válvula mariposa
*(VAHL-voo-lah
mah-ree-POH-sah)*

Valve, by-pass
Válvula de derivación
*(VAHL-voo-lah deh
deh-ree-vee-ka-SYON)*

Valve cap
Caperuza de la válvula
*(kah-peh-ROO-sa deh lah
VAHL-voo-lah)*

Valve, check
Válvula cheque
(VAHL-voo-lah CHEH-keh)

Valve, dry pipe
Válvula de tubería seca
*(VAHL-voo-lah
deh too-beh-REE-ah SEH-kah)*

V

Valve, gate
Válvula de compuerta
(*VAHL-voo-lah deh
kohm-PWER-tah*)

Valve, hub
Válvula de cubo
(*VAHL-voo-lah deh KOO-boh*)

Valve, key
Válvula de llave
(*VAHL-voo-lah deh JAH-veh*)

Valve, outside steam & yoke
(OS&Y)
Válvula de vástago ascendente
(*VAHL-voo-lah deh
VAHS-tah-goh
ah-sehn-DEHN-teh*)

Valve, pilot
Válvula piloto
(*VAHL-voo-lah pee-LOH-toh*)

Valve pit
Pozos de válvulas
(*po-sohs deh VAHL-voo-lahs*)

Valve seat
Asiento de válvula de alarma
(*ah-SYEN-to deh
VAHL-voo-lah deh
a-LAHR-ma*)

Valve, solenoid
Válvula solenoide
(*VAHL-voo-lah
soh-leh-NOY-deh*)

Venting system
Sistema de ventilación
(*sees-TEH-mah deh
ven-tee-la-SYON*)

Veneer
Revestimiento
(*reh-veh-stee-MYEHN-toh*)

Veneer plaster
Revestimiento de enlucido/
revoque
(*reh-veh-stee-MYEHN-toh
deh ehn-loo-SEE-doh/
reh-VOH-keh*)

Vent
Respiradero
(*reh-spee-rah-DEH-roh*)

Vent (v)
Ventilar
(*vehn-tee-LAR*)
Evacuar
(*eh-vah-KWAR*)
Aliviar
(*ah-lee-VYAR*)
Desahogar
(*dehs-ah-oh-GAR*)

Vent pipe
Tubo de ventilación
(*TOO-boh deh
vehn-tee-lah-SYON*)

Vent shaft
Recinto de ventilación
(*reh-SEEN-toh deh
vehn-tee-lah-SYON*)

Vent stack
Respiradero vertical
(*reh-spee-rah-DEH-roh
vehr-tee-KAHL*)

Vent system
Sistema de ventilación
(*see-STEH-mah deh
vehn-tee-lah-SYON*)

Ventilate
Ventilar
(*vehn-tee-LAR*)

Venting system
Sistema de evacuación
(*see-STEH-mah deh
eh-vah-kwah-SYON*)

Vertical pipe
Tubería vertical
(*too-beh-REE-ah
vehr-tee-KAHL*)

Vessel
Recipiente
(*reh-see-PYEHN-teh*)
Recipiente a presión
(*reh-see-PYEN-teh ah
preh-SYON*)

Vestibule
Vestíbulo
(*vehs-TEE-boo-loh*)

Vinyl siding
Revestimiento vinilo
(*reh-veh-stee-MYEHN-toh
vee-NEE-loh*)

Vise
Morsa
(*MOHR-sah*)

Void space
Espacio vacío
(*eh-SPAH-syoh vah-SEE-oh*)

Volatile memory
Memoria volátil
(*meh-MOH-ree-ah
voh-LAH-teel*)

Voltage
Voltaje
(*vohl-TAH-heh*)

Volts
Voltios
(*VOHL-tee-ohs*)

Wafer head
Cabeza plana
(kah-BEH-sah PLAH-nah)

Wainscot, Wainscoting
Friso
(FREE-soh)
Alfarje
(ahl-FAR-heh)
Material de revestimiento
*(mah-teh-RYAHL deh
reh-veh-stee-MYEHN-toh)*
Zócalos altos
(SOH-kah-lohs AHL-tohs)

Waive
Descartar
(dehs-kahr-TAHR)
Renunciar a un derecho
*(reh-noon-SYAR ah oon
deh-REH-choh)*

Walk-in cooler
Frigorífico
(free-goh-REE-fee-koh)

Walking surface
Superficie/Área peatonal
*(soo-pehr-FEE-see-eh/
AH-reh-ah pyah-toh-NAHL)*

Walks, moving
Caminos móviles
*(kah-MEE-nohs
MOH-vee-lehs)*

Walkway
Camino
(kah-MEE-noh)

Wall
Muro
(MOO-roh)
Pared
(pa-REHD)
Barda
(BAR-dah)

Wall bracket
Abrazadera de pared
*(ah-brah-sah-DEH-ra
deh pah-RHED)*

Wall, bearing
Pared portante
(pah-RHED pohr-TAHN-teh)

Wall face
Placa de pared
(PLAH-kah deh pa-REHD)

Wall frames
Estructuras de muros
*(ehs-trook-TOO-rahs
deh MOO-rohs)*

Wall, non-bearing
Pared no portante
*(pah-RHED noh
pohr-TAHN-teh)*

Wallboard
Plancha de yeso
(*PLAHN-chah deh YEH-soh*)
Cartón de yeso
(*kahr-TOHN deh YEH-soh*)

Warehouse
Depósito
(*deh-POH-see-toh*)
Bodega
(*boh-DEH-gah*)
Almacén
(*ahl-mah-SEHN*)
Galpón
(*gahl-POHN*)

Washer and Dryer
Lavadora y secadora
(*lah-vah-DOH-rah ee
seh-kah-DOH-rah*)

Washer
Arandela
(*ah-rrahn-DEH-lah*)
Planchuela de perno
(*plahn-CHWEH-lah deh
PEHR-noh*)

Water flow alarm valve
Válvula de alarma de paso
de agua
(*VAHL-voo-lah deh
a-LAHR-ma deh PAH-soh
deh AH-gwah*)

Water flow switch
Interruptor de flujo
(*een-teh-rrup-TOHR
deh FLOO-ho*)

Water hammer
Golpe de ariete
(*HOHL-peh deh
ah-ryeh-teh*)

Water heater
Calentador/Calentón de agua
(*kah-lehn-tah-DOHR/
kah-lehn-TOHN de AH-gwah*)
Calefón
(*kah-leh-FOHN*)
Termotanque
(*tehr-moh-TAHN-keh*)

Water main
Tubería principal
(*too-beh-REE-ah
preen-see-PAL*)
Tubería matriz
(*too-beh-REE-ah
mah-TREES*)
Colector de abastecimiento
(*koh-lehk-TOHR deh
ah-bahs-teh-see-MYEHN-toh*)

Water mist
Agua atomizada
(*AH-gwah
ah-toh-mee-SAH-dah*)

Water motor alarm
Alarma motorizada por agua
(*a-LAHR-ma
moh-toh-ree-SAH-dah
pohr AH-gwah*)

Water motor gong
Timbre de alarma motorizado
por agua
(*TEEM-breh deh a-LAHR-ma
moh-toh-ree-SAH-doh pohr
AH-gwah*)

Water spray
Agua pulverizada
*(AH-gwah
pool-vehr-ree-SAH-dah)*

Water supply
Abastecimiento de agua
*(ah-bahs-teh-see-MYEN-toh
deh AH-gwah)*

Watertight seal
Tapón estanco
(tah-POHN eh-STAHN-koh)

Water well
Aljibe
(ahl-HEE-beh)
Pozo de agua
(POH-soh deh AH-gwah)

Wax seal
Empaque de cera
(ehm-PAH-keh deh SEH-rah)

Weeds
Yerbajos
(jehr-BAH-hos)

Wedge
Cuña
(KOO-nyah)

Welding
Soldadura
(sohl-dah-DOO-rah)

Welding rod
Electrodo
(eh-lehk-TROH-doh)

Well, dug
Pozo excavado
*(POH-soh
ehk-SKAH-vah-doh)*

Window
Ventana
(ven-TAH-nah)

Window sill
Soporte de ventana
*(so-POR-teh deh
ven-TAH-nah)*
Repisa de ventana
*(reh-PEE-sah deh
ven-TAH-nah)*

Wire
Alambre
(ah-LAM-breh)

Wire backing
Alambre de soporte
*(ah-LAM-breh deh
soh-pohr-TEH)*

Wire, chicken
Alambre de pollo
(ah-LAM-breh deh POH-joh)

Wire connectors
Conectores de alambre
*(koh-nek-TOH-rehs deh
ah-LAM-breh)*
Cable alambre conector
*(KAH-bleh ah-LAM-breh
koh-nek-TOHR)*

Wire fabric
Malla de alambre
(MAH-jah deh ah-LAM-breh)

Wire mesh
Tela metálica
(TEH-lah meh-TAH-lee-kah)

Wire tie
Alambre de paca
(ah-LAM-breh deh PAH-kah)

Wood board
Tabla de madera
(tah-BLAH deh ma-DEH-rah)

Wood framing
Estructura en/de madera
(eh-strook-TOO-rah ehn/deh
mah-DEH-rah)
Entramado de madera
(ehn-trah-MAH-doh deh
mah-DEH-rah)
Bastidores de madera
(bah-stee-DOH-rehs deh
mah-DEH-rah)

Wood shakes
Duela de madera
(DWEH-lah deh
mah-DEH-rah)

Wood shingles
Tejas de madera
(TEH-hahs deh
mah-DEH-rah)

Wood strip flooring
Piso enlistonado de madera
(PEE-soh
ehn-lee-stoh-NAH-doh
deh mah-DEH-rah)

Wood truss
Cercha de madera
(SEHR-chah deh
mah-DEH-rah)

Woodworker
Ebanista
(eh-bah-NEES-tah)

Work
Obra
(OH-brah)
Trabajo
(trah-BAH-hoh)

Work, completion of
Terminación de obra
(tehr-mee-nah-SYON
deh OH-brah)

Working drawings
Planos
(PLAH-nohs)
Dibujos
(dee-BOO-hos)

Yoke
Horquilla
(ohr-KEE-jah)

Tools

Axe
 Hacha
 (AH-chah)

Ball-peen hammer
 Martillo de bola
 (mar-TEE-joh deh BOH-lah)

Bar
 Barreta
 (bah-RREH-tah)

Basin wrench
 Llave pico de ganso
 (JAH-veh PEE-koh deh GAHN-soh)

Blower
 Sopladora
 (soh-plah-DOH-rah)

Brace and bit
 Taladro de mano
 (tah-LAH-droh deh MAH-no)
 Berbiquí y barrena
 (ber-bee-KEE ee bah-RREH-nah)

Broom
 Escoba
 (ehs-KOH-bah)

Brush
 Pincel
 (peen-SEHL)
 Brocha
 (BROH-chah)
 Cepillo
 (seh-PEE-joh)

Bucket
 Cubeta
 (koo-BEH-tah)
 Balde
 (BALH-deh)

Carpenter's apron
 Mandil
 (mahn-DEEL)
 Delantal
 (deh-lahn-TAHL)

Carpenter's square
 Escuadra
 (ehs-KWAH-drah)

C-clamp
 Prensa en c
 (PREN-sah en seh)

Chain pipe wrench
 Llave de cadena
 (JAH-veh deh kah-DEH-nah)

Chain saw
 Sierra de cadena
 (SYEH-rrah deh kah-DEH-nah)

Chisel wood
 Escopio
 (ehs-KOH-pee-oh)
 Formón
 (for-MON)
 Cincel
 (seen-SEL)

Tools

Circular saw
Sierra circular de mano
(*SYEH-rrah seer-koo-LAR
deh MAH-noh*)

Circular saw blade
Disco
(*DEES-koh*)

Claw hammer
Martillo chivo
(*mahr-TEE-joh CHEE-voh*)

Come-along
Mordaza tiradora de alambre
(*mohr-DAH-sah
tee-rah-DOH-rah
deh ah-LAM-breh*)

Combination square
Escuadra de combinación
(*ehs-KWAH-drah deh
kohm-been-ah-SYON*)

Compound mitre saw
Sierra de corte angular
(*SYEH-rrah deh KOHR-teh
ahn-goo-LAHR*)
Sierra de ingletes compuesta
(*SYEH-rrah deh
een-GLEH-tehs
kohm-PWEHS-tah*)

Cut-off saw
Sierra para cortar
(*SYEH-rrah PAH-rah
kohr-TAHR*)
Sierra de madera
(*SYEH-rrah deh
mah-DEH-rah*)

Darby
Plana
(*PLAH-na*)
Flatacho
(*flah-TAH-choh*)

Drill
Taladro
(*tah-LAH-droh*)

Drill bit
Broca
(*BROH-kah*)
Mecha
(*MEH-cha*)

Drill, electric
Taladro eléctrico
(*tah-LAH-droh
eh-LEHK-tree-koh*)

File
Lima
(*LEE-ma*)

Flashlight
Linterna
(*leen-TEHR-nah*)

Flat head
Desarmador de hoja plana
(*des-ar-mah-DOR deh OH-ha
PLAH-na*)

Forklift
Montacargas
(*mohn-tah-CAHR-gahs*)

Framing square
Escuadra
(*ehs-KWAH-dra*)

Funnel
Embudo
(*ehm-BOO-doh*)

Goggles
Lentes de seguridad
(*LEHN-tehs deh
seh-goo-ree-DAHD*)

Gloves
Guantes
(*GWAN-tehs*)

Hammer
Martillo
(*mar-TEE-joh*)

Hand saw
Serrucho de mano
(*seh-RROO-cho
deh MAH-noh*)

Hawk
Esparavel
(*ehs-pah-ra-VEL*)

Hoe
Azadón
(*ah-sah-DOHN*)
Zapa
(*SAH-pah*)

Hose
Manguera
(*mahn-GEH-rah*)

Jigsaw
Sierra de vaivén
(*SYEH-rrah deh vahy-VEHN*)

Jointer
Cepillo automático
(*seh-PEE-yoh
ah-oo-toh-MAH-tee-koh*)

Jointer plane
Cepillo de mano
(*seh-PEE-yoh deh MAH-no*)

Knife, utility
Navaja
(*nah-VAH-hah*)
Cortapluma
(*kohr-tah-PLOO-mah*)

Ladder
Escalera de mano
(*ehs-kah-LEH-rah
deh MAH-no*)

Lawnmower
Cortadora de césped/pasto
(*kor-tah-DOH-rah deh
SEHS-pehd/PAHS-toh*)
Cortacésped
(*kor-tah-SEHS-pehd*)

Level
Nivel
(*nee-VEL*)

Mallet
Mazo
(*MAH-soh*)

Mask
Máscara
(*MAHS-kah-rah*)
Careta
(*kah-REH-tah*)

Medicine cabinet
Botiquín
(*boh-tee-KEEN*)

Mitre box
Caja de corte a ángulos
(*KAH-hah deh KOHR-teh
ah AHN-goo-lohs*)

Tools

Mitre saw
Sierra de retroceso para
ingletes
(*SYEH-rrah deh
reh-troh-SEH-soh PAH-rah
een-GLEH-tehs*)

Mixer
Mezcladora
(*mehs-klah-DOH-rah*)
Revolvedora
(*reh-vohl-veh-DOH-rah*)

Nail gun
Clavadora automática
(*klah-vah-DOH-rah
ah-oo-toh-MAH-tee-kah*)

Nail set
Botador/embutidor de clavos
(*boh-tah-DOHR/
ehm-boo-tee-DOHR
deh KLAH-vohs*)

Phillips
Desarmador de punta de cruz
(*des-ar-mah-DOR deh
POON-tah deh kroos*)

Pick
Pico
(*PEE-koh*)

Pick-axe
Zapapico
(*sah-pah-PEE-koh*)

Plane
Cepillo
(*seh-PEE-joh*)

Pliers
Alicates
(*ah-lee-KAH-tehs*)
Pinzas
(*PEEN-sas*)

Pliers, channel lock
Alicates de extensión
(*ah-lee-KAH-tehs
deh ehk-stehn-SYON*)

Pliers, vise grips
Alicates de presión
(*ah-lee-KAH-tehs
deh preh-SYON*)
Pinzas perras
(*PEEN-sas PEH-rras*)

Plumb bob
Plomada
(*ploh-MAH-dah*)

Plumb line
Hilo de plomada
(*EE-loh deh ploh-MAH-dah*)

Pump
Bomba
(*BOHM-bah*)

Punches
Punzones
(*poon-SOH-nehs*)

Radial arm saw
Serrucho guillotina
(*seh-RROO-choh
gheeh-joh-TEE-nah*)

Radial saw
Sierra fija
(*SYEH-rrah FEE-hah*)

Rake
Rastrillo
(rahs-TREE-joh)

Rebar bender
Doblador de varilla
(doh-blah-DOR
deh vah-REE-jah)

Reciprocating saw
Sierra alternativa
(SYEH-rrah
ahl-tehr-nah-TEE-vah)

Roller
Aplanadora
(ah-plah-nah-DOH-rah)

Router
Fresadora
(freh-sah-DOH-rah)
Contorneador
(kohn-tohr-neh-ah-DOHR)
Buriladora
(boo-ree-lah-DOH-rah)

Safety glasses
Gafas de seguridad
(GAH-fahs deh
seh-goo-ree-DAHD)

Sander
Lijadora
(lee-hah-DOH-rah)

Saw
Sierra
(SYEH-rrah)
Serrucho
(seh-RROO-choh)

Saw, electric
Sierra eléctrica
(SYEH-rrah
eh-LEHK-tree-ka)

Saw, hack
Sierra para metales
(SYEH-rrah PAH-rah
meh-TAH-les)

Saw, hand
Serrucho de mano
(seh-RROO-cho
deh MAH-noh)

Saw, power
Sierra eléctrica
(SYEH-rrah
eh-LEHK-tree-ka)

Sawhorse
Burro
(BOO-rroh)

Screwdriver
Destornillador
(dehs-tor-nee-jah-DOR)
Desarmador
(dehs-ar-mah-DOR)

Sheet metal shears
Tijeras para metal
(Tee-HEH-rahs PAH-rah
meh-TAHL)

Shingling hammer
Martillo para tejamanil
(mar-TEE-joh PAH-rah
teh-hah-mah-NEEL)

Shovel
Pala
(PAH-lah)

Sledgehammer
Marro
(MAH-rroh)
Mazo
(MAH-soh)

Tools

Square
Escuadra
(ehs-KWAH-drah)

Solderer
Soldador
(sohl-dah-DOHR)

Soldering torch
Soplete
(soh-PLEH-teh)

Stapler
Engrapadora
(ehn-grah-pah-DOH-rah)

Staple gun
Engrapadora automática
*(ehn-grah-pah-DOH-rah
ah-oo-toh-MAH-tee-kah)*

Strap wrench
Llave de correa
(JAH-veh deh koh-RREH-ah)
Llave de cincho
(JAH-veh deh SEEN-cho)

Table saw
Sierra fija
(SYEH-rrah FEE-hah)
Sierra de mesa
(SYEH-rrah deh MEH-sah)
Sierra circular de mesa
*(SYEH-rrah seer-koo-LAR
deh MEH-sah)*

Thread
Hilo
(EE-loh)

Tool box
Caja de herramientas
*(KAH-hah deh
eh-rrah-MYEN-tahs)*

Trowel, joint filler
Paleta de relleno
*(pah-LEH-tah
deh reh-JEH-noh)*

Trowel, mason's
Paleta de albañil
*(pah-LEH-tah
deh al-bah-NYEEL)*

Trowel, square
Llana
(JAH-nah)

T-square
Regla T
(REH-glah TEH)

Valve seat wrench
Llave de asientos de válvula
*(JAH-veh deh ah-SYEN-tohs
deh VAHL-voo-lah)*

Vice bench
Torno/tornillo de banco
*(TOR-noh/tohr-NEE-joh
deh BAHN-koh)*

Welding mask
Careta para soldar
*(kah-REH-tah PAH-rah
sohl-DAHR)*

Wheel barrow
Carretilla
(kah-rreh-TEE-jah)
Carrucha
(kah-RROO-chah)
Engarilla
(ehn-gah-REE-jah)

Worm drive circular saw
Sierra circular con tornillo
sinfin
*(SYEH-rrah seer-koo-LAR
cohn tohr-NEE-joh
seen-FEEN)*

Wrench
Llave
(JAH-veh)

Wrench, adjustable
Llave francesa
(JAH-veh frahn-SEH-sa)

Wrench, basin
Llave pico de ganso
*(JAH-veh PEE-koh
deh GAHN-soh)*

Wrench, crescent
Llave de tuercas
(JAH-ve deh TWER-kas)
Llave francesa ajustable
*(JAH-veh frahn-SEH-sa
ah-HOOS-tah-bleh)*

Wrench, plumbers
Llave inglesa
(JAH-veh een-GLEH-sa)

Work light
Lámpara de trabajo
*(LAHM-pah-rah
deh trah-BAH-hoh)*

Useful Phrases

Do you speak English?
¿Habla inglés?
[AH-blah een-GLEHS]

What is your name?
¿Cómo se llama (usted)?
[KOH-moh seh JAH-ma (oos-TEHD)]
¿Cuál es su nombre?
[KWAL ehs soo NOHM-breh]

My name is.../I am...
Mi nombre es.../ Me llamo...
[mee NOHM-breh ehs.../Meh JAH-mo...]

Pleased to meet you.
Mucho gusto (en conocerlo).
[MOO-choh GŌOS-toh (en koh-noh-SEHR-loh)]

What is your phone number?
¿Cuál es su número de teléfono?
[KWAHL ehs soo NOO-meh-roh deh teh-LEH-foh-noh]

Please fill out this application.
Por favor, complete (usted) ésta solicitud.
[pohr fah-VOR com-PLEH-teh (oos-TEHD) EHS-ta soh-lee-see-TOOD]

I need you to fill out this federal tax form.
Necesito que complete éste formulario de impuestos federales.
[neh-ceh-SEE-toh keh com-PLEH-teh EHS-teh for-moo-LAH-ree-oh deh eem-PWES-toss feh-deh-RAH-less]

...And this one for state taxes.
Y éste de impuestos estatales.
[EE EHS-teh deh eem-PWES-toss ehs-tah-TAH-less]

...Also this I-9 form from the government.
También éste formulario I-9 del gobierno.
[tam-BYEN EHS-teh for-moo-LAH-ree-oh EE-NWEH-veh dehl go-BYER-noh]

I need to see the actual identification you list on the form.
Necesito ver la identificacion que indicó (usted) en el formulario.
[neh-ceh-SEE-toh vehr la ee-den-tee-fee-kah-SEEOHN keh een-dee-KOH (oos-TEHD) ehn el for-moo-LAH-ree-oh]

Useful Phrases

...Either one from column A or one each from columns B and C.

Se requiere una de la columna A o una de cada una de las columnas B y C.

[seh reh-KYEH-reh oo-nah deh la koh-LOOM-nah AH oh oo-na deh lass koh-LOOM-nas BEH ee CEH]

Without I.D., I can't hire you.

Sin la identificación adecuada, no puedo emplearlo.

[seen la ee-den-tee-fee-kah-SEEOHN ah-deh-KWAH-dah noh PWEH-doh ehm-pleh-AR-loh]

Do you have a union card?

¿Tiene su credencial de la unión (sindicato)?

[TYEH-neh soo kreh-den-SEE-al deh la oon-YOHN (seen-dee-KAH-to)]

Can I see it please?

¿Puedo verla por favor?

[PWEH-doh VEHR-la por fah-VOHR]

Did the union send you?

¿Lo manda la unión (el sindicato)?

[loh MAHN-dah la oon-YOHN (ehl seen-dee-KAH-toh)]

Can I see the referral?

¿Puedo ver la hoja (referencia)?

[PWEH-doh VEHR-la OH-hah (reh-feh-REHN-see-ah)]

Do you have your own tools?

¿Tiene (usted) sus propias herramientas de mano?

[TYEH-neh (oos-TEHD) soos PROH-pee-as EHR-rah-MYEN-tas deh MAH-noh]

...If not, I can't use you.

Si no, entonces no puedo emplearlo.

[see NOH, ehn-TOHN-cehs noh PWEH-doh ehm-pleh-AR-loh]

Your pay is going to be per hour.

Se le va a pagar por hora.

[seh leh VAH ah pah-GAHR pohr OH-rah]

...Less tax withholding

(...benefits ...union dues).

...Menos descuentos por impuestos (...beneficios ...cuota de la unión).

[...MEH-nohs des-KWEN-tos pohr eem-PWES-toss (beh-neh-FEE-see-ohs ...KWOH-tah deh lah oon-YOHN)]

I will pay you at the end (of the day/week/month).

Le pagaré al final (del día/ semana/mes).

[leh pah-gah-REH ahl fee-NAHL (dehl DEE-ah/ seh-MAH-nah/MEHS)]

Payday is every Friday (Saturday, Sunday, etc.).

El día de pago es cada viernes (sábado, domingo, etc.).
[ehl DEE-ah deh PAH-goh
ehs KAH-dah VYEHR-nes
(SAH-bah-doh,
doh-MEEN-goh)]

Can you work tomorrow?

¿Puede trabajar mañana?
[PWEH-deh trah-bah-HAR
mah-NYAH-nah]

See you tomorrow.

Nos vemos mañana.
[nohs VEH-mohs
mah-NYAH-nah]

Please do not waste materials.

Por favor no malgaste los materiales.
[pohr fah-VOHR noh
mal-GAHS-teh lohs
mah-teh-RYAH-less]

Can you drive a car?

¿Sabe conducir?
[SAH-beh kohn-doo-SEER]

Do you have a driver's license?

¿Tiene licencia de conducir?
[TYEH-neh lee-SEHN-see-ah
deh kohn-doo-SEER]

You may use this bathroom.

Puede usar este baño.
[PWEH-deh oo-SAHR
EHS-teh BAH-nyo]

How late can you work?

¿Qué tan tarde puede trabajar?
[keh tahn TAHR-deh
PWEH-de trah-bah-HAR]

Are you hungry/thirsty?

¿Tiene hambre/sed?
[TYEH-neh AHM-breh/SEHD]

What do you want to eat/drink?

¿Qué quiere comer/tomar?
[keh KYEH-reh KOH-mehr/
toh-MAHR]

Come with me.

Venga conmigo.
[VEHN-gah kohn-MEE-goh]

Here is your job safety booklet. Read it and use it.

Aquí está su folleto de seguridad en el trabajo. Léalo y úselo.
[ah-KEE ehs-TAH soo
foh-YEH-toh deh
se-goo-ree-DAD en el
trah-BAH-ho. LEH-ah-loh
ee OO-seh-loh]

Wear these glasses (hat, gloves) for your protection.

Use estos lentes (casco, guantes) para su protección.
[OO-seh EHS-tohs LEHN-tehs
(KAHS-coh, GWAHN-tehs)
PAH-rah soo
proh-tehk-SYON]

Are you sick? You need to go home.

¿Se siente enfermo? Necesita regresar a casa.
[seh SYEHN-teh
en-FEHR-moh?
Neh-seh-SEE-tah
reh-greh-SAHR ah CAH-sah]

Useful Phrases

Are you injured? Go to the doctor/clinic now!

¿Se lesionó? ¡Vaya al doctor/a la clínica ahora mismo!
[seh leh-syoh-NOH? VAH-yah ahl dohk-TOHR/ah lah KLEE-nee-kah ah-OH-rah MEES-moh]

Bring the doctor's report when you come back.

Tráigame el reporte (la nota) del doctor cuando regrese.
[TRAHY-gah-meh el reh-POHR-teh (la NOH-tah) dehl dohk-TOHR KWAN-doh re-GREH-seh]

Don't use any tools (without asking).

No use ninguna herramienta (sin mi permiso).
[noh OO-seh neen-GOO-nah eh-rrah-MYEN-ta (seen mee per-MEE-soh)]

Whenever a building inspector shows up, let me know immediately.

Cuando llegue un inspector, avíseme inmediatamente.
[KWAHN-doh JEH-geh oon eens-pec-TOHR, ah-VEE-seh-meh een-meh-DYAH-tah-men-teh]

Be careful!

¡Ten(ga) cuidado!
[TEHN(gah) kwee-DAH-doh]

Watch out!

¡Cuidado!
[kwee-DAH-doh]
¡Ojo!
[OH-ho]
¡Aguas!
[AH-gwas]
¡Pon(ga) atención!
[POHN(gah) ah-tehn-SYON]

Follow me.

Sígame.
[SEE-gah-meh]

Pull!

¡Jale!
[HA-leh]
¡Tire!
[TEE-reh]

Push!

¡Empuje!
[ehm-POO-heh]

Bring me that 2x4 (...that fixture, ...that fitting,...that duct).

Tráigame ese dos por cuatro (...ese accesorio, ...esa conexion, ...ese conducto).
[TRAHY-gah-meh EH-seh dohs por KWAH-troh (...EH-seh ak-seh-SOH-ree-oh, ...EH-sah koh-nehk-SYON, ...EH-seh kahn-DOOK-toh]

Help me unload the truck (...lift the beam, ...install the drain).
Ayúdeme a descargar el camión (...levantar la viga, ...instalar el desagüe).
[AH-YU-deh-meh ah dehs-car-GAR el kah-MEEOHN (...leh-vahn-TAR la VEE-gah, ...een-stah-LAR el deh-SAH-gweh]

Stack the (lumber/pipe/insulation) over there.
Apile (la madera/la tubería/el aislamiento) allá.
[ah-PEE-leh (lah mah-DEH-rah/lah too-beh-REE-ah/ehl ah-ees-lah-MYEHN-to) ah-JAH]

Cut it at a 45-degree angle.
Córtelo a un ángulo de cuarenta y cinco grados.
[KOHR-teh-loh ah oon AHN-goo-loh deh kwa-REHN-tah ee SEEN-co GRAH-dos]

Hold it there and nail it.
Sosténgalo allí y clávelo.
[sohs-TEHN-gah-loh ah-GEE ee KLAH-veh-lo]

Hold it there while I nail.
Sosténgalo allí mientras lo clavo.
[sohs-TEHN-gah-loh ah-GEE MYEHN-trahs loh KLAH-vo]

Pick this up.
Levante esto.
[leh-VAHN-teh EHS-toh]

Turn it over... Turn it clockwise (counterclockwise).
Voltéelo... Gírelo a la derecha (a la izquierda).
[vohl-TEH-eh-loh... HEE-reh-loh ah la deh-REH-cha (ah la ees-KYEHR-da)]

Raise it a little.
Levántelo un poco.
[leh-VAHN-teh-loh oon POH-ko]

Lower it a little.
Bájelo un poco.
[BAH-heh-loh oon POH-co]

That is too heavy. Don't try to lift/carry it alone.
Eso es demasiado pesado. No intente levantarlo/llevarlo solo.
[EH-soh ehs deh-mah-SYAH-doh peh-SAH-do. Noh een-TEHN-teh leh-vahn-TAHR-loh/ jeh-VAHR-loh SOH-lo]

Get someone to help you.
Pida a alguien que le ayude.
[PEE-dah ah AHL-guee-ehn keh leh ah-YOO-deh]

Shovel this into the wheelbarrow.
Cargue esto en la carretilla.
[KAHR-geh EHS-toh ehn lah kah-rreh-TEE-jah]

Useful Phrases

Put it in the trash bin (or dump truck).

> Póngalo en la basura (o camión de volteo).
> *[POHN-gah-loh ehn lah bah-SOO-rah (oh kah-MYON-deh vohl-TEH-oh)]*

Clean these... (windows, doors, walls, etc.).

> Limpie estas... (ventanas, puertas, paredes, etc.).
> *[LEEM-pyeh EHS-tahs... (vehn-TAH-nahs, PWER-tahs, pah-REH-dehs)]*

Sweep this up.

> Barra esto.
> *[BAH-rrah EHS-toh]*

Hammer this.

> Martille esto.
> *[mahr-TEE-jeh EHS-toh]*

Where is the saw?

> ¿Dónde está la sierra?
> *[DOHN-deh ehs-TAH lah SYEH-rrah]*

Tie this... (with wire, rope).

> Amarre esto... (con alambre, soga).
> *[ah-MAH-rreh EHS-toh... (cohn ah-LAHM-breh, SOH-gah)]*

It is break time.

> Es hora de descanso.
> *[ehs OH-rah deh dehs-KAHN-soh]*

No. Don't do it like that. Please, do it this way.

> No. Así no lo haga. Por favor, hagalo así.
> *[NOH. Ah-SEE noh loh AH-gah. Pohr fah-VOHR AH-gah-loh ah-SEE]*

Use (the pick, the shovel, the hammer) like this.

> Use (el pico, la pala, el martillo) así.
> *[OO-seh (ehl PEE-koh, lah PAH-lah, ehl mahr-TEE-joh) ah-SEE]*

Take this to the truck, please.

> Lleve esto al camión/ camioneta, por favor.
> *[JEH-veh EHS-toh ahl kah-MYON/ kah-myo-NEH-tah, pohr fah-VOHR]*

Don't drop it, it's very fragil.

> No lo deje caer, es muy frágil.
> *[noh loh DEH-heh kah-EHR, ehs MOOY FRAH-heel]*

Watch your step.

> Cuidado al pisar.
> *[kwee-DAH-doh ahl pee-SAHR]*

I study my Means Dictionary every day to learn Spanish.

> Estudio mi Means Diccionario todos los días para aprender Español.
> *[eh-STU-dyo mee meens deek-syo-NAH-ryo to-dos lohs DEE-ahs pah-rah AH-prehn-dehr EHS-pah-nyol]*

Tables

The numbers		
Los números		
0	zero	cero
1	one	uno (una)
2	two	dos
3	three	tres
4	four	cuatro
5	five	cinco
6	six	seis
7	seven	siete
8	eight	ocho
9	nine	nueve
10	ten	diez
11	eleven	once
12	twelve	doce
13	thirteen	trece
14	fourteen	catorce
15	fifteen	quince
16	sixteen	dieciséis
17	seventeen	diecisiete
18	eighteen	dieciocho
19	nineteen	diecinueve
20	twenty	veinte
21	twenty-one	veintiuno
22	twenty-two	veintidós
30	thirty	treinta
31	thirty-one	treinta y uno
40	forty	cuarenta
50	fifty	cincuenta

Tables

60	sixty	sesenta
70	seventy	setenta
80	eighty	ochenta
90	ninety	noventa
100	one hundred	cien
101	one hundred and one	ciento uno
200	two hundred	doscientos
300	three hundred	trescientos
400	four hundred	cuatrocientos
500	five hundred	quinientos
600	six hundred	seiscientos
700	seven hundred	setecientos
800	eight hundred	ochocientos
900	nine hundred	novecientos
1,000	one thousand	mil
2,000	two thousand	dos mil
1,000,000	one million	un millón
2,000,000	two million	dos millones

The months of the year	
Los meses del año	
January	enero
February	febrero
March	marzo
April	abril
May	mayo
June	junio
July	julio
August	agosto
September	septiembre
October	octubre
November	noviembre
December	diciembre

The days of the week	
Los días de la semana	
Monday	lunes
Tuesday	martes
Wednesday	miércoles
Thursday	jueves
Friday	viernes
Saturday	sábado
Sunday	domingo

Tables

SI SYMBOLS AND PREFIXES

BASE UNITS

Quantity	Unit	Symbol
Length	Meter	m
Mass	Kilogram	kg
Time	Second	s
Electric current	Ampere	A
Thermodynamic temperature	Kelvin	K
Amount of substance	Mole	mol
Luminous intensity	Candela	cd

SI SUPPLEMENTARY UNITS

Quantity	Unit	Symbol
Plane angle	Radian	rad
Solid angle	Steradian	sr

SI PREFIXES

Multiplication Factor	Prefix	Symbol
$1\ 000\ 000\ 000\ 000\ 000\ 000 = 10^{18}$	exa	E
$1\ 000\ 000\ 000\ 000\ 000 = 10^{15}$	peta	P
$1\ 000\ 000\ 000\ 000 = 10^{12}$	tera	T
$1\ 000\ 000\ 000 = 10^{9}$	giga	G
$1\ 000\ 000 = 10^{6}$	mega	M
$1\ 000 = 10^{3}$	kilo	k
$100 = 10^{2}$	hecto	h
$10 = 10^{1}$	deka	da
$0.1 = 10^{-1}$	deci	d
$0.01 = 10^{-2}$	centi	c
$0.001 = 10^{-3}$	milli	m
$0.000\ 001 = 10^{-6}$	micro	$\propto$
$0.000\ 000\ 001 = 10^{-9}$	nano	n
$0.000\ 000\ 000\ 001 = 10^{-12}$	pico	p
$0.000\ 000\ 000\ 000\ 001 = 10^{-15}$	femto	f
$0.000\ 000\ 000\ 000\ 000\ 001 = 10^{-18}$	atto	a

SI DERIVED UNIT WITH SPECIAL NAMES			
Quantity	Unit	Symbol	Formula
Frequency (of a periodic phenomenon)	hertz	Hz	$1/s$
Force	newton	N	$kg \cdot m/s^2$
Pressure, stress	pascal	Pa	N/m^2
Energy, work, quantity of heat	joule	J	$N \cdot m$
Power, radiant flux	watt	W	J/s
Quantity of electricity, electric charge	coulomb	C	$A \cdot s$
Electric potential, potential difference, electromotive force	volt	V	W/A
Capacitance	farad	F	C/V
Electric resistance	ohm	Ω	V/A
Conductance	siemens	S	A/V
Magnetic flux	weber	Wb	$V \cdot s$
Magnetic flux density	tesla	T	Wb/m^2
Inductance	henry	H	Wb/A
Luminous flux	lumen	lm	$cd \cdot sr$
Illuminance	lux	lx	lm/m^2
Activity (of radionuclides)	becquerel	Bq	$1/s$
Absorbed dose	gray	Gy	J/kg

Tables

CONVERSION FACTORS

To convert	to	multiply by
LENGTH		
1 mile (U.S. statute)	km	1.609 344
1 yd	m	0.9144
1 ft	m	0.3048
	mm	304.8
1 in	mm	25.4
AREA		
1 mile^2 (U.S. statute)	km^2	2.589 998
1 acre (U.S. survey)	ha	0.404 6873
	m^2	4046.873
1 yd^2	m^2	0.836 1274
1 ft^2	m^2	0.092 903 04
1 in^2	mm^2	645.16
VOLUME, MODULUS OF SECTION		
l acre ft	m^3	1233.489
1 yd^3	m^3	0.764 5549
100 board ft	m^3	0.235 9737
1 ft^3	m^3	0.028 316 85
	L(dm^3)	28.3168
1 in^3	mm^3	16 387.06
	mL (cm^3)	16.3871
1 barrel (42 U.S. gallons)	m^3	0.158 9873
(FLUID) CAPACITY		
1 gal (U.S. liquid)*	L**	3.785 412
1 qt (U.S. liquid)	mL	946.3529
1 pt (U.S. liquid)	mL	473.1765
1 fl oz (U.S.)	mL	29.5735
1 gal (U.S. liquid)	m^3	0.003 785 412
*1 gallon (UK) approx. 1.2 gal (U.S.)	**1 liter approx. 0.001 cubic meter	
SECOND MOMENT OF AREA		
1 in^4	mm^4	416 231 4
	m^4	416 231 4 10^{-7}
PLANE ANGLE		
1° (degree)	rad	0.017 453 29
	mrad	17.453 29
1' (minute)	urad	290.8882
1" (second)	urad	4.848 137

126

VELOCITY, SPEED		
1 ft/s	m/s	0.3048
1 mile/h	km/h	1.609 344
	m/s	0.447 04
VOLUME RATE OF FLOW		
1 ft^3/s	m^3/s	0.028 316 85
1 ft^3/min	L/s	0.471 9474
1 gal/min	L/s	0.063 0902
1 gal/min	m^3/min	0.0038
1 gal/h	mL/s	1.051 50
1 million gal/d	L/s	43.8126
1 acre ft/s	m^3/s	1233.49
TEMPERATURE INTERVAL		
1°F	°C or K	0.555 556
		$^5/_9$°C = $^5/_9$K
EQUIVALENT TEMPERATURE ($t_{°C}$ = T_K - 273.15)		
$t_{°F}$	$t_{°C}$	$t_{°F}$ = $^9/_5 t_{°C}$ + 32
MASS		
1 ton (short ***)	metric ton	0.907 185
	kg	907.1847
1 lb	kg	0.453 5924
1 oz	g	28.349 52
***1 long ton (2,240 lb)	kg	1016.047
MASS PER UNIT AREA		
1 lb/ft^2	kg/m^2	4.882 428
1 oz/yd^2	g/m^2	33.905 75
1 oz/ft^2	g/m^2	305.1517
DENSITY (MASS PER UNIT VOLUME)		
1 lb/ft^3	kg/m^3	16.01846
1 lb/yd^3	kg/m^3	0.593 2764
1 ton/yd^3	t/m^3	1.186 553
FORCE		
1 tonf (ton–force)	kN	8.896 44
1 kip (1,000 lbf)	kN	4.448 22
1 lbf (pound–force)	N	4.448 22
MOMENT OF FORCE, TORQUE		
1 lbf·ft	N·m	1.355 818
1 lbf·in	N·m	0.112 9848
1 tonf·ft	kN·m	2.711 64
1 kip·ft	kN·m	1.355 82

Tables

FORCE PER UNIT LENGTH		
1 lbf/ft	N/m	14.5939
1 tonf/ft	kN/m	29.1878
1 lbf/in	N/m	175.1268
PRESSURE, STRESS, MODULUS OF ELASTICITY (FORCE PER UNIT AREA) (1 Pa = 1 N/m^2)		
1 tonf/in^2	MPa	13.7895
1 tonf/ft^2	kPa	95.7605
1 kip/in^2	MPa	6.894 757
1 lbf/in^2	kPa	6.894 757
1 lbf/ft^2	Pa	47.8803
Atmosphere	kPa	101.3250
1 inch mercury	kPa	3.376 85
1 foot (water column at 32°F)	kPa	2.988 98
WORK, ENERGY, HEAT(1J = 1N·m = 1W·s)		
1 kWh (550 ft·lbf/s)	MJ	3.6
1 Btu (Int. Table)	kJ	1.055 056
	J	1055.056
1 ft·lbf	J	1.355 818
COEFFICIENT OF HEAT TRANSFER		
1 Btu/(ft^2·h·°F)	W/(m^2·K)	5.678 263
THERMAL CONDUCTIVITY		
1 Btu/(ft·h·°F)	W/(m·K)	1.730 735
ILLUMINANCE		
1 lm/ft^2 (footcandle)	lx (lux)	10.763 91
LUMINANCE		
1 cd/ft^2	cd/m^2	10.7639
1 foot lambert	cd/m^2	3.426 259
1 lambert	kcd/m^2	3.183 099

General

Tools & Equipment

Adjustable Wrench
   Llave Ajustable

Wrench
   Llave

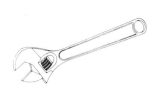

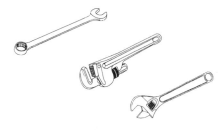

Chain
   Cadena

Clamp
   Abrazadera

Fire Extinguisher
   Extinguidor/Extintor de Incendio

Socket Wrench
   Chicharra

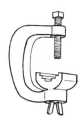

General: Tools & Equipment

Tape
   Cinta Métrica

Bench Vise
   Abrazadera

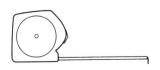

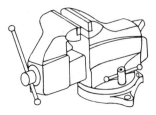

Crane
   Grúa Hidraúlica

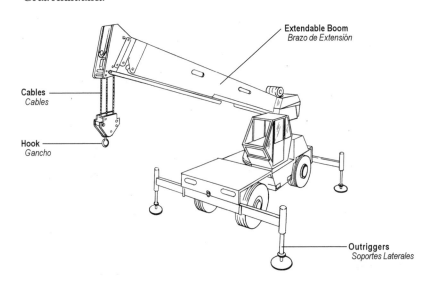

Extendable Boom
Brazo de Extensión

Cables
Cables

Hook
Gancho

Outriggers
Soportes Laterales

Ladder
   Escalera/Escala

Site Work

Tools & Equipment

Backhoe-Crawler Type
   Retroexcavadora

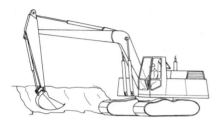

Backhoe/Loader-Wheel Type
   Retroexcavadora/Cargador con Ruedas

Tractor-Crawler Type
   Tractor Oruga

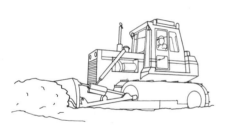

Tractor Loader-Wheel Type
   Tractor Cargador con Ruedas

Tractor Loader-Wheel Type, small
   Tractor Cargador con Ruedas, pequeño

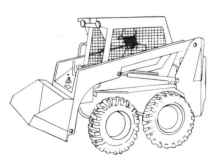

Dump Truck
   Camión de Volteo

Site Work: Tools & Equipment

Grader
Niveladora

Gradall
Camion de Excavaciones

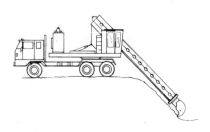

Roller
Aplanadora

Trencher
Excavadora de Zanjas

Compactor Roller
Compactadora

Compactor-Vibrator Plate
Compactadora Manual

Site Work: Systems & Components

Trench Shoring
Apuntalamiento de Zanja

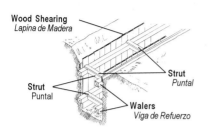

Wood Shearing
Lapina de Madera

Strut
Puntal

Strut
Puntal

Walers
Viga de Refuerzo

Septic Systems
Sistema Séptico

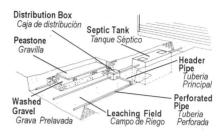

Distribution Box
Caja de distribución

Septic Tank
Tanque Séptico

Peastone
Gravilla

Header Pipe
Tuberia Principal

Washed Gravel
Grava Prelavada

Leaching Field
Campo de Riego

Perforated Pipe
Tuberia Perforada

Paving
Pavimento

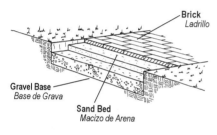

Brick
Ladrillo

Gravel Base
Base de Grava

Sand Bed
Macizo de Arena

Chain Link Fence, Industrial
Cerca de Malla Metálica, Industrial

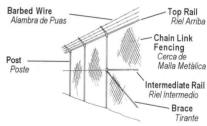

Barbed Wire
Alambra de Puas

Post
Poste

Top Rail
Riel Arriba

Chain Link Fencing
Cerca de Malla Metálica

Intermediate Rail
Riel Intermedio

Brace
Tirante

Fire Hydrant System
Sistema de Hidrante

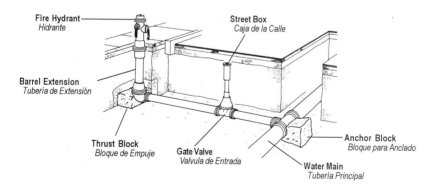

Fire Hydrant
Hidrante

Street Box
Caja de la Calle

Barrel Extension
Tubería de Extensión

Thrust Block
Bloque de Empuje

Gate Valve
Valvula de Entrada

Water Main
Tubería Principal

Anchor Block
Bloque para Anclado

Concrete

Tools & Equipment

Bull Float
　　Cuchara Toro

Magnesium Float
　　Cuchara Metalica

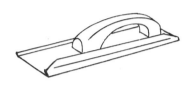

Rubber Float
　　Cuchara de Goma

Bush Hammer
　　Martillo para Texturizado

Finishing Broom
　　Cepillo de Acabado

Power Trowel
　　Palustre Eléctrico

Concrete: Tools & Equipment

Vibrator
Vibrador

Concrete Saw
Sierra para Hormigón/Concreto

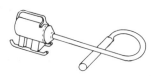

Concrete Pump
Bomba para Hormigón/Concreto

Steel Trowel
Paleta de Acero

Concrete: Systems & Components

Adjustable Horizontal Shore
Apuntalador Ajustable Horizontal/
Puntal Horizontal Ajustable

Composite Metal and Wood Shore
Puntal Compuesto de Acero y
Madera

Concrete: Systems & Components

Concrete Flat-Plate
Losa de Concreto

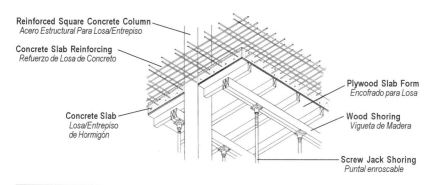

Reinforced Square Concrete Column
Acero Estructural Para Losa/Entrepiso

Concrete Slab Reinforcing
Refuerzo de Losa de Concreto

Concrete Slab
Losa/Entrepiso
de Hormigón

Plywood Slab Form
Encofrado para Losa

Wood Shoring
Vigueta de Madera

Screw Jack Shoring
Puntal enroscable

Spread Footings
Zapata/Fundación Directa

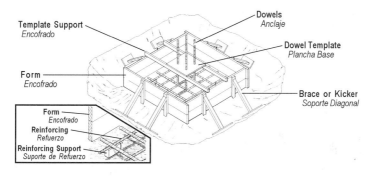

Template Support
Encofrado

Form
Encofrado

Dowels
Anclaje

Dowel Template
Plancha Base

Brace or Kicker
Soporte Diagonal

Form
Encofrado
Reinforcing
Refuerzo
Reinforcing Support
Suporte de Refuerzo

Steel Shore
Apuntalador de Acero/Puntal de
Acero

Structural Scaffolding
Estructura de Andamios

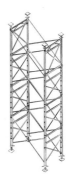

Masonry

Tools & Equipment

Mixer
Mezcladora para Hormigón/Concreto

Mason's Trowel and Jointer
Llana de Albañil y Cepillo Automático

Systems & Components

Concrete Block Wall
Pared de Bloques de
Hormigón/Concreto

Brick Chimney
Chimenea de Ladrillo

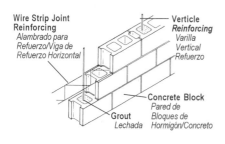

Wire Strip Joint
Reinforcing
Alambrado para
Refuerzo/Viga de
Refuerzo Horizontal

Verticle
Reinforcing
Varilla
Vertical
Refuerzo

Concrete Block
Pared de
Bloques de
Grout   Hormigón/Concreto
Lechada

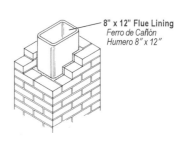

8" x 12" Flue Lining
Ferro de Cañón
Humero 8" x 12"

Brick Veneer Wall System
Muro con Recubrimiento
de Bloque de Ladrillo

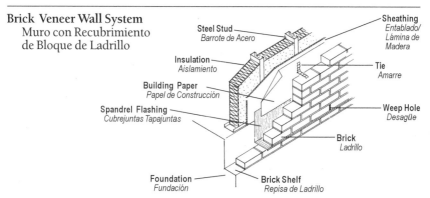

Steel Stud
Barrote de Acero

Insulation
Aislamiento

Building Paper
Papel de Construcción

Spandrel Flashing
Cubrejuntas Tapajuntas

Foundation
Fundación

Brick Shelf
Repisa de Ladrillo

Sheathing
Entablado/
Lámina de
Madera

Tie
Amarre

Weep Hole
Desagüe

Brick
Ladrillo

Structural Steel

Systems & Components

Steel Roof Deck on Joists
Cubierta Metálica Sobre Vigas

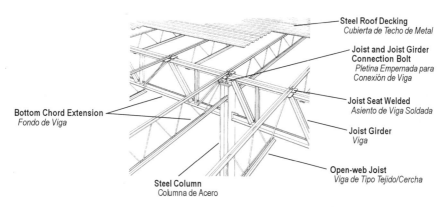

Steel Roof Decking
Cubierta de Techo de Metal

Joist and Joist Girder
Connection Bolt
*Pletina Empernada para
Conexión de Viga*

Joist Seat Welded
Asiento de Viga Soldada

Joist Girder
Viga

Open-web Joist
Viga de Tipo Tejido/Cercha

Bottom Chord Extension
Fondo de Viga

Steel Column
Columna de Acero

Deck and Joists on Bearing Walls
Cubierta y Vigas en Muralles de Soporte

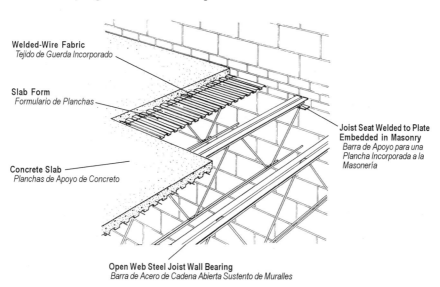

Welded-Wire Fabric
Tejido de Guerda Incorporado

Slab Form
Formulario de Planchas

Concrete Slab
Planchas de Apoyo de Concreto

Joist Seat Welded to Plate
Embedded in Masonry
*Barra de Apoyo para una
Plancha Incorporada a la
Masonería*

Open Web Steel Joist Wall Bearing
Barra de Acero de Cadena Abierta Sustento de Muralles

Carpentry

Tools & Equipment

Electrical Cord
Extensión Electrica

Air Hose
Mangas de Aire

Air Compressor
Compresor de Aire

Chalk Line
Tira Líneas de Cal

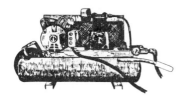

Chisel
Cincel

Crow Bar
Pata de Cabra

Carpentry: Tools & Equipment

Drill
   Taladro

Flat Bar
   Palanca, Plana

Hammer
   Martillo

Nail Gun
   Pistola para Clavos/Clavadora Automático

Nail Puller
   Saca Clavos

Speed Square
   Escuadra

Carpentry: Tools & Equipment

Tape Measure
Cinta para Medir/Cinta Métrica

Tool Pouch
Cinturón para Herramientas

Utility Knife
Cuchilla/Navaja

Chain Saw
Roto Sierra/Sierra Eléctrica

Hand Saw
Serrucho

Reciprocating Saw
Sierra Reciprocadora

Carpentry: Tools & Equipment

Worm-drive Saw
   Sierra Circular de Mano

Router
   Fresadora/Ranuradora

Sander
   Lijadora

Saber Saw
   Caladora Eléctrica

Carpentry: Systems & Components

Wood Framing Nomenclature
   Nomenclatura Para Estructuras de Madera

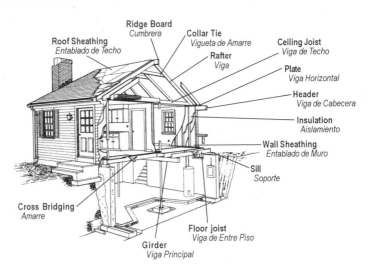

Ridge Board
Cumbrera

Collar Tie
Vigueta de Amarre

Ceiling Joist
Viga de Techo

Roof Sheathing
Entablado de Techo

Rafter
Viga

Plate
Viga Horizontal

Header
Viga de Cabecera

Insulation
Aislamiento

Wall Sheathing
Entablado de Muro

Sill
Soporte

Cross Bridging
Amarre

Floor joist
Viga de Entre Piso

Girder
Viga Principal

Carpentry: Systems & Components

Wood Deck
Cubierta de Madera

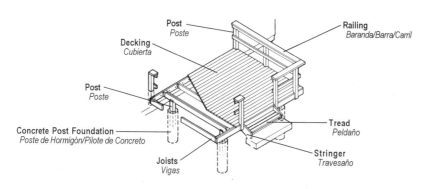

Post — *Poste*
Decking — *Cubierta*
Post — *Poste*
Concrete Post Foundation — *Poste de Hormigón/Pilote de Concreto*
Joists — *Vigas*
Railing — *Baranda/Barra/Carril*
Tread — *Peldaño*
Stringer — *Travesaño*

Kitchen Cabinets
Gabinetes de Cocina

Soffit — *Fascia/Cornisa*
Wall Cabinets — *Gabinetes de Pared*
Counter Top — *Tope de Gabinete*
Base Cabinets — *Gabinetes de Base/ Gabinetes Inferior o de Piso*

Stairs
Escalera

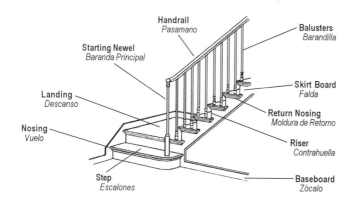

Handrail — *Pasamano*
Starting Newel — *Baranda Principal*
Landing — *Descanso*
Nosing — *Vuelo*
Step — *Escalones*
Balusters — *Barandilla*
Skirt Board — *Falda*
Return Nosing — *Moldura de Retorno*
Riser — *Contrahuella*
Baseboard — *Zócalo*

Carpentry: Systems & Components

Wall Framing
  Estructura de la Pared

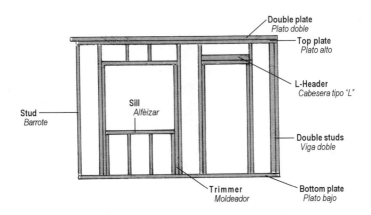

Double plate
Plato doble

Top plate
Plato alto

L-Header
Cabesera tipo "L"

Stud
Barrote

Sill
Alféizar

Double studs
Viga doble

Trimmer
Moldeador

Bottom plate
Plato bajo

Jalousie Window
  Ventana de Celosía de Aluminio

Casement Window
  Ventana Batiente

Double Hung Window
  Ventana Colgante Doble de
  Madera

Skylight
  Claraboya/Tragaluz

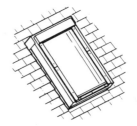

Carpentry: Systems & Components

Sliding Window
Ventana Corrediza de Madera

Door
Puerta

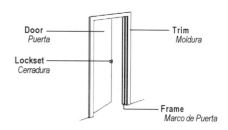

Door — Puerta
Trim — Moldura
Lockset — Cerradura
Frame — Marco de Puerta

Sliding Door
Puerta corredizas, deslizante de dobla hoja

Door Closer
Brazo de Puerta

Locksets
Cerraduras

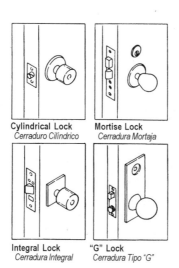

Cylindrical Lock
Cerraduro Cilíndrico

Mortise Lock
Cerradura Mortaja

Integral Lock
Cerradura Integral

"G" Lock
Cerradura Tipo "G"

Carpentry: Systems & Components

Light Gauge Steel
Acero de Bajo Calibre

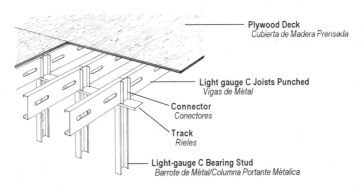

Plywood Deck
Cubierta de Madera Prensada

Light gauge C Joists Punched
Vigas de Métal

Connector
Conectores

Track
Rieles

Light-gauge C Bearing Stud
Barrote de Métal/Columna Portante Métalica

Vinyl Siding
Covertura de Vinil

Building Paper
Papel de Construcción

Vinyl
Vinil

Vinyl
Moldura de Vinil

Backer Insulation Board
Aislante Termico

Metal Framing
Estructura de Metal

Top Rack
Riel Alto/Superior

Horizontal Bridging
Puente Horizontal

Bottom Rack
Riel Bajo/Inferior

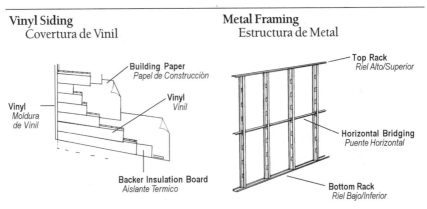

Composite Wood Joists
Viga de Madera Compuesta

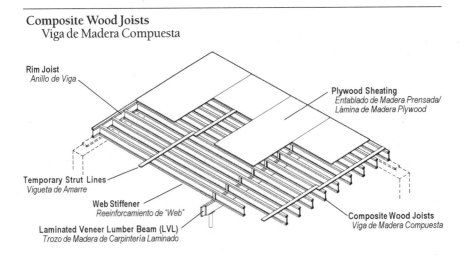

Rim Joist
Anillo de Viga

Plywood Sheating
Entablado de Madera Prensada/ Lámina de Madera Plywood

Temporary Strut Lines
Vigueta de Amarre

Web Stiffener
Reeinforcamiento de "Web"

Laminated Veneer Lumber Beam (LVL)
Trozo de Madera de Carpintería Laminado

Composite Wood Joists
Viga de Madera Compuesta

Roofing

Systems & Components

Clay Tile
    Teja de Arcilla

Asphalt Shingles
    Tejas de Asfalto

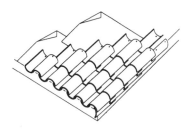

Wood Shingles
    Tejas de Madera

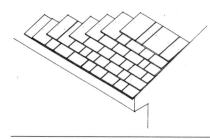

Single Ply Roofing
    Lámina Separada de Techumbre

Insulation
Aislamiento

Metal Fascia
Cubrefaltas de Metal

Treated Wood Blocking
Bloque de Madera Procesada

Membrane Roofing
Techo de Membrana

Treated Wood Blocking
Listón de Madera Tratada
Quimicamente

Steel Roof Deck
Lámino de Acero Corrugado

Roofing: Systems & Components

Roofing System
Sistema de Techo

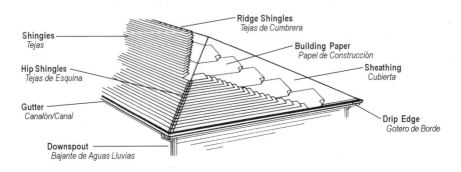

Ridge Shingles
Tejas de Cumbrera

Shingles
Tejas

Building Paper
Papel de Construcción

Hip Shingles
Tejas de Esquina

Sheathing
Cubierta

Gutter
Canalón/Canal

Drip Edge
Gotero de Borde

Downspout
Bajante de Aguas Lluvias

Exterior Trim
Molduras Exterior

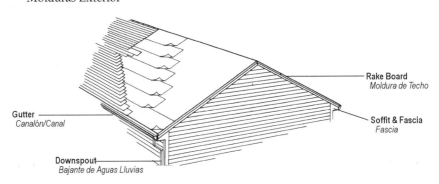

Rake Board
Moldura de Techo

Gutter
Canalón/Canal

Soffit & Fascia
Fascia

Downspout
Bajante de Aguas Lluvias

Finishes

Tools & Equipment

Rolling Scaffold
   Andamio Con Ruedas

Corner Tool
   Herramienta de Esquina

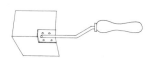

Finishing Knife
   Espátula

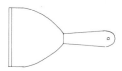

Paint Brush
   Brocha

Drywall Trowel
   Llana de Tabla de Yeso

Roller Frame
   Rodilla de Pintar

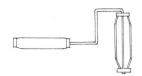

Finishes: System & Components

Gypsum Plasterboard
Panel de Yeso/Tablero de Yeso

Suspended Ceiling System
Sistema de Cieloraso/Cielo Falso de
Suspensión Visible

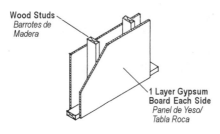

Wood Studs
Barrotes de
Madera

1 Layer Gypsum
Board Each Side
Panel de Yeso/
Tabla Roca

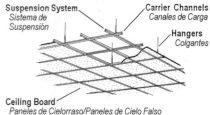

Suspension System
Sistema de
Suspensión

Carrier Channels
Canales de Carga

Hangers
Colgantes

Ceiling Board
Paneles de Cielorraso/Paneles de Cielo Falso

Mechanical

Tools & Equipment

Box Wrench
    Llave

Pipe Hanger
    Soporte para Tuberías

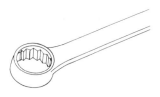

Pipe Wrench
    Llave Tirso/Llave Stilson

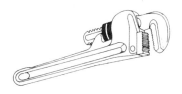

Systems & Components

Bathtub
    Bañera/Tina

Sink
    Lavamanos/Lavabo

Mechanical: Systems & Components

Toilet
Pocera/Inodoro/Sanitario

Heelproof Floor Drain
Drenaje de Piso

Shower Drain
Drenaje de Ducha

Tee-Plain End Pipe
T para Tuberia de Acabado Simple

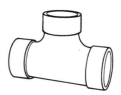

45° Elbow-malleable Iron
Codo de Hierro de 45°

Valve
Válvula

156

Mechanical: Systems & Components

Side Beam Bracket
    Soporte de Viga Lateral

Medium Welded Steel Bracket
    Soporte de Acero Mediano-Soldado

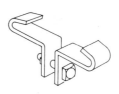

C-Clamp
    Abrazadera Tipo "C"

I-Beam Clamp
    Abrazadera para Vigas Tipo "I"

Extension Pipe or Riser Clamp
    Extensión para Tuberias

Split Ring Pipe Clamp
    Abrazadera de Anillo Separado

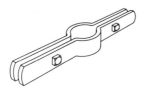

Mechanical: Systems & Components

Alloy Steel Pipe Clamp
Abrazadera para Tubería de Metal

Medium Pipe Clamp
Abrazadera para Tubería Mediana

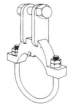

Pipe Supports
Soporte de Tuberías

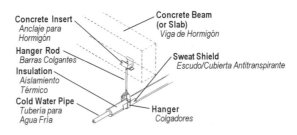

Concrete Insert
Anclaje para
Hormigón

Concrete Beam
(or Slab)
Viga de Hormigón

Hanger Rod
Barras Colgantes

Sweat Shield
Escudo/Cubierta Antitranspirante

Insulation
Aislamiento
Térmico

Cold Water Pipe
Tubería para
Agua Fría

Hanger
Colgadores

Heating System
Sistema de Calefacción

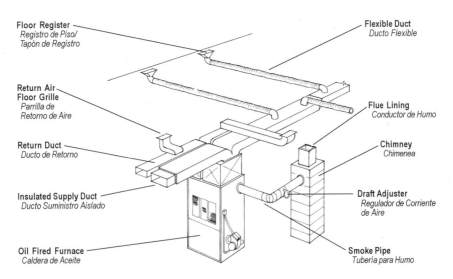

Floor Register
Registro de Piso/
Tapón de Registro

Flexible Duct
Ducto Flexible

Return Air
Floor Grille
Parrilla de
Retorno de Aire

Flue Lining
Conductor de Humo

Return Duct
Ducto de Retorno

Chimney
Chimenea

Insulated Supply Duct
Ducto Suministro Aislado

Draft Adjuster
Regulador de Corriente
de Aire

Oil Fired Furnace
Caldera de Aceite

Smoke Pipe
Tubería para Humo

Mechanical: Systems & Components

Ductwork
Sistema de Conducto

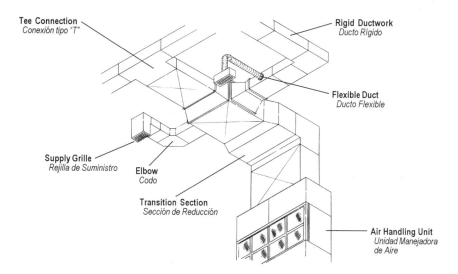

Tee Connection
Conexión tipo "T"

Rigid Ductwork
Ducto Rígido

Flexible Duct
Ducto Flexible

Supply Grille
Rejilla de Suministro

Elbow
Codo

Transition Section
Sección de Reducción

Air Handling Unit
Unidad Manejadora de Aire

Electrical

Tools & Equipment

Hand Bender
    Dobla Tubos Manual
    (para Tubo Metálico)

"Hot Box" PVC Bender
    Dobla Tubos Para PVC

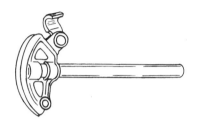

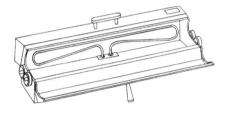

Compression Hand Tool
    Herramienta de Compresión Manual

Screwdriver
    Destornillador

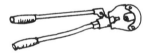

Electrical: Systems & Components

Electrical Service
Servicio Electrico

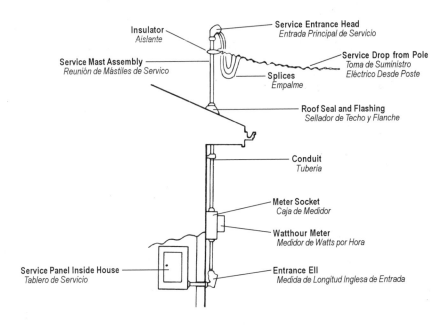

Insulator
Aislante

Service Mast Assembly
Reunión de Màstiles de Servico

Service Entrance Head
Entrada Principal de Servicio

Service Drop from Pole
Toma de Suministro
Eléctrico Desde Poste

Splices
Empalme

Roof Seal and Flashing
Sellador de Techo y Flanche

Conduit
Tuberia

Meter Socket
Caja de Medidor

Watthour Meter
Medidor de Watts por Hora

Service Panel Inside House
Tablero de Servicio

Entrance Ell
Medida de Longitud Inglesa de Entrada

Electrical Switch
Interruptor/Switch

Duplex Receptacle
Toma Corriente Doble

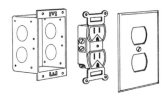

Electrical: Systems & Components

PVC Jacket Connector
    Conector Adaptable de PVC

SER, Insulated, Aluminum
    Conector de Aluminio Aislado Tipo SER

600 Volt, Armored
    Reforzado Para 600 Voltios

5 KV Armored
    Conector de Cable Reforzado Para 5 KV

Cable Support
    Soporte de Cable

Service Entrance Cap
    Topa/Caja de Acometida

Electrical: Systems & Components

EMT Set Screw Connector
Conector Con Tornillos para
Tuberia EMT

EMT Connector
Conector para Tuberia EMT

EMT to Conduit Adapter
Conector para Tuberia EMT y
Tuberia Conduit

EMT to Greenfield Adapter
Adaptador de Tuberia EMT a
Tuberia Greenfield

Aluminum Conduit
Tuberia de Aluminio "Conduit"

Aluminum Elbow
Codo de Aluminio

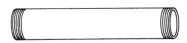

Means
Diccionario
Inglés/
Español de la
Construccion

RSMeans
CMDGROUP

HOME
BUILDER
PRESS
Books to Build On

NAHB

Means
Diccionario Inglés/ Español de la Construcción

Una Herramienta Esencial en el Lugar
de Trabajo y Oficina

Incluye:

- Los Términos de Construcción más Usados
- Frases Útiles
- Ilustraciones Sobre los Sistemas
  de Construcción
- Una Sección de Herramientas de Uso Fácil
- Tablas Prácticas
- . . . con un Sistema de Pronunciación Fonética

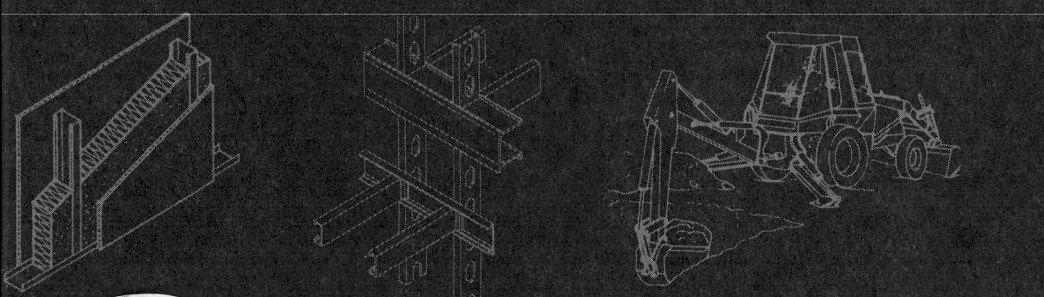

Derechos de Autor 2000

R.S. Means Company, Inc.
Editorial y Consultores de Construcción
Construction Plaza
63 Smiths Lane
Kingston, MA 02364-0800
(781) 585-7880

El editor de éste libro fue Danielle Georges. El encargada de edición fue Mary Greene. El director de producción fue Mike Kokernak. La coordinadora de producción fue Marion Schofield. La composición fue revisada por Paula Reale-Camelio. Robin Richardson fue asistente de correcion y traduccion. El libro y portada fueron diseñados por Norman R. Forgit.

Impreso en los Estados Unidos de América

1 0 9 8 7 6 5 4 3 2 1

Biblioteca del Congreso: Depósito legal número

ISBN 0-87629-578-2

Tabla de Contenido

Prefacio

Hoy en día, el español o castellano es la primera lengua de más de 17 millones de personas en los E.U.A. Según la oficina de censo ("U.S. Census Bureau"), dentro de cinco años, la población hispana será el grupo étnico más grande del país. De allí, mientras más gente habla español en el campo laboral, mayor es la necesidad por crear herramientas que faciliten la comunicación entre los hablantes de español e inglés.

Los clientes de Means nos han hecho saber a través de conversaciones telefónicas, seminarios y proyectos de consultoría, la enorme necesidad de un diccionario ilustrado de uso fácil y organizado de tal modo que sea provechoso para la industria de la construcción.

El *Diccionario Means Inglés/Español de la Construcción* es el resultado de la colaboración entre la empresa R.S. Means Co., Inc., la International Conference of Building Officials (ICBO) y los destacados consultores de normas para construcciones Rolf Jensen & Associates (RJA).

Este diccionario compila los términos más utilizados en la construcción junto con un sistema de pronunciación fonética desarrollado por ICBO. Este mismo diccionario incluye más de 300 expresiones referentes a las normas de construcción y protección contra incendios. Incluso más, este diccionario se caracteriza por mostrar una serie de ilustraciones relacionadas con los sistemas de construcción más comunes y a sus especialidades, indicando no tan sólo los nombres de sus componentes sino también las relaciones entre ellos. También se incorporan dibujos adicionales de herramientas y equipos, organizados según su especialidad: carpintería, concreto, electricidad, masonería, techumbre, trabajos de campo y otros.

Este trabajo es el producto de una extensa investigación llevada a cabo en distintas áreas de la industria de la construcción. Es de utilidad tanto para las personas cuya primera lengua es el español y están aprendiendo el inglés, como para los anglo-hablantes que desean

aprender el español, de modo que sea posible romper las barreras de comunicación que pueden poner en peligro la seguridad y van en deterioro de la productividad, calidad y buenas relaciones laborales. Por ello, este diccionario es una herramienta esencial para las labores diarias de contratistas, personal de obra, arquitectos, inspectores, tanto en la oficina como en el terreno, o en programas de entrenamiento o pasantías laborales. Asimismo, se busca unificar la terminología usada en la construcción en Hispanoamérica con la del sector de habla hispana en los E.U.A.

No obstante, comprendemos que las lenguas evolucionan y por ende, los diccionarios que las compilan lo hacen del mismo modo. De tal manera, querríamos recibir sus opiniones sobre nuestro trabajo. Por favor, háganos llegar sus comentarios y cualquier sugerencia sobre términos que desea incluir en nuestra edición futura del *Diccionario Means Inglés/Español de la Construcción* a la siguiente dirección: Reference Department, R.S. Means Company, Inc., 63 Smiths Lane, Kingston, MA 02364-0800.

Reconocimientos

El primer reconocimiento debe ser dado al equipo de ICBO cuyo *Constructionary* es la base del *Diccionario Means Inglés/Español de la Construcción*. Se reconoce el trabajo de Terry Eddy, gerente de recursos humanos de ICBO, que concibió la idea del *Constructionary*. Reconocimientos para el director de programas y servicios internacionales, Sergio Barrueto; David Jamieson, Editor; Maria Aragon, especialista en mercadeo; Suzane Nunes, coordinadora de desarrollo de productos; y Alberto Herrera, editor, quienes cooperaron en el desarrollo de *Constructionary* de ICBO. Asimismo, se reconoce la colaboración de Philip Ramos, encargado de la construcción en la ciudad de Stanton, California; Mark Stevens, contratista independiente de construcción; Benjamin Rodriguez, representante del sindicato de carpinteros; David Bautista, representante de ventas de productos de la construcción; y Miguel Lamas, inspector de construcción de la ciudad de Pomona, California.

El equipo de Rolf Jensen & Associates contribuyó con más de 300 términos pertinentes a las normas de construcción y protección contra incendios. Se agradece a George Toth, vice presidente de Mercadeo, Jaime Moncado, ingeniero; y Berta Sabogal, traductor técnico de la ciudad de Bogotá, Colombia.

Se da especial agradecimiento a Francisco Polanco, presidente de R.M. Technologies de la ciudad de Lawrence, Massachusetts, por proporcionar una valiosa asistencia en la traducción de las ilustraciones. Un reconocimiento á Scot Simpson por ilustraciones de *Framing & Rough Carpentry*.

El diccionario ha sido completamente revisado por el Profesor Raymond Issa y su equipo de estudiantes de postgrado, Zorina Montiel, Rodrigo Castro y Hector Valdez, de la Escuela de Construcción, M.E. Rinker, Sr. de la Universidad de Florida.

Nota: las guías de pronunciación tanto en inglés como en español fueron desarrolladas en base a los principios simples de comunicación y no en base al Sistema Fonético Internacional empleado en la mayoría de los diccionarios de idiomas.

Guía de Pronunciación

Vocales

A   es una vocal abierta entre la *a* y le *e*. No existe en español

A   es una *a* cerrada que resuaena en la parte posterior de la cavidad bucal. No existe en español.

E   es una *e* cerrada y que resuena en la parte posterior de la cavidad bucal. No existe en español.

U   es una *u* cerrada. Después de la *o* solo se usa para cerrar el diptongo rápidamente.

O   vocal abierta casi como para decir *a*.

IY   es una *i* larga.

Otros simbolos usados

DY   es una sonido fuerte de la *y* o *ll*.

S   suena como el zumbido de la abeja.

TH   como la *z* castellana (thin) o *th* como *d* en (then)

A

Abanico
Fan
(fan)

Abastecimiento de agua
Water supply
(WA-ter se-PLAI)

Abertura
Opening
(O-pen-ing)

Abertura de limpieza
Cleanout (chimney)
(KLI-naut (CHEM-ni))

Abrazadera de carga central
Clamp, center load
(klamp, CENT-r loud)

Abrazadera de pared
Wall bracket
(wal BRAK-et)

Abrazadera en C
C-clamp
(SI-klamp)

Abrazadera grande con brida
Clamp, large flange
(klamp lardsh fleindsh)

Abrazadera para viga doble T
Clamp, T beam
(klamp, TI-bim)

Abrazadera universal de viga superior e inferior
Clamp, universal top and bottom beam
(klamp, iu-ni-VER-sal tap and BAT-m bim)

Acabado
Finish
(FE-nesh)

Acanalado
Splined
(splin-d)
Riffled
(REF-ld)

Acanaladura de chimenea
Chimney chase
(CHEM-ni cheis)

Acceso
Access
(AK-ses)

Acceso para bomberos
Fire department access
(faier d-PART-ment AK-ses)

Accesorio
Fitting
(FE-ting)
Fixture
(FEX-tiur)

Accesorio de tubería
Pipe fitting
(paip FE-ting)

Accesorios
Trimmings
(*TRE-mings*)

Accionado por pólvora
Powder driven
(*PAUD-r DREV-n*)

Acera
Sidewalk
(*SAID-wak*)

Acero
Steel
(*stil*)

Acero fundido/moldeado/colado
Cast steel
(*kast stil*)

Acero galvanizado
Galvanized steel
(*GAL-va-naizt stil*)

Acero inoxidable
Stainless steel
(*STEIN-les stil*)

Acoplamiento
Coupling
(*KAP-ling*)

Acoplamiento de compresión
Compression coupling
(*kam-PRE-shwn KAP-ling*)

Acoplamiento para barras (varillas)
Rod-coupling
(*rad KAP-ling*)

Acoplamiento roscado
Screwed fitting
(*scru-d FE-ting*)

Adherido en secciones
Spot mopped
(*spat MAP-d*)

Aditivos y mezclas
Additives and admixtures
(*AD-e-tevs and ad-MEK-stiurs*)

Adosado
Doubled
(*DAB-ld*)

Agarradera
Handle
(*JAND-l*)

Agarre
Grip
(*grep*)

Agente halogenado
Halogenated agent
(*JA-lodsh-en-AIT-d EIDSH-ent*)

Agente limpio
Clean agent
(*klin EIDSH-ent*)

Aglutinante
Binder
(*BAIND-r*)

Agua atomizada
Water mist
(*WA-ter mest*)

Agua caliente
Hot water
(*jat WA-ter*)

Agua no potable
Nonpotable water
(*nan-PO-tab-l WA-ter*)

Agua potable
Potable water
(PO-tab-l WA-ter)

Agua pulverizada
Water spray
(WA-ter sprei)

Agua templada
Tempered water
(TEM-perd WA-ter)

Aguas negras
Sewage
(SU-eidsh)

Aguas residuales
Waste water
(weist WA-ter)

Aguja
Spire
(SPA-ier)

Agujero
Hole
(joul)

Agujero ciego
Knockout
(NAK-aut)

Aire libre
Open air
(O-pen ER)

Aislamiento, Aislante
Insulation
(en-se-LEI-shwn)
Insulating
(en-se-LEI-ting)

Aislante plástico
Plastic insulator
(PLAS-tek en-se-LEI-tor)

Alambre
Wire
(waier)

Alambre conductor
Conductor wire
(kan-DAKT-r WA-ier)

Alambre de paca
Wire tie
(WA-ier tai)

Alambre de pollo
Chicken wire
(CHEK-n WA-ier)

Alambre de relleno
Filler wire
(FE-ler WA-ier)

Alambre de soporte
Wire backing
(WA-ier BA-king)

Alambre para amarres
Tie wire
(tai WA-ier)

Alambre rastreador/testigo
Tracer
(TREIS-r)

Alarma de incendio manual
Manual pull station
(MAN-iual pul STEI-shwn)

Alarma de incendios
Fire alarm
(FA-ier a-LARM)

Alarma motorizada por agua
Water motor alarm
(WA-ter MOT-r a-LARM)

Alas (columna/viga)
Flanges (column/beam)
(FLEIN-dyes (KA-lem/bim))

Albañil
Mason
(MEI-son)

Albañilería
Masonry
(MEI-sn-ri)

Albardilla
Coping
(KOU-ping)

Alberca
Swimming pool
(SWE-ming pul)

Alcance
Scope
(skoup)

Alcantarilla
Culvert
(KAL-vert)
Sewer drain
(SU-er drein)
Conduit
(KAN-duit)
Storm drain
(storm drein)

Aleación para soldar
Brazing alloy
(BREI-sing A-loy)

Aleación principal
Parent alloy
(PE-rent A-loy)

Alero
Eave
(iv)

Aleros voladizos
Eave overhangs
(iv O-ver-jangs)

Alfarje
Wainscot
(WEIN-skat)
Wainscoting
(WEIN-skat-ing)

Alféizar
Sill
(sel)
Splay
(spley)

Alimentación eléctrica para estufa/cocina
Range power outlet
(reindsh PA-uer AUT-let)

Aliviar
To vent
(tu vent)

Aljibe
Cistern
(SES-tern)

Alma (columna/viga)
Web (column/beam)
(web (KA-lemn/bim))

Almacén
Warehouse
(WER-jaus)

Almacén de líquidos
Liquid storage warehouse
(LE-kuid STO-redsh
WER-jaus)

Almacenamiento apilado
High-piled storage
(jai-pail-d STO-redsh)

Almacenamiento en estanterías
High rack storage
(jai STO-redsh rak)

Almacenamiento en estantes
Rack storage
(*rak STO-redsh*)

Almacenamiento en pilas altas
High-piled storage
(*jai-paild STO-redsh*)

Alquitrán
Tar
(*tar*)

Altura
Height
(*jait*)

Aluminio
Aluminum
(*a-LU-me-nam*)

Alzada (de mortero de cemento)
Grout lift
(*graut left*)

Alzado
Façade
(*fa-SAD*)
Front (of a building)
(*front (av ei BEL-ding)*)

Amarre, Amarra
Binder
(*BAIND-r*)
Tie
(*tay*)

Amortiguador
Suppressor
(*se-PRES-r*)

Ampliación
Addition
(*a-DE-shwn*)

Ancho de la salida
Exit width
(*EX-et wedth*)

Ancianato
Nursing home
(*NER-sing joum*)

Ancla de retención
Hold-down anchor
(*jold daun EN-ker*)

Anclaje
Anchor
(*EN-ker*)
Anchorage
(*EN-ke-redsh*)
Fastener
(*FAS-n-r*)

Anclaje mecánico
Mechanical anchorage
(*me-KAN-ek-l EN-ke-redsh*)

Anclajes para tubería
Pipe clamps
(*paip klamps*)

Andamiaje
Scaffolding
(*SKA-fol-ding*)

Andamio
Scaffold
(*SKA-fold*)

Anillo, bucle
Loop
(*lup*)

Anticorrrosivo
Corrosion-resistant
(*ka-RO-shwn ri-SES-tent*)

Antisifonaje
Antisiphon
(AN-ti-sai-fen)

Antorcha
Torch
(torch)

Anulación
Abatement
(a-BEIT-ment)

Anular
Override
(O-ver-raid)
Abate
(a-BEIT)

Apagador
Circuit breaker
(SER-ket BREI-kr)
Switch
(swetch)

Aparato de ensayo/prueba
Test apparatus
(test a-pa-RA-tus)

Apartamento residencial
Apartment house
(a-PART-ment jaus)

Apoyo
Support
(su-PORT)

Aprobado
Approved
(a-PRUV-d)

Arandela
Grommet
(GRA-met)
Washer
(WASH-r)
Gasket
(GAS-ket)

Arcilla
Clay
(kley)

Área bruta/total
Gross area
(gros E-re-a)

Área cargada/sometida a carga
Loaded area
(LOU-ded E-re-a)

Área ilimitada
Unlimited area
(an-LE-me-ted E-re-a)

Área de refugio
Refuge area
(RE-fiudsh E-re-a)

Área segura de dispersión
Safe dispersal area
(seif dis-PER-sal E-re-a)

Arena
Sand
(sand)

Areniscas
Sandstone
(sand-stoun)

Argamasa
Mortar
(MORT-r)

Armado
Framed
(freimd)

Armadura
Truss
(tras)
Reinforcement
(ri-en-FORS-ment)

Armario de exhibición
Showcase
(SHOU-keis)

Armazón
Framework
(FREIM-wark)
Frame
(freim)

Arquitecto
Architect
(AR-ke-tekt)

Arraigado
Embeded
(em-BE-ded)

Arriostramiento
Bracing
(BREI-sing)

Artefacto
Fixture
(FEX-tiur)

Artefacto de combinación
Combination fixture
(kam-be-NEI-shwn FEX-tiur)

Artefacto de iluminación
Light fixture
(lait FEX-tiur)

Artefacto eléctrico
Electrical fixture
(i-LEK-tre-kal FEX-tiur)

Artefacto sanitario
Bathroom/Plumbing fixture
*(BATH-rum/PLA-ming
FEX-tiur)*

Ascensor
Elevator
(e-le-VEI-tor)

Asentamiento
Slump
(slamp)

Aserradero
Lumber mill
(LAM-ber mel)

Asfalto
Asphalt
(AS-falt)

Asiento de drenaje
Drain seat
(drein sit)

Asiento de válvula (de alarma)
Valve seat
(valv sit)

Asilo de ancianos
Nursing home
(NER-sing joum)

Áspero
Coarse
(kors)

Aspirador
Aspirator
(AS-pe-rei-tor)

Aspiradora
Vacuum
(VA-kium)

Astilladuras
Spalling
(SPA-ling)

Astrágalo
Astragal
(AS-tra-gal)

Atado
Bundle
(BAN-d-l)

Atarjea
Sewer
(SU-er)

Atiesador
Stiffener
(STE-fe-ner)

Atmósfera común
Common atmosphere
(KA-m-n AT-mos-fir)

Atrio
Atrium
(EI-tri-am)

Autocierre
Self-closing
(self-KLO-sing)

Autoenrasado
Self-furring
(self-FE-ring)

Autoignición
Self-ignition
(self-eg-NE-shwn)

Autoluminoso
Self-luminous
(self-LU-mi-nas)

Automático
Automatic
(au-to-MA-tik)

Autoridad competente
Building official
(BEL-ding a-FESH-l)
Code official
(coud a-FESH-l)

Azotado
Plaster
(PLAS-t-r)
Plastering
(PLAS-t-ring)

Azotea
Roof (flat)
(ruf (flat))
Terrace
(TE-ras)

B

Bajante
Stack
(stack)

Bajante de aguas negras
Soil pipe
(soil paip)

Bajante sanitaria
Soil stack
(soil stack)

Bajopiso
Subfloor
(sab-flor)
Underlayment
(an-der-LEI-ment)

Balcón
Balcony
(BAL-ke-ni)

Baldosas
Floor tile
(flor tail)

Baldosas cerámicas
Ceramic tile
(si-RA-mik tail)

Bandeja de carga
Hot bus bar
(jat bas bar)

Bandeja neutra/a tierra
Ground/neutral bus bar
(graund/NIU-tral bas bar)

Bandeja portacables
Cable tray
(KEI-b-l trei)

Banqueta
Sidewalk
(SAID-wak)

Bañera, Bañadera
Bathtub
(BATH-tab)

Baño
Bathroom
(BATH-rum)
Restroom
(REST-rum)
Toilet compartment
(TOI-let kam-PART-ment)
Water closet
(WA-ter KLA-set)

Baranda
Guardrail
(gard-reil)
Railing
(REI-ling)
Rail
(reil)

Barandilla
Rail
(reil)

B

Barda
Wall
(wal)
Fence
(fens)

Barra
Railing
(REI-ling)
Bar
(bar)

Barra de emergencia
Panic bar
(PA-nek bar)

Barra de refuerzo
Rebar
(RI-bar)

Barra de anclaje
Stud anchor
(stad EN-ker)

Barra ómnibus de carga
Hot bus bar
(jat bas bar)

Barras de apoyo/soporte
Grab bars
(grab bars)

Barras desviadas
Offset bars
(AF-set bars)

Barrera antihumo
Smoke barrier
(smouk be-RI-er)

Barrera contra corriente de aire
Draft stop
(draft stap)

Barreta
Bar
(bar)

Barro
Clay
(kley)

Barrote
Stud
(stad)

Base de techo
Subroof
(sab-ruf)

Bastidor
Frame
(freim)

Bastidores de madera
Wood framing
(wud FREI-ming)

Basura
Rubbish
(RA-besh)

Batería
Battery
(BA-te-ry)

Bienestar público
Public welfare
(PA-blek WEL-fer)

Bisagra
Hinge
(jendsh)

Bloque, Bloquear
Block
(blak)
Blocking
(BLA-king)

Bloque antifuego
Fireblock
(*faier-blak*)

Boca
Outlet
(*AUT-let*)

Boca de acceso
Manhole
(*MAN-jol*)

Boca de incendio
Hydrant
(*JAI-drent*)

Boca de inspección
Manhole
(*MAN-jol*)

Boca de salida
Water outlet
(*WA-ter AUT-let*)

Bodega
Storeroom
(*STOR-rum*)
Storage room
(*STO-redsh rum*)

Boiler
Boiler
(*BOI-ler*)

Bola de fuego
Fireball
(*FAIER-bal*)

Bomba
Pump
(*pamp*)

Bomba contra incendios centrífuga
Fire pump, centrifugal
(*FAIER pamp, sen-tri-FIOU-gal*)

Bomba contra incendios de carcasa partida
Fire pump, split-case
(*FAIER pamp, splet keis*)

Bomba de sumidero
Sump pump
(*samp pamp*)

Bombilla
Lightbulb
(*LAIT-bulb*)

Boquete
Hole
(*joul*)

Boquilla
Nozzle
(*NAZ-l*)

Boquilla de neblina
Nozzle, water fog
(*NAZ-l, WA-ter fag*)

Boquilla de rociador
Sprinkler head
(*SPRIN-kler jed*)

Borde
Rim
(*rem*)
Edge
(*edsh*)

Bordes del entablado
Sheating edges
(*SHI-ting ED-yes*)

B

Bordillo
Curb
(kerb)

Borne de enlace
Bonding jumper
(BAN-ding DYAM-per)

Botaguas
Flashing
(FLA-shing)

Botiquín
Medicine cabinet
(ME-des-n KA-be-net)

Bóveda
Vault
(valt)

Brazo
Bracket
(BRA-ket)
Handle
(JAND-l)

Brazo horizontal
Armover
(ARM-o-ver)

Brea
Tar
(tar)

Brida
Flange
(fleindsh)

Brigada de incendios
Fire brigade
(faier bre-GAID)

Bronce
Brass
(bras)

Buharda
Dormer
(DOR-m-r)

Bujía pie (medida de
iluminación)
Foot candles
(fut KAN-dls)

Bulto
Bundle
(BAN-d-l)

Buscador de montantes
Stud finder
(stad FAIN-der)

Buzón
Mail box
(meil bax)

C

Caballete
Coping
(KOU-ping)
Truss
(tras)

Cabeza de pilote
Pile cap
(pail kap)

Caja de alarma de incendios
Manual fire alarm box
(MAN-iual faier a-LARM bax)

Cabeza del rociador
Sprinkler head
(SPRIN-kler jed)

Cabeza plana
Wafer head
(WEI-fer jed)

Cabezal
Header
(JE-der)

Cabio, Cabrio
Rafter
(RAF-t-r)

Cable alambre conector
Wire connector
(waier ka-NEKT-r)

Cable a tierra
Ground wire
(graund waier)

Cable de alimentación
Feeder cable
(FI-d-r KEI-b-l)

Cable de enlace
Ground bond
(graund band)

Cable de extensión
Extension cord
(ex-TEN-shwn kord)

Cable principal
Main power cable
(mein PA-uer KEI-b-l)

Cable neutro
Neutral wire
(NIU-tral waier)

Cable principal neutro
Neutral service wire
(NIU-tral SER-ves waier)

Cabreada
Truss
(tras)

Cadena
Chain
(chein)

**Caja de conexiones
de empalme/union**
Junction box
(DYANK-shwn bax)

Caja de enchufe/tomacorriente
Outlet box
(AUT-let bax)

Caja de fusibles
Fuse box
(fius bax)

Cajones de aire comprimido
Caissons
(*KEI-sans*)

Cálculo hidráulico
Hydraulic calculation
(*jai-DRO-lik
kal-kiou-LAI-shen*)

Cal hidráulica
Hydrated lime
(*jai-DREI-ted laim*)

Cal viva
Quicklime
(*kuek-laim*)

Caldera
Boiler
(*BOI-ler*)
Kettle
(*KE-t-l*)

Calefacción
Heating
(*JI-ting*)

Calefactor, Calentador
Heater
(*JI-ter*)

Calentador de agua
Water heater
(*WA-ter JI-ter*)
Boiler
(*BOI-ler*)

Calhidra
Hydrated lime
(*jai-DREI-ted laim*)

Calibre
Gage/Gauge
(*geidsh*)

Calificación climática
Climatic rating
(*klai-MA-tek REI-ting*)

Caliza
Limestone
(*LAIM-stoun*)

Callejón
Alley
(*A-li*)

Cámara de aire
Air gap
(*er gap*)

Cámara de cebado
Priming chamber
(*PRAI-ming CHEM-b-r*)

Cámara de distribución de aire
Plenum
(*PLE-nam*)

Camara de espuma
Foam maker
(*foum MEI-ker*)

Camino
Walkway
(*WAK-wey*)

Camino peatonal
Pedestrian walkway
(*pe-DES-tri-an WAK-wey*)

Caminos móviles
Moving walks
(*MU-ving waks*)

Camisa
Sleeve
(*sliv*)

Campana (chimenea/cocina)
Hood
(jud)

Campana de cocina
Kitchen hood
(KE-chen jud)

Campanario
Steeple
(STI-p-l)

Canal
Gutter
(GA-ter)
Rib
(reb)
Raceway
(REIS-wey)

Canaleta
Chase
(cheis)
Gutter
(GA-ter)

Canalizaciones
Masonry chase
(MEI-sn-ri cheis)

Cancelar
Override
(O-ver-raid)

Candado
Lock
(lak)

Canilla
Spigot
(SPE-gat)

Cañón de espuma
Foam monitor
(foum MA-net-r)

Canto (a canto)
Edge (on edge)
(edsh (an edsh))

Cañería, Caño
Pipe
(paip)
Piping
(PAI-ping)
Tubing
(TIU-bing)

Cañería principal de gas
Gas main
(gas mein)

Capa
Ply
(plai)

Capa base
Underlayment
(an-der-LEY-ment)

Capa bituminosa debajo del piso de madera
Underlayment
(an-der-LEY-ment)

Capa de colada/vaciado
Pour coat
(por kout)

Capa de cubierta de techo compuesta
Built-up roofing ply
(BELT-ap RU-fing plai)

Capa de humo
Smoke layer
(smouk LEY-r)

Capa de soporte
Underlayment
(an-der-LEY-ment)

Capa intermedia
Interlayment
(en-ter-LEY-ment)

Capataz
Foreman
(FOR-man)

Caperuza
Cap
(kap)

Caperuza de la válvula
Valve cap
(valv kap)

Carbón
Coal
(col)
Charcoal
(CHAR-col)
Carbon
(KAR-bn)

Carga
Load
(loud)

Carga muerta
Dead load
(ded loud)

Carga nominal
Nominal load
(NA-men-l loud)

Carga permanente
Dead load
(ded loud)

Carga sísmica
Earthquake load
(ERTH-kueik loud)

Carga variable
Live load
(laiv loud)

Cargas no balanceadas
Unbalanced loads
(an-BA-lansd louds)

Cargas vivas
Live loads
(laiv louds)

Carpintero
Carpenter
(KAR-pent-r)

Carril
Railing
(REI-ling)

Carro de bomberos
Fire engine
(faier EN-dshen)

Cartela
Bolster
(BOL-st-r)
Haunch
(jaunch)

Cartelera
Tackboard
(TAK-bord)

Cartón de yeso
Wallboard
(WAL-bord)

Casa de convalecencia
Nursing home
(NER-sing joum)

Cascajo
Gravel
(GRAV-l)

Cáscara
Shell
(shel)

Casco
Helmet
(JEL-met)

Casco de seguridad
hard hat
(jard jat)

Caseta de rociado
Spray booth
(sprei buth)

Casquete
Cap
(kap)

Caudal
Flow
(flou)

Caudal
Rate
(reit)

Cavidades ocultas
Concealed spaces
(kan-SIL-d SPEI-ses)

Celda
Cell
(sel)

Celosía
Louver
(LU-ver)

Centro comercial
Mall
(mal)

Cerramiento, recinto
Enclosure
(en-KLO-shiur)

Cerrar
Shut off
(shat af)

Cepa
Trench
(trench)

Cerca
Fence
(fens)

Cercha
Truss
(tras)

Cercha de madera
Wood truss
(wud tras)

Cerradura
Lock
(lak)

Cerrajería de emergencia
Panic hardware
(PA-nek JAR-duer)

Cerramiento
Enclosure
(en-KLO-shiur)

Cerrojo
Latch
(latch)
Lock
(lak)

Certificado de uso
Certificate of occupancy
(ser-TE-fe-keit av
a-kiu-pen-si)

Césped
Lawn
(lahn)

Chapa
Sheet
(*shiyt*)

Chapa metálica
Sheet metal
(*shiyt me-tal*)

Chapopote
Tar
(*tar*)

Chimenea
Chimney
(*CHEM-ni*)

Chimenea de mampostería
Masonry chimney
(*MEI-sn-ri CHEM-ni*)

Chimenea prefabricada
Factory-built chimney/
fireplace
(*FAK-te-ri-belt CHEM-ni/
FAIER-pleis*)
Pre-fab chimney/fireplace
(*PRI-fab CHEM-ni/
FAIER-pleis*)

Cielorraso
Ceiling
(*SI-ling*)

Cielorraso suspendido
Suspended ceiling
(*ses-PEN-ded SI-ling*)

Cierre de tiro
Draft stop
(*draft stap*)

Cimiento, Cimentación
Foundation
(*faun-DEY-shwn*)
Footing
(*FU-ting*)

Cincho
Strap
(*strap*)

Circuito
Circuit
(*SER-ket*)

Circuito a tierra
Ground fault circuit
(*graund falt SER-ket*)

Cisterna
Cistern
(*SES-tern*)

Clapeta
Clapper
(*KLA-p-r*)

Claraboya
Skylight
(*SKAI-lait*)

Claro
Span
(*span*)

Claro de puerta
Doorway
(*DOR-wey*)

Clasificación
Rating
(*REI-ting*)
Occupancy
(*A-kiu-pen-si*)

Clasificación por temperatura
Temperature rating
(*TEM-pra-chour REI-ting*)

Clavado
Spiked
(*spaikt*)

Clave
Keystone
(*KI-stoun*)

Clavija
Plug
(*plag*)

Clavo
Nail
(*neil*)

Clavo afilado
Barbed nail
(*BAR-b-d neil*)

Clavo anular
Annular grooved nail
(*AN-iu-ler GRUV-d neil*)

Clavo con fuste corrugado
Ring shank nail
(*ring sheink neil*)

Clavo de cabeza grande plana
Box nail
(*bax neil*)

Clavo de cabeza perdida
Casing nail
(*KEI-sing neil*)

Clavo largo especial para madera
Spike
(*spaik*)

Clavo oblicuo
Toenail
(*TOU-neil*)

Clavo para madera
Box nail
(*bax neil*)

Clavo sin cabeza
Finishing nail
(*FE-ne-shing neil*)

Cloaca
Sewer
(*SU-er*)

Cloruro de calcio
Calcium chloride
(*KAL-si-am KLO-raid*)

Cobre
Copper
(*KA-per*)

Cobre estirado en frío
Hard drawn copper
(*jard dran KA-per*)

Cobre forjado
Wrought copper
(*rat KA-per*)

Coche de ascensor
Elevator car
(*e-le-VEI-tor KAR*)

Cochera
Garage
(*ga-RADSH*)

Cociente, Coeficiente
Ratio
(*REI-shi-o*)

Código
Code
(*koud*)

Código Uniforme
Uniform Code
(*IU-ne-form koud*)

Codo
Elbow
(*EL-bo*)

Colada de mortero de cemento
Grout pour
(*graut pour*)

Colar
Pour/Cast concrete
(pour/kast KAN-krit)

Colada
Lift
(left)

Colector
Header
(JED-r)

Colector de aba stecimiento
Water main
(WA-ter mein)

Colector de grasas
Grease trap
(gris trap)

Colgadero
Hanger
(JANG-r)
Hanging
(JANG-ing)

Colgante ajustable para vigas laterales
Hanger, side beam adjustable
*(JANG-r, said bim
ad-SHAS-tab-l)*

Colgante de bucle ajustable y oscilante
Hanger, adjustable swivel
*(JANG-r, ad-SHAS-tab-l
SWEV-l)*

Colgante de horquilla
Hanger, clevis type
(JANG-r KLE-vis taip)

Colgante giratorio y elástico
Hanger, malleable swivel
(JANG-r, MAL-ya-b-l SWEV-l)

Colgante para tubería
Pipe hanger
(paip JANG-r)

Columna
Column
(KA-lem)

Columna de agua
Standpipe
(stand-paip)

Columna hidrante
Standpipe
(stand-paip)

Combinación de cargas
Load combination
(loud kam-ben-EI-shwn)

Combustible
Fuel
(fiul)

Combustión
Burning
(BAR-ning)

Comerciable
Marketable
(MAR-ke-tab-l)

Compensar
To offset
(tu AF-set)

Comportamiento
Performance
(per-FOR-mans)

Compresor
Air compressor
(er kam-PRES-or)

Compresor de aire
Air pump
(er pamp)

Compuerta
Hatch
(jatch)

Con clavos ocultos
Blind nailed
(blaind neild)

Con clavos sumidos
Nailing, face
(NEI-ling feis)

Concesión
Trade-off
(treid af)

Concreto
Concrete
(KAN-krit)

Condominio residencial
Condominium
(kan-do-MEN-ium)

Conducto
Duct
(dakt)
Conduit
(KAN-du-it)

Conducto de humo
Passageway (chimney)
(PA-sedsh-wey (CHEM-ni))

Conducto eléctrico
Raceway
(REIS-wey)

Conducto principal de gas
Gas main
(gas mein)

Conducto portacables flexible
Flex conduit
(flex KAN-du-it)

Conductor
Conductor
(kan-DAKT-r)

Conductos de humo
Flue
(flu)

Conector
Connector
(ko-NEKT-r)

Conector con tornillo
Screw connector
(scru ko-NEKT-r)

Conector de alambre
Wire connector
(waier ko-NEKT-r)

Conector de chimenea
Chimney connector
(CHEM-ni ko-NEKT-r)

Conexión
Connection
(ka-NEK-shwn)
Linkage
(LENK-edsh)
Fitting
(FE-ting)

Conexión a tierra
Ground connection
(graund ka-NEK-shwn)

Conexión cruzada
Cross connection
(kras ka-NEK-shwn)

Conexión para bomberos
Fire department connection
(faier d-PART-ment ka-NEK-shwn)

Conexión roscada
Pipe thread connection
(*paip thred ka-NEK-shwn*)

Conexión urbana
Street main
(*strit mein*)

Conjunto
Assembly
(*a-SEM-bli*)

Construcción a dos aguas
Gable construction
(*geib-l kan-STRAK-shwn*)

Construcción apuntalada/no apuntalada
Shored/Unshored construction
(*shord/AN-shord kan-STRAK-shwn*)

Constructor
Contractor
(*kan-TRAKT-r*)

Contaminación
Contamination
(*kan-tam-e-NEI-shwn*)

Contención
Containment
(*kan-TEIN-ment*)

Contracción
Shrinkage
(*SHRINK-edsh*)

Contrachapa de escurrimiento
Counterflashing
(*KAUNT-er-FLA-shing*)

Contrachapar
Interlay
(*EN-ter-ley*)

Contracorriente
Backwater
(*BAK-wa-ter*)

Contraflujo
Backflow
(*BAK-flou*)

Contragrano
Cross-grain
(*KRAS-grein*)

Contrahuella
Riser, rise
(*RAI-s-r, rais*)
Stair
(*ster*)

Contrapeso esférico
Ball weight
(*bal weit*)

Controlador de la bomba contra incendios
Fire pump, controller
(*faier pamp, kan-TROL-r*)

Contrapiso
Subfloor
(*sab-flor*)

Contrapresión
Backpressure
(*BAK-pre-shur*)

Contrasifonaje
Backsiphonage
(*bak-SAI-fon-edsh*)

Contratista
Contractor
(kan-TRAKT-r)

Copa de drenaje
Drip cup
(drep kap)

Copa de llenado
Fillcup
(fel-kap)

Copla
Coupling
(KAP-ling)

Cordón
Curb
(kerb)

Corneta
Horn
(jorn)

Cornisa
Cornice
(KOR-nes)

Cornisa inclinada
Gable rake
(GEIB-l reik)

Corona (grapas)
Crown
(kraun)

Corredor ciego
Dead-end corridor
(ded-end KOR-ri-dor)

Corrediza
Sliding
(SLAI-ding)

Corredor de servicio
Service corridor
(SER-ves KOR-ri-dor)

Corrimiento
Displacement
(des-PLEIS-ment)

Corrosivo
Corrosive
(ko-RO-sev)

Cortacircuito
Circuit breaker
(SER-ket BREI-k-r)

Corte (de una casa)
Section
(SEK-shwn)

Cortina
Curtain
(KERT-n)

Cortina antihumo
Smoke curtain
(smouk KERT-n)

Cortinajes
Hangings
(JANG-ings)

Costilla
Rib
(reb)

Cremallera
Rack
(rak)
Rail
(reil)

Cresta
Ridge
(redsh)

Criterios de carga
Loading criteria
(LOU-ding krai-TE-ria)

Criterio de funcionamiento
Performance criteria
(per-FOR-mans krai-TE-ria)

Cronograma de construcción
Construction schedule (CPM)
(kan-STRAK-shwn SKE-dyul)

Croquis
Lay out
(LEI-aut)

Cuadro
Table
(TEIB-l)

Cuadro de cortacircuito
Circuit breaker panel
(SER-ket BREI-k-r PAN-l)

Cuadro de cubierta de techo
Roofing square
(RU-fing skuer)

Cuarto
Room
(rum)

Cuarto de almacenamiento
Storage room
(STO-redsh rum)

Cuarto de azotea
Penthouse
(PENT-jaus)

Cuarto de baño
Bathroom
(BATH-rum)

Cuarto de calderas
Boiler room
(BOI-ler rum)

Cuarto de huéspedes
Guest room
(GEST rum)

Cuarto interior
Interior room
(en-TE-ri-or rum)

Cuarto de regadera
Shower stall
(SHA-uer stal)

Cuarto intermedios
Intervening room
(en-ter-VIN-ing rum)

Cubierta
Decking
(DEK-ing)
Deck
(dek)
Casing
(KEI-sing)
Canopy
(KAN-e-py)
Cover
(KA-ver)
Shell
(shel)

Cubierta de acceso
Access covering
(AK-ses KA-ve-ring)

Cubierta de azotea/techo
Roof covering
(ruf KA-ve-ring)
Roof deck
(ruf dek)

Cubierta de hormigón/concreto
Concrete cover
(KAN-krit KA-ver)

Cubierta de techo compuesta
Built-up roofing
(BELT-ap RU-fing)

Cubierta de techo de asfalto
Built-up roof covering
(BELT-ap ruf KA-ve-ring)

Cubierta metálica para techos
Metal roof covering
(MET-l ruf KA-ve-ring)

Cubrejuntas
Flashing
(FLA-shing)
Batten
(BA-tn)

Cuerpo/Departamento de bomberos
Fire department
(faier d-PART-ment)

Cuezo
Hod
(jad)

Cumbrera
Coping
(KOU-ping)
Ridge
(redsh)
Ridge cap
(redsh kap)
Ridgepole
(REDSH-poul)

Cuña
Wedge
(uedsh)
Quoin
(kuoin)

Cuota
Quota
(KUO-ta)

Curado con humedad
Moist curing
(moist KIU-ring)

D

Dañino
Hazardous
(JA-ser-des)

De bucles
Tufted
(TAFT-d)

De centro a centro
On center
(an SENT-r)

Declive
Incline
(IN-klain)

Deflector
Deflector
(di-FLECT-r)

Delantal
Apron
(EI-pron)

Densidad de humo
Smoke density
(smouk DEN-se-ti)

**Departamento/Cuerpo
de bomberos**
Fire department
(faier d-PART-ment)

**Departamento de obras/de
construcción/de edificación**
Building department
(BEL-ding d-PART-ment)

Depósito
Storeroom
(stor-rum)
Storage room
(STO-redsh rum)

Depósito a presión
Tank, pressure
(teink PRE-shur)

Depósito enterrado
Tank, underground
(teink, AN-der graund)

Deposito por gravedad
Tank, gravity
(teink, GRA-ve-ti)

Depósito
Reservoir
(RE-se-vouar)

Derivación
Bypass
(BAI-pas)

Desagüe
Drain
(drein)
Drainage
(DREIN-edsh)

Desagüe de área/patio
Area drain
(E-re-a drein)

Desagüe de techo
Roof drain
(ruf drein)

D

Desagüe pluvial
Storm drain
(storm drein)

Desagüe (sanitario) de la edificación/del edificio
Building drain
(BEL-ding drein)

Desahogar
To vent
(tu vent)

Desatascador
Plunger
(PLAN-dsh-r)

Descanso de ascensoreso de escaleras
Landing
(LAN-ding)

Descarga
Release
(ri-LIS)

Descartar
To waive
(tu WEIV)

Descongelación
Thawing
(THA-ing)

Desempeño
Performance
(per-FOR-mans)

Desenganchador
Release
(ri-LIS)

Desenganchar
To release
(tu ri-LIS)

Desfogue de alivio de emergencia
Emergency relief venting
(e-MER-dshen-si ri-LIF VEN-ting)

Despiece
Detailing
(DI-teil-ing)

Desplazamiento
Offset
(AF-set)
Drift
(dreft)
Displacement
(des-PLEIS-ment)

Destino
Occupancy
(A-kiu-pen-si)

Desviación
Offset
(AF-set)

Desvío
Offset
(AF-set)

Detector de calor
Detector, heat
(di-TEKT-r, jit)

Detector de calor termovelocimetro
Detector, rate of rise heat
(di-TEKT-r, reit af rais jit)

Detector de gas
Detector, gas
(di-TEKT-r, gas)

Detector de haz de luz
Detector, lineal beam
(di-TEKT-r, LE-nial bim)

Detector de humo
Smoke detector
(smouk di-TEKT-r)

Detector de múltiples sensores y criterios
Detector, multisensor multicriteria
(di-TEKT-r, MAL-ti-SEN-sor MAL-ti-krai-TE-ri-a)

Detector fotoeléctrico
Detector, photoelectric
(di-TEKT-r, fo-to-i-LEK-trek)

Detector iónico
Detector, ionization
(di-TEKT-r ai-o-nai-zei-shen)

Detector por muestreo de aire
Detector, air sampling
(di-TEKT-r er SEM-pling)

Detector ultravioleta/infrarrojo
Detector, UV/IR
(di-TEKT-r, iou-vi/ai-ar)

Deterioro
Dilapidation
(di-la-pe-DEI-shwn)

Determinar las dimensiones
To proportion
(tu pro-POR-shwn)

Dibujante
Draftsman
(DRAFTS-man)

Dibujos
Working drawings
(WAR-king DRA-ings)

Dimensionado
Proportioned
(pro-POR-shwn-d)

Dimensionar
To proportion
(tu pro-POR-shwn)

Dintel (de la puerta)
Lintel
(LEN-tel)
Header (door frame)
(JE-der (dor freim))

Dioxido de carbono
Carbon dioxide
(KAR-bon dai-OX-aid)

Director de obras
Building official
(BEL-ding a-FESH-l)
Code official
(koud a-FESH-l)

Discapacidad
Disability
(des-a-BEL-e-ti)
Handicap
(JAN-di-kap)

Discapacitado
Handicapped
(JAN-di-kapt)

Diseño
Lay out
(LEI aut)

Diseño basado en criterios de desempeño
Performance based design
(per-FOR-mans beis-d de-SAIN)

Diseñador
Designer
(di-SAI-ner)

D

Disparador
Release
(*ri-LIS*)

Dispensadores de papel
Paper dispensers
(*PEI-per des-PEN-sers*)

Disposición
Provision
(*pro-VE-shwn*)
Proviso
(*pro-VAI-so*)

Dispositivo
Device
(*di-VAIS*)

Dispositivo activador
Initiating device
(*e-ne-shi-EI-ting di-VAIS*)

Dispositivo adaptador
Adapter fitting
(*a-DAP-ter FE-ting*)

**Dispositivo autocerrante/de
cierre automático/mecanizado**
Self-closing device
(*self-KLOU-sing di-VAIS*)
Automatic closing device
(*au-to-MA-tik KLOU-sing
di-VAIS*)

Dispositivo de activación
Tripping device
(*TRE-ping di-VAIS*)

Dispositivo de presión
Pressure operated switch
(*PRE-shur a-pe-REIT-d
swetch*)

Dispositivo de traba
Latching device
(*LA-ching di-VAIS*)

Dispositivo termosensible
Thermosensitive device
(*THER-mo-SEN-se-tev
di-VAIS*)

Distancia a recorrer
Travel distance
(*TRAV-l DES-tens*)

División
Partition
(*par-TE-shwn*)

Doble enclavamiento
Double interlock
(*DOB-l EN-ter-lak*)

**Documentación de obra/
ingeniería**
Building documentation
(*BEL-ding
DA-kiu-men-TEI-shwn*)

Dormitorio
Bedroom
(*bed-rum*)

Dormitorio estudiantil
Dormitory
(*DOR-me-tor-y*)

Drenaje
Drainage
(DREIN-edsh)

Drenaje de bola
Ball drip
(bal drep)

Ducha
Shower stall
(SHA-uer stal)

Ducto
Chute
(shut)

Ducto de basura
Chute, rubbish
(shut, RA-besh)

Ducto de lencería
Chute, linen
(shut, LI-nen)

Duela de madera
Wood shakes
(wud sheiks)

Durmientes
Sleepers
(SLI-pers)

E

Ebanista
Cabinetmaker
(*ka-be-net-MEI-ker*)
Woodworker
(*wud-WAR-ker*)

Edificaciones esenciales
Essential facilities
(*i-SEN-shal fa-SE-le-tis*)

Edificio de un piso
Building, single story
(*BEL-ding, SIN-gl STO-ri*)

Edificio de varias plantas
Building, multistory
(*BEL-ding, MAL-ti-STO-ri*)

Edificación, Edificio
Building
(*BEL-ding*)

Edificaciones inseguras
Unsafe buildings
(*an-SEIF BEL-dings*)

Edificación separada
Detached building
(*di-TACHD BEL-ding*)

**Edificio de apartamentos/
departamantos**
Apartment house
(*a-PART-ment jaus*)

Edificio de gran altura
High rise building
(*jai rais BEL-ding*)

Efecto de golpe de ariete
Toggle effect
(*TOG-gl i-FEKT*)

Electricidad
Electricity
(*i-lek-TRE-se-ti*)

Electricista
Electrician
(*i-lek-TRE-shwn*)

Electrodo
Welding rod
(*UEL-ding rad*)

Electrodoméstico
Appliance
(*a-PLAI-ans*)

Elemento termosensible
Fusible link
(*FIOU-sib-l lenk*)

Elevador
Elevator
(*e-le-VEI-tor*)

Eliminación
Removal
(*ri-MU-val*)

Embridada
Flanged
(*fleindshd*)

Emisión de calor
Rate of heat release
(*reit af JIT ri-LIS*)

E

Empalme
Junction
(DYANK-shwn)
Splice
(splais)

Empalme de compresión
Compression coupling
(kam-PRE-shwn KAP-ling)

Empanelado
Paneling
(PA-nel-ing)

Empaque
Gasket
(GAS-ket)

Empaque de cera
Wax seal
(UAX sil)

Empotrados
Embedded
(em-BED-ed)

Empotrado
Recessed
(RI-ses-d)

Empotradura
Embedment
(em-BED-ment)

Empotramiento
Bedding
(BED-ing)

Encerrado
Enclosed
(en-KLOUSD)

Encerrar
To enclose
(tu en-KLOUS)

Enchufe
Electrical outlet
(e-LEK-tri-kal AUT-let)
Plug
(plag)

Enchufe para estufa/cocinas
Range power outlet
(reindsh PA-uer AUT-let)

Enclavamiento
Interlocking
(en-ter-LA-king)

Encofrado
Formwork
(FORM-wark)

Encofrados
Forms (concrete)
(forms (KAN-krit))

Encogimiento
Shrinkage
(SHRINK-edsh)

Encristalado
Glazed
(GLEIS-d)
Glazing
(GLEI-sing)

Enjarre
Plaster
(PLAST-r)

Enjuta
Spandrel
(SPAN-dr-l)

Enlace
Link
(lenk)
Linkage
(LENK-edsh)

Enlace fusible
Solder link
(SOL-der lenk)

Enlucido
Plaster
(PLAS-t-r)
Plastering
(PLAS-t-ring)
Stucco
(STA-ko)
Putty coat
(PA-ty kout)

Enrasado
Furred out
(ferd aut)
Furring
(FE-ring)

Ensayo
Test
(test)

Escalera de evacuación
Exit stair
(EX-et ster)

Escalera de incendios
Fire escape
(faier es-KEIP)

Escudo de techo
Escutcheon
(es-KA-chen)

Entablado
Sheathing
(SHI-thing)

Entablonado
Planking
(PLEN-king)

Entarimado de tejado
Roof sheeting
(ruf SHI-ting)

Entrada
Doorway
(DOR-wey)

Entramado de madera
Wood framing
(wud FREI-ming)

Entrelazados
Intertied
(en-ter-TAID)

Entrepiso
Attic
(A-tik)

Entubado
Casing
(KEI-sing)

Enyesar
To plaster
(tu PLAS-t-r)

Equiviscosa
Equiviscous
(E-kui-VES-kas)

Escalera
Stairway
(STER-wei)
Stairs
(sters)

Escalera de mano
Ladder
(LA-der)

Escalera mecánica
Escalator
(es-ka-LEI-t-r)

E

Escalera privada
Private stairway
(PRAI-vet STER-wey)

Escaleras circulares
Circular stairs
(SER-kiu-ler sters)

Escaleras de caracol
Spiral stairs
(SPAI-r-l sters)

Escalones
Steps
(steps)

Escape
Exhaust
(ex-AST)

Escombro
Rubble
(RAB-l)

Escopio
Chisel wood
(CHES-l wud)

Escorias
Slags
(slags)

Esfuerzo
Stress
(stres)

Espacio angosto
Crawl space
(kral speis)

Espacio habitable
Habitable space
(JA-be-tab-l speis)

Espacio vací-o
Void space
(void speis)

Espacios ocultos
Concealed spaces
(kan-SIL-d SPEI-ses)

Espuma de baja expansión
Foam, low expansion
(foum, lo ex-PAN-shwn)

Espuma de formación
de capa acuosa
Foam, aqueous film forming
(AFFF)
(foum, AK-wias felm
FOR-ming)

Espuma fluoroproteínica
Foam, fluoroprotein
(foum, flou-ro-PRO-tin)

Espesor
Thickness
(THEK-nes)

Espiga
Spigot
(SPE-gat)

Espirales
Spirals
(SPAIR-ls)

Espuma de plástico
Plastic foam
(PLAS-tek foum)

Estación de bomberos
Fire station
(faier STEI-shwn)

Estancamiento de agua
Ponding
(*PAN-ding*)
Pooling
(*PU-ling*)

Estante
Pallet
(*PA-let*)
Rack
(*rak*)

Esterilizador
Sterilizer
(*STE-re-lai-ser*)

Estipulación
Provision
(*pro-VE-shwn*)
Proviso
(*pro-VAI-so*)

Estrados
Stands
(*stands*)

Estribo para vigueta
Joist hanger
(*dyoist JANG-r*)

Estribos
Stirrups
(*STE-raps*)

Estructura
Frame
(*freim*)
Structure
(*STRAK-tiur*)
Structural Frame
(*STRAK-tiu-ral freim*)
Framing
(*FREI-ming*)

Estructura armada
Framed structure
(*freimd STRAK-tiur*)

Estructura arriostrada
Braced frame
(*breist freim*)

Estructura de gunita/hormigón proyectado
Shotcrete structure
(*SHAT-krit STRAK-tiur*)

Estructura en/de acero
Steel framing
(*stil FREI-ming*)

Estructura en/de madera
Wood framing
(*wud FREI-ming*)

Estructura de muro/pared
Wall frame
(*wal freim*)

Estuco
Stucco
(*STA-ko*)

Estufa
Stove
(*stouv*)
Heater
(*JI-ter*)

Etiqueta
Tag
(*tag*)

Evacuar
To vent
(*tu vent*)

Excavar
Dig
(*deg*)

E

Excusado
Toilet
(TOI-let)

Expansión
Swelling
(SUE-ling)
Addition
(a-DE-shwn)

Explosión
Explosion
(ex-PLO-shen)

Exposición a la intemperie
Exposure
(ex-PO-shiur)

Extinguidor, Extintor
Fire extinguisher
(faier ex-TIN-guish-er)

Extracción
Exhaust
(ex-AST)

Extracción de humo
Smoke exhaust
(smouk ex-AST)

Extremidades
Limbs
(lembs)

Extremos cerrados
Dead end
(ded end)

Eyector de aguas negras
Sewage ejector
(SU-edsh i-DSCHEKT-r)

F

Fachada
Façade
(fa-SAD)
Front (of a building)
(frant (av a BEL-ding))

Falla a tierra
Ground fault
(graund falt)

Falso plafón
Suspended ceiling
(ses-PEN-ded SI-ling)

Fiabilidad
Reliability
(re-lai-a-BEL-e-ti)

Fibra transversal
Cross-grain
(kras-grein)

Fibroso afieltrado
Fibrous-felted
(FAID-res FEL-ted)

Fieltro
Felt
(felt)

Fijadores
Restraints
(RI-streints)

Fila
Row
(rou)

Filtro
Strainer
(STREIN-r)

Flanco
Curb
(kerb)

Fleje
Strap
(strap)

Flejes
Strapping
(STRA-ping)

Flexión
Bending
(BEN-ding)

Flotador
Ball cock
(bal kak)

Fluorescente
Fluorescent
(flo-RES-ent)

Foco
Lightbulb
(LAIT-bulb)

Foco industrial
Floodlight
(FLAD-lait)

Fogón
Firebox
(faier-bax)

Forjados
Plastering
(PLAS-te-ring)

F

Formón
Chisel wood
(*CHES-l wud*)

Franja de tableros
Panel zone
(*PAN-l soun*)

Fregadero
Sink
(*sink*)

Fregadero de cocina
Kitchen sink
(*KE-chen sink*)

Frigorífico
Walk-in cooler
(*WAK-en KU-ler*)

Friso
Wainscot
(*WEIN-skat*)

Fuego con obstáculos
Fire, shielded
(*faier, SHIL-ded*)

Fuego de gran intensidad
High challenge fire
(*jai CHE-lendsh faier*)

Fuego rápido y generalizado
Flash fire
(*flash faier*)

Fuente de alimentación
Power supply
(*PA-uer se-PLAI*)

Fuerza de estiramiento
Jacking force
(*DYA-king fors*)

Función
Occupancy
(*A-kiu-pen-si*)

Fundación
Foundation
(*faun-DEI-shwn*)

Fundente para soldar
Brazing flux
(*BREI-sing flax*)
Welding flux
(*WEL-ding flax*)

Fusible
Fuse
(*fius*)

Fusible de bayoneta
Knife-blade cartridge fuse
(*NAIF-bleid KAR-tredsh fius*)

Fusible de cartucho
Cartridge fuse
(*KAR-tredsh fius*)

Fusible de rosca
Plug fuse
(*plag fius*)

G

Gabinete
Cabinet
(KA-be-net)

Galones por minuto
Gallons per minute (GPM)
(GA-lons per ME-nut)

Gancho
Hanger
(JANG-r)

Gancho en U
U-hook
(IU juk)

Garaje
Garage
(ga-RADSH)

Gases
Fumes
(fiums)

Generador
Generator
(dye-ne-REI-tor)

Generador a motor
Engine driven
(EN-dshen DRE-ven)

Gerente
Manager
(MA-ne-dyer)

Golpe de ariete
Water hammer
(WA-ter JAM-r)

Gotera
Gutter
(GA-ter)

Gradas, Graderías
Bleachers
(BLI-chers)
Grandstands
(grand-stands)
Stands
(stands)

Grava
Gravel
(GRA-v-l)

Grieta
Crack
(kraks)

Grifo
Spigot
(SPE-gat)
Faucet
(FA-set)

Grifo de cierre automático
Self-closing faucet
(self-KLOU-sing FA-cet)

Grifo de manguera
Sill cock
(sel kak)

Grifo de purga
Flood drain
(flud drein)

G

Grosor
Depth
(depth)

Grueso
Coarse
(kors)

Guardaesquinas
Cornerite
(KOR-ne-rait)

Guarnición
Curb
(kerb)

Gunita
Gunite
(GA-nait)
Shotcrete
(SHAT-krit)

H

Habitación
Bedroom
(BED-rum)
Dwelling
(DUE-ling)

Hacha
Axe
(ax)

Hastial
Gable
(GEI-b-l)

Haya
Beech
(bich)

Hembrilla
Eye rod
(AI rad)

Hermético
Tightfitting
(tait FE-ting)

Herrajes antipánico/de
emergencia
Panic hardware
(PA-nek JAR-duer)

Herramienta
Tool
(tul)

Herramienta cuadrada
Square drive
(skuer draiv)

Herramienta para hidrantes
Hydrant wrench
(JAI-drant rench)

Hidrante de pared
Hydrant, wall
(JAI-drant, wal)

Hidrante húmedo
Hydrant, wet
(JAI-drant, wet)

Hidrante seco
Hydrant, dry
(JAI-drant, drai)

Higiene
Sanitation
(sa-ne-TEI-shwn)

Higiene y seguridad
en la construcción
Construction Health and
Safety
(kan-STRAK-shwn JELTH
and SEIF-ti)

Hilada
Wythe
(uayth)

Hilera
Tier
(ti-r)
Aisle
(aiel)

Hogar
Fireplace
(FAIER-pleis)

Hogar de mampostería
Masonry fireplace
(mei-sn-ri FAIER-pleis)

Hogar prefabricado
Factory-built fireplace
(FAK-te-ri-belt FAIER-pleis)
Pre-fab fireplace
(PRE-fab FAIER-pleis)

Horario
Schedule
(SKE-dyul)

Hormigón
Concrete
(KAN-krit)

Hormigón de yeso
Gypsum concrete
(DYEP-sam KAN-krit)

Hormigón liviano
Lightweight concrete
(LAIT-weit KAN-krit)

Hormigón postensado
Posttensioned concrete
(post-TEN-shwnd KAN-krit)

**Hormigón preesforzado/
precargado/pretensado/
precomprimido/prefatigado**
Prestressed concrete
(pri-STRESD KAN-krit)

Hormigón premezclado
Ready-mixed concrete
(RE-di-mixt KAN-krit)

Hormigón premoldeado
Precast concrete
(pri-KAST KAN-krit)

Hormigón proyectado
Shotcrete
(SHAT-krit)

Hormigón reforzado
Reinforced concrete
(ri-en-FORSD KAN-krit)

Hormigonada
Lift
(left)

Hormigón simple estructural
Structural plain concrete
*(STRAK-tiu-ral plein
KAN-krit)*

Horquilla
Fork
(fork)
Yoke
(iouk)

Hospedaje
Lodging house
(LAD-shing jaus)

Hoyo
Hole
(joul)

Huella
Tread
(tred)
Step
(step)

Hueco del elevador
Elevator hoistway
(e-le-VEI-tor JOIST-wey)

Huecos del eslabón
Link eye holes
(lenk AI jouls)

Huella
Stair, tread
(ster, tred)

Huésped
Guest
(guest)

Hulla
Coal
(kol)

Humo
Smoke
(smouk)

Iluminación de emergencia
Emergency lighting
(*e-MER-dshen-si LAI-ting*)

Iluminación industrial
Floodlight
(*FLAD-lait*)

Impermeabilizació
Waterproofing
(*WA-ter-PRU-fing*)

Impermeables al humo
Smoke tight
(*smouk tait*)

Imprimado
Primed
(*praim-d*)

Imprimador
Primer
(*PRAI-mer*)

Impulsado
Driven
(*DRE-ven*)

Incendio
Fire
(*faier*)

Incendio generalizado
Flashover
(*flash-over*)

Incendio premeditado
Arson
(*ar-son*)

Inclinación
Incline
(*EN-klain*)

Incluir
Encompass
(*en-KAM-pas*)

Incombustible
Fireproof
(*FAIER-pruf*)

Incrustado
Embedded
(*em-BE-ded*)

Indicador
Gauge/Gage (instrument)
(*geidsh*)

Indice de tiempo de respuesta (ITR)
Response Time Index (RTI)
(*re-SPANS taim EN-dex*)

Inferior a lo normal
Substandard
(*sab-STAND-rd*)

Informes
Reports
(*re-PORTS*)

Ingeniero
Engineer
(*en-DYE-nir*)

Ingeniero licenciado
Professional engineer
(*pro-FE-sio-nel en-DYE-nir*)

Inodoro
  Toilet
  (TOI-let)
  Water closet
  (WA-ter KLA-set)

Inquilino
  Tenant
  (TE-nent)

Inspector (de obras/ construcción)
  Inspector
  (en-SPEK-tor)

Instalación
  Facility
  (fa-SE-le-ty)

Instalación en obra negra o gruesa
  Rough-in
  (RAF-en)

Instalaciones esenciales
  Essential facilities
  (i-SEN-shal fa-SE-le-tis)

Instalaciones hidráulicas y sanitarias
  Plumbing
  (PLA-ming)

Integridad estructural
  Structural integrity
  (STRAK-tiu-ral en-TE-gre-ti)

Intemperización
  Weathering
  (WE-the-ring)

Interceptor de grasas
  Grease interceptor
  (gris en-ter-SEPT-r)

Interconexión
  Cross connection
  (kras ka-NEK-shwn)

Interruptor
  Switch
  (swetch)

Interruptor automático
  Circuit breaker
  (SEK-ket BREI-k-r)

Interruptor automático bipolar
  Double pole breaker
  (DOB-l poul BREI-k-r)

Interruptor automático principal
  Main breaker
  (mein BREI-k-r)

Interruptor automático unipolar
  Single pole breaker
  (sing-l poul BREI-k-r)

Interruptor de circuito
  Circuit breaker
  (SER-ket BREI-k-r)

Interruptor de flujo
  Water flow switch
  (WA-ter flo swetch)

Interruptor de supervisión
  Supervisory switch
  (su-per-VAI-so-ry swetch)

Interruptores de resorte
  Snap switches
  (snap swetch-s)

Interruptor fusible de seguridad a tierra
  Ground fault circuit
  (graund falt SER-ket)

Interruptor de vac-o
  Vacuum breaker
  (VA-kium BREI-k-r)

J

Jácena
Girder
(GER-der)

Jácena exterior
Spandrel
(SPAN-dr-l)

Jaharro
Plaster
(PLAS-t-r)
Plastering
(PLAS-te-ring)

Jamba
Jamb (door frame)
(dyamb (dor freim))

Jaula (rociador)
Guard
(gard)

Jefe de bomberos
Fire chief
(faier chif)

Jefe de obras
Building official
(BEL-ding a-FESH-l)
Code official
(koud a-FESH-l)

Juego de accesorios
Trim
(trem)

Junta
Joint
(dyoint)
Union
(IU-nion)
Overlap
(O-ver-lap)
Splice
(splais)
Gasket
(GAS-ket)

Junta de aislamiento
Isolation joint
(ai-so-LEI-shwn dyoint)

Junta de collar
Collar joint
(KAL-r dyoint)

Junta de construcción
Construction joint
(kan-STRAK-shwn dyoint)

Junta de control
Control joint
(kan-TROL dyoint)

Junta de dilatación/expansión
Expansion joint
(ex-PAN-shwn dyoint)

Junta horizontal
Bed joint
(bed dyoint)

J

Junta movediza
    Slip joint
      (slep dyoint)

Junta vertical
    Head joint
      (jed dyoint)

L

Ladera
Incline
(EN-klain)

Ladrillo
Brick
(brek)

Ladrillo cerámico
Masonry tile
(MEI-sn-ri tail)

Ladrillo de fuego
Firebrick
(FAIER-brek)

Ladrillo para frentes
Facing brick
(FEI-sing brek)

Lámina, Laminado
Sheeting
(SHI-ting)
Sheet metal
(shiyt ME-tal)

Lámina de cobre
Sheet copper
(shiyt KA-per)

Laminadora
Mill
(mel)

Lámpara
Flashlight
(FLASH-lait)

Larguero central
Mullion (door)
(MAL-ion (dor))

Larguero
Runner
(RAN-r)
Stringer
(STRING-r)

Latón
Brass
(bras)

Lavabo
Sink
(senk)

Lavadora y secadora
Washer and Dryer
(WASH-r and DRAI-r)

Lazadas
Loop
(lup)

Lazo
Hoop
(jup)

Lechada
Laitance
(LEI-tens)

Lechada de cemento
Grout
(graut)

Levantamiento
Lift
(left)

Levantamiento (por viento)
Uplift
(AP-left)

L

Liberación
Release
(ri-LIS)

Libras por pulgadas cuadradas
Pounds per square inch (PSI)
(paunds per skuer ench)

Ligadura
Tie
(tai)

Lima (hoya/tesa)
Hip
(jep)

Lindero
Property line
(PRA-per-ti lain)

Linea
Line
(lain)

Línea de alimentación
Feeder
(FID-r)

Línea de centro
Center line
(SENT-r lain)

Linea de gis/de marcar
Chalk line
(chak lain)

Línea de propiedad
Property line
(PRA-per-ti lain)

Línea media
Center line
(SENT-r lain)

Líquido combustible
Combustible liquid
(kam-BAS-tab-l LE-kuid)

Líquido inflamable
Flammable liquid
(FLAM-a-bl LE-kuid)

Listón
Strip
(strep)
Lath
(lath)

Listón de enrasado
Furring strip
(FA-ring strep)

Listón para clavar
Nailing strip
(NEI-ling strep)

Listón travesaño
Batten
(BAT-n)

Listón yesero
Gypsum lath
(DYEP-sam lath)

Llave
Faucet
(FA-set)
Spigot
(SPE-gat)

Llave de alivio
Relief valve
(re-LIF valv)

Llave de contraflujo
Check valve
(check valv)

Llave de flotador
Ball cock
(bal kak)

Llave de flujo
Ball valve
(bal valv)

Llave de mezcla
Mixing valve
(MEX-ing valv)

Llave de paso
Gate valve
(geit valv)

Lobby
Lobby
(LA-bi)

Local
Premises
(PRE-me-ses)

Localización de averías
Trouble shooting
(TRAB-l SHU-ting)

Lona
Tarp
(tarp)

Losa
Slab
(slab)

Loseta
Floor tile
(flor tail)
Small slab
(smal slab)

Lote
Lot
(lat)
Lift
(left)

Lugar de la obra/en la obra
Site
(sait)
Jobsite
(DYOB-sait)

Luz
Span
(span)

Luz de emergencia
Emergency light
(e-MER-dshen-si lait)

Luz estroboscópica
Strobe light
(STROUB lait)

M

Machihembrado
Tongue and groove
(*tang and gruv*)

Madera aglomerada
Particleboard
(*PAR-tek-l bord*)

Madera clasificada/elaborada
Graded lumber
(*GREI-ded LAMB-r*)

Madera contrachapada
Plywood
(*PLAI-wud*)

Madera de construcción
Timber
(*TEMB-r*)
Lumber
(*LAMB-r*)

Madera de secoya
Redwood
(*RED-wud*)

Madera estacionada
Seasoned wood
(*SI-sond wud*)

Madera prensada
Plywood
(*PLAI-wud*)

Madera tratada
Treated wood
(*TRI-ted wud*)

Maderos
Timber
(*TEMB-r*)

Maderos aserrados
Sawn timber
(*sahn TEMB-r*)

Maderos estructurales
Heavy timber
(*JE-vi TEMB-r*)

Malla de alambre
Wire fabric
(*waier FA-brik*)

Malla de enlucir
Lath
(*lath*)

Mampara
Bulkhead
(*BALK-jed*)

Mampara, barrera, muro de contención
Bulk head
(*BALK-jed*)

Mampara de ducha
Shower door
(*SHA-uer dor*)

Mampostería
Masonry
(*MEI-sn-ri*)

Mampostería reforzada
Reinforced masonry
(*ri-en-FORS-d MEI-sn-ri*)

Manchón de manguito
Compression coupling
(*kam-PRE-shwn KA-pling*)

M

Manga
Sleeve
(sliv)

Mango
Handle
(JAND-l)

Manguera
Hose
(jous)

Manguera manual
Hand hose
(jand jous)

Manguito
Coupling
(KAP-ling)
Sleeve
(sliv)

Manguito y tapa
Nip and caps
(nep and caps)

Manguito, niple
Nipple
(NEP-l)

Manija
Handle
(HAND-l)

Manipulación
Handling
(JAND-ling)

Manipular
Handle
(JAND-l)

Mano de obra
Workmanship
(WARK-man-shep)

Manómetro
Gauge/Gage (instrument)
(geidsh)

Manómetro de inspección
Inspector's test gage
(en-SPEK-tors test geidsh)

Mansarda
Mansard roof
(MAN-sard ruf)

Marco
Frame
(freim)

Marco de puerta
Door frame
(dor freim)

Marco de ventana
Window frame
(WEN-dou freim)

Marquesina
Marquee
(mar-KI)

Masillado, Masillar
Caulking
(KA-king)

Mástil metálico
Metal flagpole
(ME-tal FLAG-poul)

Mastique
Mastic
(MAS-tik)

Mastique de cal
Lime putty
(laim PA-ty)

Matafuegos
Fire extinguisher
(faier ex-TEN-gui-sher)

Material altamente tóxico
Highly toxic material
(JAI-li TAX-ek ma-TE-ri-al)

Material de revestimiento
Wainscoting
(WEIN-sca-ting)

Material para pisos
Flooring
(FLO-ring)

Material peligroso
Hazardous material
(JA-ser-des ma-TE-ri-al)

**Materiales resistentes
a la corrosión**
Corrosion-resistant materials
*(ka-RO-shwn ri-SES-tent
ma-TE-ri-al)*

Matriz
Main
(mein)

Mediera
Fence
(fens)

Medidor
Meter
(MI-ter)

Medios de salida
Means of egress
(mins av I-GRES)

Memoria volátil
Volatile memory
(VO-la-tail MEM-ri)

Mezcla
Mortar
(MORT-r)

Mezcla aditiva
Admixture
(ad-MEX-tiur)

Mezcladora
Mixer
(MEX-er)

Miembros
Limbs
(lembs)
Members
(MEM-br-s)

Mingitorio
Urinal
(IUR-i-nal)

Minusválido
Handicapped
(JAN-di-kapt)

Modificar
Alter
(AL-ter)

Modificación
Alteration
(al-te-REI-shwn)

Mojinete
Coping
(KOU-ping)

Moldura
Molding
(MOL-ding)
Trim
(trem)

Monitor de agua
Monitor nozzle
(MA-net-r NOZ-l)

M

Montacargas
Forklift
(fork-left)
Dumbwaiter
(DAM-wei-ter)

Montaje
Assembly
(a-SEM-bli)
Installation
(en-sta-LEI-shwn)
Mounting
(MOUN-ting)

Montante
Stud
(stad)
Gable stud
(GEIB-l stad)

Montante de acero
Steel stud
(stil stad)

Montaplatos
Dumbwaiter
(DAM-wei-ter)

Morsa
Vise
(vais)

Mortero
Mortar
(MORT-r)

Mortero de cemento
Grout
(graut)

Movido por motor
Motor driven
(MOT-r DRE-ven)

Mueble de combinación
Combination fixture
(kam-be-NEI-shwn FEX-tiur)

Mueble sanitario
Plumbing appliance
(PLA-ming a-PLAI-ans)

Muesca
Rabbet
(RA-bet)
Chase
(cheis)

Muro
Wall
(wal)

Muro cortafuego
Fire rated assembly
(faier REIT-d a-SEM-bli)

Muro cortante/de corte
Shear wall
(shir wal)

Muro con montantes
Stud wall
(stad wal)

Muro de carga
Bearing wall
(BE-ring wal)

Muro de contención/retención
Retaining wall
(re-TEI-ning wal)

Muro de fundación
Foundation wall
(*faun-DEI-shwn wal*)

Muro de parapeto
Parapet wall
(*PA-ra-pet wal*)

Muro de retención en voladizo
Cantilever retaining wall
(*kan-te-LI-ver ri-TEI-ning
wal*)

Muro de relleno
Spandrel
(*SPANDR-l*)

Muro doble
Wythe
(*waith*)

Muro en seco
Dry wall
(*drai wal*)

Muro exterior
Exterior wall
(*ex-TE-ri-or wal*)

Muro hueco
Cavity wall
(*KA-ve-ti wal*)

Muro no portante
Nonbearing wall
(*nan-BE-ring wal*)

Muro portante
Bearing wall
(*BE-ring wal*)

Muro portante con montante
Stud bearing wall
(*stad BE-ring wal*)

Muro subterráneo
Below-grade wall
(*bi-LO-greid wal*)

Muro revestido
Faced wall
(*feist wal*)

Muro sismorresistente
Shear wall
(*shir wal*)

Muros rajados
Cracked walls
(*krakt wals*)

N

Niple montante
Riser niple
(RAIS-r NEP-l)

Nivel (de terreno)
Level
(LEV-l)
Floor
(flor)
Grade
(greid)

Nivel de inundación
Flood level rim
(flad LEV-l rem)

Nivel de piso
Floor
(flor)

Nivel de piso terminado
Finished floor level
(FE-neshd flor LEV-l)

Nivelación, nivelación de terreno
Grading
(GREI-ding)

Nocivo
Hazardous
(JA-sar-des)

No tejido
Nonwoven
(nan UOV-n)

Notificación de incendios
Fire notification
(faier no-te-fe-KE-shen)

Número de ocupantes
Occupant load
(A-kiu-pant loud)

O

Obra
Work
(wark)
Field
(fi-ld)

Obra de construcción
Building site
(BEL-ding sait)

Oficina principal
Headquarters
(JED-kuar-ters)

Oficial de códigos
Code official
(coud a-FESH-l)

Ojal
Grommet
(GRA-met)

Oleaje de las mareas
Tidal surge
(TAID-l serdsh)

Orificio de entrada
Inlet
(EN-let)

Oxidantes
Oxidizers
(ax-e-DAIS-rs)

P

Palanca
Lever
(LE-ver)

Palanca de trinquete
Latch lever
(latch LE-ver)

Palco de prensa
Press box
(pres bax)

Pandeo
Buckling
(BAK-ling)
Crippling
(KREP-ling)

Panel
Board
(bord)

Panel acústico
Acoustical tile
(a-KUS-te-kal tail)

Panel de yeso
Gypsum board
(DYEP-sam bord)
Gypsum wallboard
(DYEP-sam WAL-bord)

Paneles colocados
Lay-in panels
(LEI-en PAN-ls)

Papel de brea
Tar paper
(tar PEI-per)

Papel Kraft
Kraft paper
(kraft PEI-per)

Parante
Stud
(stad)

Parcela
Property
(PRA-per-ti)
Parcel
(PAR-sel)

Pared
Wall
(wal)

Pared exterior
Exterior wall
(ex-TE-ri-or wal)

Pared de barrotes
Stud wall
(stad wal)

Paredes rajadas
Cracked walls
(kract wals)

Pared no portante
Wall, non-bearing
(wal, nan-BE-ring)

Pared portante
Wall, bearing
(wal, BE-ring)

Pared tipo cortina
Curtain wall
(KERT-n wal)

P

Parlante
Speaker
(SPIK-r)

Parrilla
Barbecue
(BAR-be-kiu)

Partidas
Cracks
(kraks)

Pasador
Pin
(pen)
Drift pin
(dreft pen)
Dowel pin
(DA-ul pen)

Pasamanos
Handrail
(JAND-reil)

Pasillo
Passageway
(PA-sedsh-wey)
Hallway
(JAL-wey)
Aisle
(aiel)

Paso
Run
(ran)

Pasta de muro
Joint compound
(dyoint KAM-paund)
Taping compound
(TE-ping KAM-paund)

Pasto
Lawn
(lon)

Patín
Flange
(fleindsh)

Patio externo
Yard
(yard)

Patio interno
Court
(kourt)

Pavimento
Pavement
(PEIV-ment)

Pedestales
Sills
(sels)

Pegamento
Glue
(glu)

Peldaños
Steps
(steps)

Peligro
Hazard
(JA-serd)

Peligros especiales
Special hazards
(SPE-shal JA-serds)

Peligroso
Hazardous
(JA-ser-des)

Pendiente
Slope
(sloup)
Incline
(EN-klain)
Pitch
(petch)

Peralte
Riser
(RAI-s-r)

Perforación
Drilling
(DRE-ling)

Perjuicio
Nuisance
(NIU-sens)

Perlita
Perlite
(PERL-ait)

Permiso (de construcción)
Permit
(PER-met)

Perno
Bolt
(bolt)

Perno de anclaje
Anchor bolt
(EN-ker bolt)

Perno de expansión
Expansion bolt
(ex-PAN-shwn bolt)

Perno de seguridad
Lock bolt
(lak bolt)

Piedra
Rock
(rak)
Stone
(stoun)

Piedra angular
Quoin
(kuoin)

Piedra arenisca
Sandstone
(sand-stoun)

Piedra de sillar
Cast stone
(kast stoun)

Piedra moldeada
Cast stone
(kast stoun)

Pieza de inflexión
Offset
(AF-set)

Pieza de refuerzo
Stiffener
(stef-ner)

Pieza de unión
Binder
(BAIND-r)

Pieza en S
Offset
(AF-set)

Pila
Battery
(BA-te-ri)

Pileta de cocina
Kitchen sink
(KE-chen senk)

P

Pilotes
Piles
(pails)

Pilotes sin encamisar/sin camisa
Uncased concrete piles
(an-KEIST KAN-krit pails)

Pincel
Brush
(brash)

Pintor
Painter
(PEIN-ter)

Piscina (de natación)
Swimming pool
(SWE-ming pul)

Piso
Floor
(flor)
Story
(STO-ri)

Piso blando
Soft story
(saft STO-ri)

Piso cerámico
Ceramic floor
(si-RA-mek flor)

Piso enlistonado de madera
Wood strip flooring
(wud strep FLO-ring)

Piso flexible
Soft story
(saft STO-ri)

Placa
Plate
(pleit)

Placa de base
Sole plate
(soul pleit)

Placa de cartela
Gusset plate
(GE-set pleit)

Placa de pared
Wall face
(wal feis)

Placa de refuerzo
Doubler plate
(DA-bler pleit)

Placa de solera
Sill plate
(sel pleit)

Placa de solera de fundación
Foundation sill plate
(faun-DEI-shwn sel pleit)

Placa de unión
Gusset plate
(GE-set pleit)

Placa del interruptor
Switch plate
(swetch pleit)

Placa plegada
Folded plate
(FOL-ded pleit)

Plafón de yeso
Gypsum board
(DYEP-sam bord)

Plan de avance de la obra
Construction schedule (CPM)
(kan-STRAK-shwn SKE-dyul)

Plancha
Sheet
(shiyt)

Plancha de blindaje
Shield plate
(*shild pleit*)

Plancha de escurrimiento
Flashing
(*FLASH-ing*)

Plancha de yeso
Gypsum board
(*DYEP-sam bord*)
Gypsum wallboard
(*DYEP-sam WAL-bord*)
Wallboard
(*WAL-bord*)

Planchas de empalme
Splice plates
(*splais pleits*)

Planchuela de perno
Washer
(*WASH-r*)

Planos
Design drawings
(*di-SAIN DRA-ings*)
Working drawings
(*WAR-king DRA-ings*)

Planos de ejecución
Shop drawings
(*shap DRA-ings*)

Planta
Floor
(*flor*)
Story
(*STO-ri*)
Floor level
(*flor LEV-l*)
Plant
(*plant*)

Planta baja
Ground level
(*graund LEV-l*)

Planta central de calefacción
Central heating plant
(*CEN-tral JI-ting plant*)

Plantillas
Templates
(*TEM-pleits*)

Plataforma
Floor deck
(*flor dek*)

Plataforma de carga
Pallet
(*PA-let*)

Plataforma metálica
Metal deck
(*ME-tal dek*)

Pleno
Plenum
(*PLE-nam*)

Pleno de aire con entrada externa de aire
Outside air intake plenum
(*AUT-said er EN-taik PLE-nam*)

Pliego
Sheet
(*shiyt*)

Plomada
Plumb bob
(*plam bab*)

Plomería
Plumbing
(*PLAM-ing*)

P

Plomero
Plumber
(*PLAM-r*)

Polvo químico seco
Dry chemical powder
(*drai KE-mi-kal PAU-der*)

Portal
Doorway
(*DOR-wei*)

Portante
Bearing
(*BE-ring*)

Portátil
Portable
(*POR-tab-l*)

Pórtico
Frame
(*freim*)

Pórtico arriostrado
Braced frame
(*breist freim*)

Postes
Poles
(*pouls*)
Posts
(*pousts*)

Pozo
Well
(*wel*)

Pozos de válvulas
Valve pit
(*valv pet*)

Pozo de agua
Water well
(*WA-ter wel*)

Pozo de confluencia/de entrada
Manhole
(*MAN-jol*)

Pozo excavado
Dug well
(*dag wel*)

Pozo hincado
Driven well
(*DREV-n wel*)

Pozo perforado
Bored well
(*BOR-d wel*)

Pozo taladrado
Drilled well
(*DREL-d wel*)

Presion
Pressure
(*PRE-shur*)

Presión de retorno
Back pressure
(*bak PRE-shur*)

Prevención de incendios
Fire prevention
(*faier pri-VEN-shen*)

Pretil
Parapet
(*PA-ra-pet*)
Concrete (stone/brick) railing
(*KAN-krit (stoun/brek)
REI-ling*)

Primer piso
First story
(*ferst STO-ri*)
First floor
(*ferst flor*)

Principal
Main
(mein)

Privado
Private
(PRAI-vet)

Propiedad
Property
(PRA-per-ti)

Proporción
Rate
(reit)
Proportion
(pro-POR-shwn)

Proporcionador de espuma
Foam proportioner
(foum pro-POR-shwn-r)

Protección al público
Public safety
(PAB-lek SEIF-ti)

Protección contra incendios
Fire protection
(faier pro-TEK-shen)

Protección contra la humedad
Dampproofing
(damp-PRU-fing)

Provisional
Temporary
(TEM-po-RE-ry)

Prueba de aceptación
Acceptance test
(ak-SEP-tens test)

Prueba de copa cerrada
Tag closed cup tester
(tag kloust kap TEST-r)

Puerta
Door
(dor)

Puerta con bisagras laterales
Side-hinged door
(SAID-jindsht dor)

Puerta/ventana deslizante/ corrediza
Sliding door/window
(SLAI-ding dor/WEN-dou)

Puerta de evacuación, salida
Exit door
(EX-et dor)

Puerta de salida
Exit door
(EX-et dor)

Puerta giratoria
Revolving door
(ri-VALV-ing dor)

Puerta pivotante
Swinging door
(SWING-ing dor)

Puertas mecánicas
Power doors
(pa-uer dor)

Puesta a tierra de equipos
Equipment grounding
(e-KUEP-ment GRAUN-ding)

Pulsador de alarma
Alarm box
(a-LARM bax)

Pulsador de alarma
Pull station
(poul STEI-shwn)

P

Pulsador manual de alarma
Manual pull station
(MAN-iual poul STEI-shwn)

Puntal
Strut
(strat)

Puntal de empuje
Thrust blocks
(thrast blaks)

Puntales
Shores
(shors)
Shoring
(SHOR-ing)

Puntales de refuerzo
Reshores
(RI-shors)
Bridging
(BRE-dying)

Punto de actuación, activación
Trip point
(TREP point)

Purga tipo clapeta
Clapper-type drip
(KLAP-r taip drep)

Q

Quebrada
Ditch
(detch)
Ravine
(ra-VIN)
Gulch
(galch)

Quebradizo
Brittle
(BRET-l)

Querosén, Querosín
Kerosene
(ke-RO-sin)

Quicio, Quicial
Jamb (door frame)
(dyamb (dor freim))

Quiosco
Kiosk
(KI-osk)

R

Rajaduras
Cracking
(*KRAK-ing*)

Ramal
Branch
(*branch*)
Branch line
(*branch lain*)

Ramal lateral
Lateral pipe
(*LA-te-ral paip*)

Ranura
Rabbet
(*RA-bet*)
Groove
(*gruv*)
Mortise
(*MOR-tis*)

Ranurado
Riffled
(*REF-ld*)

Rasante
Grade (ground elevation)
(*greid (graund
e-le-VEI-shwn)*)

Rascacielos
Skyscraper
(*skai-SKREI-per*)
Building, high-rise
(*BEL-ding jai-rais*)

Razón
Rate
(*reit*)
Ratio
(*REI-shio*)

Reanimar (fuego)
Rekindle
(*re-KEND-l*)

Rebajo a media madera
Shiplap
(*shep-lap*)

Recámara
Bedroom
(*BED-rum*)

Recinto
Shaft
(*shaft*)

Recinto de ascensor
Elevator shaft
(*e-le-VEI-tor shaft*)

Recinto de escaleras
Stairwells
(*ster-wels*)
Enclosed stairway
(*en-klousd STER-wei*)

Recinto de ventilación
Vent shaft
(*vent shaft*)

Recipiente
Vessel
(*VE-sel*)

R

Recipiente a presión
  Vessel
  (VE-sel)

Recojegotas
  Weep screed
  (wip skrid)

Recubrimiento
  Cover
  (KA-ver)
  Lining
  (LAI-ning)

Red de abastecimiento publico
  Public main
  (PAB-lek mein)

Reducción
  Shrinkage
  (SHRINK-edsh)

Reformatorio
  Reformatory
  (re-FORM-a-to-ri)

Refuerzo
  Reinforcement
  (ri-en-FORS-ment)
  Stiffener
  (STEF-ner)

Regadera
  Showerhead
  (SHA-uer-jed)
  Shower stall
  (SHA-uer stal)

Región
  Region
  (RID-sh-n)

Registro
  Cleanout
  (KLIN-aut)

Regulador cortafuego
  Damper, fire
  (DEMP-r, faier)

Regulador estanco al humo
  Damper, smoke
  (DEMP-r, smouk)

Regleta
  Reglet
  (REG-let)

Regulador
  Damper
  (DAM-per)
  Regulator
  (reg-iu-LEI-tor)

Reja, Rejilla
  Grille
  (gril)

Rejilla (pared/techo)
  Register (wall/ceiling)
  (RE-dyis-ter (wal/SI-ling))

Rejilla de piso
  Baseboard register
  (BEIS-bord RE-dyis-ter)

Relación
  Ratio
  (REI-shio)
  Rate
  (reit)

Relé temporizador
  Time relay
  (taim RI-lei)

Rellano
Stair, landing
(*ster LAND-ing*)

Rellenado
Filled
(*feld*)

Relleno
Backfill
(*BAK-fel*)

Relleno sin consolidar
Unbalanced fill
(*an-BAL-ansd fel*)

Remache
Rivet
(*RE-vet*)

Remanso
Backwater
(*BAK-WA-ter*)

Remate de borde
Return lip
(*ri-TERN lep*)

Remoción
Removal
(*re-MU-v-l*)
Abatement
(*a-BEIT-ment*)

Remonte
Uplift
(*AP-left*)

Remover
Abate
(*a-BEIT*)

Rendimiento
Performance
(*per-FOR-mans*)

Renunciar a un derecho
To waive
(*tu weiv*)

Reparación, Reparo
Repair
(*ri-PEIR*)
Overhaul
(*O-ver-jaul*)

Repello
Plastering
(*PLAS-te-ring*)

Repisa
Apron
(*E-pran*)
Shelf
(*shelf*)

Repisa de ventana
Window sill
(*WEN-dou sel*)

Reportes
Reports
(*ri-PORTS*)

Resaltar
Set out
(*set aut*)

Residencia
Dwelling
(*DUEL-ing*)
Residence
(*RE-se-dens*)
Mansion
(*MAN-shwn*)

Residencia comunitaria
Congregate residence
(*KAN-gre-geit re-se-dens*)

Residencias para estudiantes
Dormitory
(DOR-me-to-ri)

Resistir
To support
(tu sa-PORT)

Resistente a la corrosión
Corrosion-resistant
(ka-RO-shwn ri-SES-tent)

Resistente al fuego (en tiempo)
Fire rated (time)
(faier reit-d taim)

Resistente al fuego
Fire resistance
(faier re-SIS-tans)

Respiradero de compensación
Compensating vents
(kom-pen-SAI-ting vents)

Resorte
Spring
(spreng)

Respaldo
Backing
(BAK-ing)

Respiradero
Vent
(vent)

**Respiradero con codo
de 180 grados**
Return bend vent pipe
(ri-TURN bend vent paip)

Respiradero de bajante
Stack vent
(stack vent)

Respiradero de sumidero
Sump vent
(samp vent)

Respiradero en circuito
Circuit vent
(SER-ket vent)

Respiradero matriz
Main vent
(mein vent)

Respiradero vertical
Vent stack
(vent stack)

Resquicio
Undercut
(AN-der-kat)

Resumidero
Building drain
(BEL-ding drein)
Area drain
(E-re-a drein)

Retardante al fuego
Fire retardant
(faier ri-TAR-dent)

Retardo térmico
Thermal lag
(THER-mal lag)

Reticulado
Truss
(tras)

Retiro
Setback
(SET-bak)

Retrete
Toilet
(TOI-let)

Retroajuste
Retrofitting
(re-tro-FE-ting)

Revestido
Faced
(feisd)

Revestimiento
Veneer
(ve-NIR)
Siding
(SAID-ing)
Facing
(FEIS-ing)
Covering
(KA-ver-ing)
Lining
(LAI-ning)

Revestimiento de chimenea
Chimney liner
(CHEM-ni LAI-ner)

Revestimiento de enlucido/revoque
Veneer plaster
(ven-IR PLAS-t-r)

Revestimiento de tablas con traslape/solape
Lap siding
(lap SAID-ing)

Revestimiento de tableros
Panel sheathing
(PAN-l SHITH-ing)

Revestimiento de techo
Roof covering
(ruf KA-ve-ring)

Revestimiento vinilo
Vinyl siding
(VAIN-l SAID-ing)

Revestimientos para pisos
Flooring
(FLOR-ing)

Revisión/Revisor de planos
Plan review/reviewer
(plan RE-viu/RE-viuer)

Revoque
Plaster
(PLAS-tr)
Plastering
(PLAS-te-ring)
Stucco
(STA-ko)
Brown coat
(braun kout)

Revoque de yeso
Gypsum plaster
(DYEP-sam PLAST-r)

Riel de guía
Guide rail
(gaid reil)

Rigidez
Stiffness
(STEF-nes)

Ripia
Wood shingle/shake
(wud SHING-l/sheik)

Ripio
Gravel
(grav-l)

Roca
Rock
(rak)
Stone
(stoun)

Rociador
Sprinkler
(SPRINK-ler)

Rociador abierto (sin elemento activo)
Sprinkler, open
(SPRINK-ler, O-pen)

Rociador automático aprobado y certificado
Sprinkler, listed
(SPRINK-ler, LES-ted)

Rociador colgante
Sprinkler, pendent
(SPRINK-ler, PEN-dent)

Rociador colgante de tubería seca
Sprinkler, dry pendent
(SPRINK-ler, drai PEN-dent)

Rociador de ampolla
Sprinkler, bulb
(SPRINK-ler, bulb)

Rociador de apertura y cierre automático
Sprinkler, on-off
(SPRINK-ler, on-af)

Rociador de cobertura extendida
Sprinkler, extended coverage
(SPRINK-ler, ex-TEN-ded KAV-redsh)

Rociador de gota gorda
Sprinkler, large drop
(SPRINK-ler, lardsh drap)

Rociador de nivel intermedio de pantalla
Sprinkler, intermediate level
(SPRINK-ler, en-ter-MID-yet lev-l)

Rociador de pared
Sprinkler, sidewall
(SPRINK-ler, SAID-wal)

Rociador de respuesta rápida
Sprinkler, fast response
(SPRINK-ler, fest RI-spans)

Rociador de respuesta ultra rápida
Sprinkler, quick response
(SPRINK-ler, kuek RI-spans)

Rociador de rocío normalizado
Sprinkler, standard spray
(SPRINK-ler STAND-rd sprei)

Rociador de supresión temprana y respuesta rápida
Sprinkler, early suppression fast response (ESFR)
(SPRINK-ler, er-LI se-PRE-shen fest RI-spans)

Rociador de techo para empotrar

Rociador empotrado
Sprinkler, flush type
(SPRINK-ler, flash taip)

Rociador empotrado
Sprinkler, recessed
(SPRINK-ler, RI-ses-d)

Rociador en estanterías
Sprinkler, in-rack
(SPRINK-ler, EN-rak)

Rociador montante
Sprinkler, upright
(SPRINK-ler, AP-rait)

Rociador normalizado
Sprinkler, standard
(SPRINK-ler, STAND-rd)

Rociador oculto
Sprinkler, concealed
(SPRINK-ler, con-SIL-d)

Rociador tipo ampolla frágil
Sprinkler, frangible bulb style
*(SPRINK-ler, FRANDSH-ib-l
BULB stail)*

Rosca de manguera
Hose threads
(JOUS threds)

Rozamiento
Scouring
(SKAU-ring)

S

Sala (de conferencias)
Assembly/Conference room
(a-SEM-bli/KAN-fer-ens rum)

Salida
Egress
(I-gres)
Exit
(EX-et)

Salida de un hidrante
Hydrant bott
(JAI-drant bot)

Salida horizontal
Horizontal exit
(jo-re-SAN-tal EX-et)

Saliente
Abutment
(a-BAT-ment)

Salón
Assembly room
(a-SEM-bli rum)

Salto de corriente
Current draw
(KE-rent dra)

Sanitario
Restroom
(REST-rum)
Bathroom
(BATH-rum)
Toilet compartment
(TOI-let kam-PART-ment)
Water closet
(WA-ter KLA-set)
Toilet
(TOI-let)

Seguridad contra incendios
Fire safety
(faier SEIF-ti)

Seguridad física
Security
(se-KIOU-ri-ti)

Seguridad humana
Life safety
(laif SEIF-ti)

Seguridad industrial
Safety
(SEIF-ti)

Seguridad pública
Public safety
(PA-blek SEIF-ti)

Selladores
Sealants
(SIL-ents)

Sello de trampa hidráulica
Trap seal
(trap sil)

Señal acústica
Audible signal
(O-dib-l SEG-nal)

Señal de evacuación
Exit sign
(EX-et sain)

Señal de salida
Output signal
(AUT-put SEG-nal)

Sensibilizador
Sensitizer
(sen-se-TAI-s-r)

Sensor de humo
Smoke detector
(smouk di-TEKT-r)

Separación
Partition
(par-TE-shwn)

Separación de atmósfera
Atmosphere separation
(AT-mos-fir se-pa-REI-shwn)

Separación, distanciamiento
Spacing
(SPEI-sing)

Servicios públicos
Utilities
(iu-TE-le-tis)
Public services
(PA-blek SER-ve-ses)

Sifón
Trap
(trap)

Sillar
Cast stone
(kast stoun)

Sin plomo
Lead-free
(led-fri)

Sin salida
Dead end
(ded end)

Sistema
Assembly
(a-SEM-bli)

Sistema automático de extinción de incendios
Automatic fire extinguishing system
(au-to-MA-tik faier ex-TEN-gui-shing SES-tem)

Sistema de alarma contra incendios
Fire alarm system
(faier a-LARM SES-tem)

Sistema de arriostramiento horizontal
Horizontal bracing system
(jo-re-SAN-tal BREI-sing SES-tem)

Sistema de columna hidrante
Standpipe system
(*stand-paip SES-tem*)

Sistema de detección de humo
Smoke-detection system
(*smouk di-TEK-shwn SES-tem*)

**Sistema de diluvio
o inundación total**
Deluge system
(*DEI-ludsh SES-tem*)

Sistema de evacuación
Venting system
(*VENT-ing SES-tem*)

Sistema de extracción de humo
Smoke exhaust system
(*smouk ex-AST SES-tem*)

**Sistema de preacción,
acción previa**
Preaction system
(*pre-AK-shan SES-tem*)

Sistema de puertas
Door assembly
(*dor a-SEM-bli*)

Sistema de rociadores
Sprinkler system
(*SPRINK-ler SES-tem*)

**Sistema de rociadores
automáticos**
Automatic fire sprinkler system
(*au-to-MA-tik faier SPRINK-ler SES-tem*)

Sistema de ventilación
Vent system
(*vent SES-tem*)
Venting system
(*VENT-ing SES-tem*)

**Sistema direccional de alarma
de incendios**
Fire alarm adressable system
(*faier a-LARM a-DRES-a-bl SES-tem*)

Sistema doble
Dual system
(*dual SES-tem*)

Sitio
Premises
(*PRE-me-ses*)
Site
(*sait*)

Sitio de construcción
Building site
(*BEL-ding sait*)
Jobsite
(*DYOB-sait*)

Sobrecarga de nieve transportada
Drift surcharge
(*dreft SER-charsh*)

Sobrerresistencia
Overstrength
(*O-ver-strength*)

Sobresolapar
To overlap
(*tu O-ver-lap*)

Sobresolape
Overlap
(O-ver-lap)

Sobrestante
Foreman
(FOR-man)
Overseer
(O-ver-si-r)
Supervisor
(su-per-VAI-s-r)

Sofito
Soffit
(SA-fit)

Soldador
Solderer
(SOD-e-rer)

Soldadura
Welding
(uel-ding)

Soldadura y fundente sin plomo
Lead-free solder and flux
(LED-fri SOD-er and flax)

Soldar en fuerte
Braze
(breis)

Solera
Ledger
(LED-yer)

Solera doble
Double plate
(DOB-l pleit)

Solera inferior
Sill plate
(sel pleit)

Someter a ensayo/a prueba
To test
(tu test)

Soporte
Support
(sa-PORT)
Backing
(BAK-ing)
Shoulder
(SHOULD-r)
Sill
(sel)
Clamp
(klamp)

Soporte de ventana
Window sill
(wendou sel)

Soporte para forjados
Plaster backing
(plast-r BAK-ing)

Sostener, Soportar
Support
(se-PORT)

Sótano
Basement
(BEIS-ment)

Sótano de poca altura
Crawl space
(kral speis)

Subpiso
Subfloor
(sab-flor)

Subsolape
Underlap
(AN-der-lap)

Substrato
Underlayment
(an-der-LEI-ment)
Substrate
(sab-STREIT)

Subterráneo
Basement
(BEIS-ment)
Underground
(AN-der-graund)

Suelo expansivo
Expansive soil
(ek-SPAN-sef soil)

Suite
Suite (hotel)
(suit (jo-TEL))

Sujetadores
Restraints
(ri-STREINTS)

Sumidero
Sump
(samp)

Superficie exterior/interior
Exterior/Interior surface
*(ex-TE-ri-or/en-TE-ri-or
SAR-fes)*

Superficie/Área peatonal
Walking surface
(WA-king SER-fes)

Superponer, Superposición
Overlap
(O-ver-lap)

Superintendente
Foreman
(FOR-man)
Overseer
(O-ver-SI-r)

Supervisor
Supervisor
(SU-per-VAI-s-r)
Inspector
(en-SPEK-tor)

Suspendido
Overhead
(O-ver-jed)

T

T, injerto
TEE
(ti)

Tabique
Partition
(par-TE-shwn)

Tabique movible
Movable partition
(MU-vab-l par-TE-shwn)

Tabique plegable
Folding partition
(FOLD-ing par-TE-shwn)

Tabique portátil
Portable partition
(PORT-ab-l par-TE-shwn)

Tabiques
Gutter partition
(GA-ter par-TE-shwn)

Tabla
Board
(bord)
Table
(TEIB-l)

Tabla de cumbrera
Ridge board
(REDSH bord)

Tabla de madera
Wood board
(WUD bord)

Tabla de pie
Toeboard
(TOU-bord)

Tabla de piso
Footboard
(FUT-bord)

Tablero de cortacircuito
Circuit breaker panel
(SER-ket BREIK-r PAN-l)

Tablero de fibra
Fiberboard
(FAIB-r bord)

Tablero de largueros
Ribbon/ledger board
(RE-bon/LED-yer bord)

Tablero de madera prensada
Plywood
(PLAI-wud)

Tablero de muro arriostrado
Braced wall panel
(BREIST wal PAN-l)

Tablero de soporte
Backer board
(BAK-er bord)

Tabla de tubería
Pipe schedule
(paip SKED-yul)

Tablero de activación
Trip panel
(trep PAN-l)

Tablero de yeso
Gypsum board
(*DYEP-sam bord*)
Dry wall
(*DRAI wal*)

Tablero duro
Hardboard
(*HARD-bord*)
Plywood
(*PLAI-wud*)

Tablilla de fibrocemento
Asbestos cement shingle
(*as-BES-tos si-MENT SHING-l*)

Tablón
Plank
(*pleink*)

Tablones
Planking
(*PLEINK-ing*)

Taller
Shop
(*shap*)

Talud
Slope
(*sloup*)

Tambor
Drums
(*drams*)

Tanque
Tank
(*teink*)

Tapa de acceso
Access cover
(*AK-ses KA-ver*)

Tanque de techo cónico
Tank, conic roof
(*teink, KA-nik ruf*)

Tanque de techo suspendido
Tank, floating roof
(*teink, FLOAT-ing ruf*)

Tapa de rociador en forma de disco
Sprinkler, cover plate assembly
(*SPRINK-ler, KA-ver pleit a-SEM-bli*)

Tapadera
Cover
(*KA-ver*)
Covering
(*KA-ver-ing*)

Tapajuntas
Flashing
(*FLASH-ing*)

Tapanco
Attic
(*AT-ik*)

Tapón de drenaje del cuerpo
Body drain plug
(*BA-dy drein plag*)

Tapón estanco
Watertight seal
(*WA-ter-tait sil*)

Tapón fusible
Plug fuse
(*plag fius*)

Tapón que saltan con facilidad
Blow-off cap
(*BLO-af cap*)

Tarima
Pallet
(PA-let)
Rack
(rak)

Tarja de cocina
Kitchen sink
(KE-chen sink)

Tasa de liberación de calor
Heat release rate
(jit ri-LIS rait)

Techado
Roofing
(RUF-ing)

Techado de asfalto
Built-up roof
(BELT-ap ruf)

Techo
Roof
(ruf)

Techo a aguas múltiples
Multiple gabled roof
(MAL-tip-l geib-ld ruf)

Techo a dos aguas
Gable roof
(GEIB-l ruf)

Techo a cuatro aguas
Hip roof
(jep ruf)

Techo en pendiente
Sloped roof
(sloupt ruf)

Techo plano
Flat roof
(flat ruf)

Técnico
Technician
(tek-NE-shian)
Technical
(TEK-ne-kal)

Teja
Shingle
(SHING-l)
Roof tile
(RUF tail)
Tile
(tail)

Teja de asfalto
Asphalt shingle
(AS-falt SHING-l)

Teja de cemento de asbestos
Asbestos cement shingle
(as-BES-tos si-MENT SHING-l)

Teja de madera
Wood shake/shingle
(wud sheik/SHING-l)

Teja de pizarra
Slate shingle
(sleit SHING-l)

Tejas para bordes
Rake tile
(reik tail)

Teja para cumbreras
Ridge tile
(REDSH tail)

Teja para limas
Hip tile
(jep tail)

Tejamanil
Roof tile
(ruf tail)
Shingle
(SHING-l)

Tejas entrelazadas para techo
Interlocking roofing tiles
(en-ter-LAK-ing RU-fing tails)

Tela metálica
Wire mesh
(waier mesh)

Teléfono transmisor receptor
Handset
(JAND-set)

Tendel
Chalk line
(chak lain)

Tendido de tubería
Piping layout
(PAI-ping LEI-aut)

Tendones
Tendons
(TEN-dans)

Tenencia
Occupancy
(A-kiu-pen-si)

Tensión
Tension
(TEN-shwn)
Stress
(stres)

Tensores
Tendons
(TEN-dans)

Terminación de obra
Completion of work
(kam-PLI-shwn av wark)

Terminado
Finish
(FE-nesh)

Terminado interior
Interior finish
(en-TE-ri-or FE-nesh)

Terminal
Terminal
(TER-mi-nal)

Terminal de enlace
Dead-end bonding jumper
(ded end BAND-ing DYAMP-r)

Termita
Termite
(TER-mait)

Termopar
Thermocouple
(THER-mo-KAP-l)

Termotanque
Water heater
(WA-ter JI-ter)

Terraplén
Earth work
(erth wark)
Embankment
(em-BANK-ment)

Terraza cubierta
Porch
(porch)

Terreno
Lot
(lat)

Terreno de obra
Building site
(BEL-ding sait)

Terreno inestable
Unstable ground
(an-STEI-b-l graund)

Textura
Texture
(TEX-tiur)

Tienda
Store
(stor)

Timbre
Doorbell
(DOR-bel)

Timbre de alarma motorizado por agua
Water motor gong
(WA-ter MOT-r gong)

Tímpano
Spandrel
(SPAN-drl)

Tina de baño
Bathtub
(BATH-tab)

Tipo clapeta con trinquete
Latched clapper type
(latch-d KLAP-r taip)

Tira
Lath
(lath)
Strip
(strep)
Stripe
(straip)

Tirante
Tie
(tai)
Link
(link)
Brace
(breis)

Tirante de diafragma
Diaphragm strut
(DAI-a-fram strat)

Tiras metálicas
Stripping
(STREP-ing)

Tiras de yeso
Lath
(lath)

Toldo
Awning
(A-ning)
Canopy
(KAN-o-pi)

Toma de bomberos siamesa
Fire department siamese connection
(faier d-PART-ment SAI-mis ka-NEK-shwn)

Toma fija de agua para manguera
Standpipe hose connection
(*stand-paip JOUS
ka-NEK-shwn*)

Tomacorriente
Electrical outlet
(*i-LEK-tre-kal AUT-let*)

Tomacorriente para estufa/cocina
Range power outlet
(*reindsh PA-uer AUT-let*)

Toma de impulsión
Fire department connection
(*faier d-PART-ment
ka-NEK-shwn*)

Toma con traba
Locking receptacle
(*LA-king re-SEP-te-kl*)

Topes (de puerta)
Stops (door frame)
(*staps (dor freim)*)

Tornillo
Screw
(*skru*)
Bolt
(*bolt*)

Tornillo autoperforante
Self-drilling screw
(*self-DRE-ling skru*)

Tornillo autorroscante
Self-tapping screw
(*self-TAP-ing skru*)

Tornillo de anclaje
Anchor bolt
(*EN-ker bolt*)

Tornillo de expansión
Expansion bolt
(*ex-PAN-shwn bolt*)

Tornillo pasante
Screw
(*skru*)

Trabado
Blocked
(*blakt*)
Bonded
(*BAN-ded*)

Trabajo
Work
(*wark*)

Trabar
Block
(*blak*)

Trabas
Blocking
(*BLAK-ing*)

Trabazón
Binder
(*BAIND-r*)

Tragaluz
Skylight
(*SKAI-lait*)

Tramo
Region
(*RIDSH-n*)

Trampa doméstica
House trap
(*JAUS trap*)

Trampa hidráulica/de artefacto
Fixture trap
(*FEX-tiur trap*)

Trampa para chispas
Spark arrester
(*spark a-REST-r*)

Transformador
Transformer
(*trans-FORM-r*)

Traslapar
To overlap
(*tu o-ver-LAP*)

Traslape
Lap splice
(*lap splais*)
Shiplap
(*SHIP-lap*)
Overlap
(*o-ver-LAP*)

Traslapo
Lapping
(*LAP-ing*)

Trasvasando
Dispensing
(*des-PENS-ing*)

Trasvasar
Dispense
(*des-PENS*)

Travesaño
Ledger
(*LED-yer*)

Travesaño superior
Top plate
(*tap pleit*)

Traviesa
Sleeper
(*SLI-per*)

Trazar y nivelar
Line and grade
(*lain and greid*)

Trazo
Stroke
(*strouk*)

Tribunas
Grandstands
(*GRAND-stands*)
Bleachers
(*BLI-chers*)
Stands
(*stands*)

Trinquete
Latch
(*latch*)

Trinquete
Ratchet
(*RA-chet*)

Triturador de basura/ desperdicios
Garbage disposal
(*GAR-besh dis-PO-sal*)

Tubería
Conduit
(*KAN-duit*)
Plumbing
(*PLAM-ing*)
Tubing
(*TUB-ing*)
Pipe
(*paip*)
Piping
(*PAI-ping*)

Tubería ascendente
Riser
(*RAIS-r*)

Tubería ascendente a los rociadores
Sprinkler riser
(*SPRINK-ler RAIS-r*)

Tubería bajante
Stack
(*stak*)

Tubería bajanta de respiradero
Stack vent
(*stak vent*)

Tubería de alimentación
Supply piping
(*se-PLAI PAIP-ing*)

Tubería de distribución principal
Feed main
(*fid mein*)

Tubería de drenaje entrapada
Trapped drain pipe
(*trap-d drein paip*)

Tubería de revestimiento
Casing
(*KEIS-ing*)

Tubería de sobrellenado
Pipe, overflow
(*paip, O-ver-flo*)

Tubería en bucle cerrado
Closed loop pipe
(*cloust lup paip*)

Tubería en forma de bucle
Looped piping
(*lup-d PAIP-ing*)

Tubería en forma de parrilla
Gridded piping
(*gred-d PAIP-ing*)

Tubería hidráulica
Water pipe
(*WA-ter paip*)

Tubería principal
Water main
(*WA-ter mein*)

Tubería principal transversal
Cross main
(*kras mein*)

Tubería vertical
Stack
(*stack*)
Standpipe
(*stand-paip*)
Vertical pipe
(*VER-te-kal paip*)

Tubería y accesorios sin plomo
Lead-free pipe and fittings
(*led fri paip and FE-tings*)

Tuberías/Cañerías de protección contra incendios
Fire-protection piping
(*faier-pro-TEK-shwn PAIP-ing*)

Tubo
Pipe
(*paip*)
Piping
(*PAIP-ing*)

Tubo bajante de aguas negras
Soil pipe
(*soil paip*)

Tubo de bajada
Leader (pipe)
(*LI-der (paip)*)

Tubo de descarga
Discharge pipe
(*DES-chardsh paip*)

Tubo de prueba
Pipe test
(*paip test*)

Tubo de ventilación
Vent pipe
(*vent paip*)

**Tubo de ventilación
con codo doble**
Return bend vent pipe
(*ri-TURN bend vent paip*)

Tubo horizontal
Horizontal pipe
(*jo-re-SAN-tal paip*)

Tubo "Pitot"
Pitot tube
(*PE-to tub*)

Tubo vertical
Riser pipe
(*RAIS-r paip*)

Tubo vertical de evacuación
Stack
(*stak*)

Tubo vertical de ventilación
Local vent stack
(*LOK-l vent stak*)

Tuerca
Nut
(*nat*)

Tuerca de ojete
Eye nut
(*AI nat*)

Tuerca de seguridad o fijación
Lock nut
(*LAK nat*)

U

Umbral
Door sill
(*DOR sel*)
Threshold
(*THRESH-jold*)

Unidad habitacional/Unidad de vivienda
Dwelling unit
(*DUEL-ing IU-net*)

Unidad de inspección
Inspector test assembly
(*en-SPEK-tor test a-SEM-bli*)

Unión
Binder
(*BAIND-r*)
Connection
(*ka-NEK-shwn*)
Joint
(*dyoint*)
Union
(*IU-nion*)

Urinal, Urinario
Urinal
(*IU-ri-nal*)

Uso
Occupancy
(*a-kiu-pen-si*)
Use
(*ius*)

Uso general
Utility
(*iu-TE-le-ti*)

Utilidad
Utility
(*iu-TE-le-ti*)

Utilizar
To use
(*tu ius*)

Utilizar en sistema abierto
Use, open system
(*ius, O-pen SES-tem*)

Utilizar en sistema cerrado
Use, closed system
(*ius, cloust SES-tem*)

V

Vaciado en sitio
Cast in place
(*kast en pleis*)

Vacío
Vacuum
(*VA-kium*)

Valor
Value
(*VA-liu*)

Valuación
Valuation
(*va-liu-EI-shwn*)

Válvula cheque
Valve, check
(*valv, chek*)

Válvula de alarma de paso
de agua
Water flow alarm valve
(*WA-ter flo a-LARM valv*)

Válvula de alivio
Relief valve
(*ri-LIF valv*)

Varilla de anclaje
Anchor rod
(*EN-ker rad*)

Válvula de cierre
Cut-off valve
(*KAT-of valv*)
Shutoff valve
(*SHAT-of valv*)

Válvula de combinación
Mixing valve
(*MEX-ing valv*)

Válvula de compuerta
Valve, gate
(*valv, geit*)

Válvula de contraflujo
Backflow preventer
(*BAK-flou pri-VENT-r*)
Check valve
(*chek valv*)

Válvula de contrapresión
Backwater valve
(*bak-WA-ter valv*)

Válvula de cubo
Hub valve
(*hab valv*)

Válvula de derivación
Valve, by-pass
(*valv, BAI-pas*)

Válvula de disparo
Tripping valve
(*TREP-ing valv*)

Válvula de drenaje
Drip valve
(*drep valv*)

Válvula de escape
Valve, blow-off
(*valv, BLO-of*)

Válvula de flotador
Ball cock
(*bal kak*)

V

Válvula de llave
  Key valve
  (ki valv)

Válvula de paso angular
  Valve, angle
  (valv, ENG-l)

Válvula de poste indicador
  Vale, post indicator (PIV)
  (val, post IN-de-KEI-tor)

Válvula de purga
  Bleeder valve
  (BLI-der valv)

Válvula de purga del deflector
  Valve, ball drip
  (valv, bal drep)

Válvula de remanso
  Backwater valve
  (bak-WA-ter valv)

Válvula de retención del flotador
  Exhauster
  (eks-AST-r)

Válvula de tubería seca
  Valve, dry pipe
  (valv, drai paip)

Válvula de vástago ascendente
  Valve, outside steam and yoke
  (OS&Y)
  (valv, AUT-said stim and jok)

Válvula fluxómetro
  Flushometer valve
  (flash-O-mi-ter valv)

Válvula mariposa
  Valve, butterfly
  (valv, BA-tr-flai)

Válvula piloto
  Valve, pilot
  (valv PAI-let)

Válvula solenoide
  Solenoid valve
  (SO-le-noid valv)

Válvulas para grifos
de mangueras
  Hose bibb valves
  (jous beb valvs)

Vano
  Span
  (span)

Vapor
  Steam
  (stim)

Varilla
  Rebar
  (RI-bar)

Varilla de empuje
  Push-rod
  (push-rad)

Varilla de sujeción
  Strut
  (strat)

Varillas en aro
  Ringed shanks
  (rendsh shanks)

Velocidad de incremento
  Rate of rise
  (reit af rais)

Ventana
  Window
  (wen-dou)

Ventilador
Fan
(fan)

Ventilador de extracción
Exhaust fan
(ex-AST fan)

Ventilar
To ventilate
(tu VEN-te-leit)
To vent
(tu vent)

Vereda
Path
(path)
Sidewalk
(SAID-wak)

Vestíbulo
Vestibule
(VES-te-biul)

Vestidor
Dressing room
(DRE-sing rum)

Veta superficial
Face grain
(feis grein)

Vía pública
Public way
(PA-blek WEI)

Vías de evacuación
Means of egress
(mins of I-gres)

Vidriado
Glazed
(gleist)
Glazing
(GLEIS-ing)

Vidriado de seguridad
Safety glazing
(SEIF-ti GLEIS-ing)

Vierteaguas
Flashing
(FLASH-ing)

Viga
Girder
(GER-der)
Joist
(dyoist)
Beam
(bim)

Viga de alma abierta
Open-web girder
(O-pen-web GER-der)

Viga de alma llena
Plate girder
(pleit GER-der)

Viga de carga
Load-bearing joist
(loud BE-ring dyoist)

Viga de celosía
Bar joist
(bar dyoist)

Viga de enlace
Link beam
(link bim)

Viga de fundación
Grade beam
(greid bim)

Viga maestra/principal
Girder
(GER-der)
Joist girder
(dyoist GER-der)

V

Vigas de acoplamiento
Coupling beams
(KAP-ling bims)

Vigas discontinuas
Discontinuous beams
(des-kon-TEN-iuas bims)

Vigueta
Joist
(dyoist)
Purlin
(PER-len)

Vigueta de piso
Floor joist
(flor dyoist)

Vigueta esquinera
End joist
(end dyoist)

Vitrina
Show window
(shou WEN-dou)

Vivienda
Dwelling
(DUEL-ing)

Vivienda bifamiliar
Two-family dwelling
(tu-FAM-li DUEL-ing)

Vivienda unifamiliar
Single-family dwelling
(seng-l FAM-li DUEL-ing)

Voladizo
Overhang
(o-ver-JANG)
Cantilever
(KANT-te-li-ver)

Voltaje
Voltage
(VOLT-eidsh)

Volteo, Vuelco, Volcamiento
Overturning
(O-ver-TERN-ing)

Voltios
Volts
(volts)

Volver a graduar
Reset
(RE-set)

Vuelo
Overhang
(o-ver-JANG)

Vuelos
Nosings
(NOU-sings)

y

Yarda
Yard
(iard)

Yerbajos
Weeds
(uids)

Yesca
Punk
(pank)
Tinder
(TEN-der)

Yeso
Gypsum
(DYEP-sam)
Plaster
(PLAST-r)

Yugo
Yoke
(iouk)

Yunque
Anvil
(AN-vel)

Yunque de banco
Bench anvil
(bench AN-vel)

Yunque de tornillo
Anvil vise
(AN-vel vais)

Yodo
Iodine
(AI-o-dain)

Z

Zanja
Trench
(trench)

Zapata
Footing
(FU-ting)

Zapatas invertidas
Turned-down footings
(turn-d daun FU-tings)

Zapatilla eléctrica
Power strip
(PA-uer strep)

Zarpa
Footing
(FU-ting)

Zócalo
Baseboard
(BEIS-bord)

Zócalos altos
Wainscoting
(WEIN-ska-ting)

Zona
Occupancy
(A-kiu-pen-si)

Zona de control de humo
Smoke-control zone
(Smouk-kan-TROL soun)

Zona de evacuación
Exit discharge
(EX-et DES-chardsh)

Zonas de inundación
Flood zones
(flad souns)

Zonas sísmicas
Seismic zones
(SAIS-mik souns)

Herramientas

Alicates
Pliers
(PLA-iers)

Alicates de extensión/presiónó
Channel lock pliers
(chan-l lak PLA-iers)

Aplanadora
Roller
(RO-ler)

Azadón
Hoe
(jou)

Balde
Bucket
(BA-ket)

Barreta
Bar
(bar)

Berbiquí y barrena
Brace and bit
(breis and bet)

Bomba
Pump
(pamp)

Botador/embutidor (de clavos)
Nail set
(neil set)

Botiquín
Medicine cabinet
(ME-des-n KA-be-net)

Broca
Drill bit
(drel bet)

Brocha
Brush
(brash)

Buriladora
Router
(RAU-ter)

Burro
Sawhorse
(sah-jors)

Cadena
Chain
(chein)

Caja de corte a ángulos
Mitre box
(MAI-t-r bax)

Caja de herramientas
Tool box
(tul bax)

Careta
Mask
(mask)
Face shield
(feis shild)

Careta para soldar
Welding mask
(WELD-ing mask)

Carretilla, Carrucha
Wheelbarrow
(juil-BA-rou)

Herramientas

Cepillo
  Plane
  (plein)
  Brush
  (brash)
Cepillo automático
  Jointer
  (DYOIN-ter)
Cepillo de mano
  Jointer plane
  (DYOIN-ter plein)
Cincel
  Chisel
  (CHES-l)
Cinta de medir
  Measuring tape
  (ME-shu-ring teip)
Cinta de pescadora
  Fish tape
  (fesh teip)
Clavadora automática
  Nail gun
  (neil gan)
Contorneador
  Router
  (RAU-ter)
Cortacésped
  Lawnmower
  (LAN-mou-er)
Cortadora de césped/pasto
  Lawnmower
  (LAN-mou-er)
Cortapluma
  Utility knife
  (iu-TE-le-ty naif)

Cubeta
  Bucket
  (BA-ket)
Cuchara de albañil
  Mason's trowel
  (MEI-sons TROU-l)
Delantal
  Apron
  (EI-pron)
Desarmador/Destornillador
  Screwdriver
  (SCRU-draiv-r)
Desarmador plano
  Flathead
  (flat-jed)
Desarmador de punta de cruz
  Phillips
  (FEL-eps)
Disco
  Circular saw blade
  (SER-cu-lar sah bleid)
Doblador de varilla
  Rebar bender
  (RI-bar bender)
Embudo
  Funnel
  (fan-l)
Engarilla
  Wheelbarrow
  (juil-BA-rou)
Engrapadora
  Stapler
  (STEI-pler)
Engrapadora automática
  Stapler gun
  (STEI-pler gan)

Escalera de mano
Ladder
(LA-der)

Escoba
Broom
(brum)

Escopio
Chisel wood
(CHES-l wud)

Esparavel
Hawk
(jak)

Escuadra
Square
(skuer)
Framing square
(FREIM-ing skuer)
Carpenter's square
(KAR-pen-ters skuer)

Escuadra de combinación
Combination square
(kam-be-NEI-shwn skuer)

Excavadora
Back hoe
(bak jou)

Flatacho
Darby
(DAR-bi)

Fresadora
Router
(RAU-ter)

Formón
Chisel wood
(CHES-l wud)

Gafas/lentes de seguridad
Safety glasses
(SEIF-ty GLAS-es)
Goggles
(GAG-ls)

Guantes
Gloves
(glavs)

Hacha
Axe
(ax)

Hilo
Thread
(thred)

Hilo de plomada
Plumb line
(plam lain)

Lámpara de trabajo
Work light
(wark lait)

Linterna
Flashlight
(flash-lait)

Llana
Square trowel
(skuer trou-l)

Llave
Wrench
(rench)
Key
(ki)

Llave de asientos de válvula
Valve seat wrench
(valv sit rench)

Herramientas

Llave de cadena
Chain pipe wrench
(*chein paip rench*)

Llave de correa/cincho
Strap wrench
(*strap rench*)

Llave de tuercas
Crescent wrench
(*KRE-sent rench*)

Llave española/de astrias/de dado
Wrench
(*rench*)

Llave francesa ajustable
Crescent wrench
(*KRE-sent rench*)

Llave inglesa
Plumber's wrench
(*PLA-mers rench*)

Llave pico de ganso
Basin wrench
(*BEIS-n rench*)

Lijadora
Sander
(*SAN-der*)

Lima
File
(*fai-l*)

Mandil de carpintero
Carpenter's apron
(*KAR-pen-ters EI-pron*)

Manguera
Hose
(*jous*)

Marro
Sledgehammer
(*sledsh-JA-mer*)

Martillo
Hammer
(*JA-mer*)

Martillo de bola
Ball-peen hammer
(*bal piyn JA-mer*)

Martillo chivo
Claw hammer
(*klah JA-mer*)

Martillo para tejamanil
Shingling hammer
(*SHING-l-ing JA-mer*)

Máscara
Mask
(*mask*)

Mazo
Sledgehammer
(*sledsh JA-mer*)
Mallet
(*MA-let*)

Mezcladora
Mixer
(*MEK-ser*)

Mecha
Drill bit
(*drel bet*)

Mordaza tiradora de alambre
Come-along
(*KAM-a-lang*)

Navaja
Utility knife
(*iu-TE-le-ty naif*)

Nivel
  Level
  (LEV-l)

Pala
  Shovel
  (SHAV-l)

Paleta de albañil
  Mason's trowel
  (MEI-sons TROU-l)

Paleta de relleno
  Joint filler trowel
  (dyoint FEL-er TROU-l)

Pico
  Pick
  (pek)

Pincel
  Brush
  (brash)

Pinzas
  Pliers
  (PLAI-ers)

Pinzas de canto de panel
  Panel edge clips
  (pan-l edsh cleps)

Pinzas perras
  Vise grip pliers
  (vais grep PLAI-ers)

Plomada
  Plumb bob
  (plam bab)

Plana
  Darby
  (DAR-bi)

Prensa
  Clamp
  (klamp)

Prensa en C
  C-Press
  (si-pres)
  C-Clamp
  (si-klamp)

Punzones
  Punches
  (PAN-ches)

Rastrillo
  Batten
  (BAT-n)
  Rake
  (reik)

Regla T
  T-square
  (ti skuer)

Retroexcavadora
  Back hoe
  (bak jou)

Revolvedora
  Mixer
  (MEK-ser)

Secadora
  Dryer
  (DRAI-er)

Segueta
  Hacksaw
  (JAK-sah)

Serrucho
  Saw
  (sah)

Serrucho de mano
  Handsaw
  (JAND-sah)

Herramientas

Serrucho guillotina
Radial arm saw
(REI-di-al arm sah)

Sierra
Saw
(sah)

Sierra alternativa/reciprocante
Reciprocating saw
(re-CE-pro-KEI-ting sah)

Sierra circular de mesa
Table saw
(TEIB-l sah)

Sierra circular de mano
Circular saw
(SER-ku-lar sah)

Sierra circular con tornillo sinfin
Worm drive circular saw
(warm draiv SER-ku-lar sah)

Sierra de cadena
Chain saw
(chein sah)

Sierra de corte angular
Compound mitre saw
(KAM-paund MAI-t-r sah)

Sierra de disco
Circular saw blade
(SER-ku-lar sah bleid)

Sierra de ingletes compuesta
Compound mitre saw
(KAM-paund MAI-t-r sah)

Sierra de madera
Cut-off saw
(kat-af sah)

Sierra de retroceso para ingletes
Mitre saw
(MAI-t-r sah)

Sierra de vaivén
Jigsaw
(DYEG-sah)

Sierra eléctrica
Electric saw
(i-LEK-trek sah)
Power saw
(PAU-er sah)

Sierra fija
Table saw
(TEIB-l sah)
Radial saw
(REI-di-al sah)

Sierra para metales
Hacksaw
(JAK-sah)

Sierra para cortar
Cut-off saw
(kat-af sah)

Sopapa
Plunger
(PLAN-dyer)

Sopladora
Blower
(BLO-uer)

Soplete
Soldering torch
(SA-der-ing torch)

Taladro
Drill
(drel)

Taladro de mano
Brace and bit
(breis and bet)

Taladro eléctrico
　Electric drill
　　(i-LEK-trek drel)

Tijeras para metal
　Sheet metal shears
　　(SHIYT me-tal shirs)

Torno/tornillo de banco
　Vice bench
　　(vais bench)

Trazador de metal
　Metal scribe
　　(me-tal scraib)

Zapa
　Hoe
　　(jou)

Zapapico
　Pick-axe
　　(PEK-ax)

Frases Utiles

Busco trabajo.
> I am looking for work.
> *[ai em LU-king for wark]*

¿Cómo se llama (usted)?
> What is your name?
> *[WAT es yor NEM]*

Mi nombre es.../ Me llamo...
> My name is.../I am...
> *[mai NEM es/ai em]*

Mucho gusto (en conocerlo).
> Pleased to meet you.
> *[plizd tu MIT iu]*

¿Cuál es su número de teléfono?
> What is your phone number?
> *[wat es yor FOUN NAMB-r?]*

Tengo experiencia como carpintero (plomero, electricista, jornalero, albañil).
> I have experience as a carpenter (plumber, electrician, laborer, bricklayer).
> *[ai jav ex-PE-ri-ens as ei CAR-pen-ter (PLA-mer, i-lek-TRI-shan LEI-bor-r, BREK–lei-r)]*

Soy buen trabajador.
> I am a good worker.
> *[ai em ei gud WARK-r]*

Tengo mi tarjeta verde.
> I have my green card.
> *[ai jav mai GRIN card]*

Soy socio (miembro) del sindicato (la unión)—aquí esta mi credencial.
> I am a member of the union—here is my membership card.
> *[ai em a MEM-ber av the IU-nion—jir es mai MEM-ber-shep card]*

Tengo mis propias herramientas.
> I have my own tools.
> *[ai jav mai OUN tuls]*

He trabajado por varios años en los Estados Unidos (México, Guatemala).
> I have worked for years in the U.S. (Mexico, Guatemala).
> *[ai jav WORKT for YIRS in the IU–ES (MEKS-i-ko, gwa-te-MA-la)]*

Tengo transportación (carro, camioneta).
> I have transportation (a car, a pick–up).
> *[ai jav trans-por-TEI-shwn (ei car, ei PIK-ap)]*

Puedo trabajar todos los dias.
> I can work every day.
> *[ai can wark EV-ry dei]*

Frases Utiles

Haré muy buen trabajo para usted.
>I will do a very good job for you.
>*[ai wil du ei VE-ry gud DSHOB for iu]*

¿Tiene hambre/sed?
>Are you hungry/thirsty?
>*[ar iu JAN-gri/THAR-sti?]*

¿Qué quiere comer/tomar?
>What do you want to eat/drink?
>*[wat du iu want tu it/drank?]*

Venga conmigo.
>Come with me.
>*[com with mi]*

¡Ten(ga) cuidado!
>Be careful!
>*[bi KER-ful]*

¡Cuidado!

¡Ojo!

¡Aguas!

¡Pon(ga) atención!
>Watch out!
>*[wach aut]*

Sígame.
>Follow me.
>*[FA-lo mi]*

¡Jale!
>Pull!
>*[pul]*

¡Empuje!
>Push!
>*[push]*

Tráigame ese dos por cuatro (...ese accesorio, ...esa conexion, ...ese conducto).
>Bring me that two by four (...that fixture, ...that fitting,...that duct).
>*[bring mi that TU bai for (that FIX-chur, ...that FI-teng,... that dact)]*

Ayúdeme a descargar el camión (...levantar la viga, ...instalar el desagüe).
>Help me unload the truck (...lift the beam, ...install the drain).
>*[halp mi un-LOD the trak (left the bim, en-STAL the dren)]*

Eso es demasiado pesado. No intente levantarlo/llevarlo solo.
>That is too heavy. Don't try to lift/carry it alone.
>*[that is tu JE-vi. Dont trai tu left/KE-ri it a-LOUN]*

No. Así no lo haga. Por favor, hagalo así.

No. Don't do it like that.
Please, do it this way.
*[no. don't du it laik that.
Plis, du it this wai.]*

¿Se lesionó? ¡Vaya al doctor/a la clínica ahora mismo!

Are you injured? Go to the
doctor/clinic now!
*[ar iu ind-SHUR-d? Go tu the
DOKT-r/KLE-nek nau]*

No lo deje caer.

Don't drop it.
[dont drap it]

Cuidado al pisar.

Watch your step.
[wach yor step]

Nos vemos mañana.

See you tomorrow.
[si iu tu-MA-ro]

Estudio mi Means Diccionario todos los días para aprender Inglés.

I study my Means Dictionary
every day to learn English.
*[ai STA-di mai MINS
DIK-sho-ne-ri EV-ry dei tu
lern ING-lesh]*

Tablas

Los números		
The numbers		
0	cero	zero
1	uno (una)	one
2	dos	two
3	tres	three
4	cuatro	four
5	cinco	five
6	seis	six
7	siete	seven
8	ocho	eight
9	nueve	nine
10	diez	ten
11	once	eleven
12	doce	twelve
13	trece	thirteen
14	catorce	fourteen
15	quince	fifteen
16	dieciséis	sixteen
17	diecisiete	seventeen
18	dieciocho	eighteen
19	diecinueve	nineteen
20	veinte	twenty
21	veintiuno	twenty-one
22	veintidós	twenty-two
30	treinta	thirty
31	treinta y uno	thirty-one
40	cuarenta	forty
50	cincuenta	fifty

Tablas

60	sesenta	sixty
70	setenta	seventy
80	ochenta	eighty
90	noventa	ninety
100	cien	one hundred
101	ciento uno	one hundred and one
200	doscientos	two hundred
300	trescientos	three hundred
400	cuatrocientos	four hundred
500	quinientos	five hundred
600	seiscientos	six hundred
700	setecientos	seven hundred
800	ochocientos	eight hundred
900	novecientos	nine hundred
1,000	mil	one thousand
2,000	dos mil	two thousand
1,000,000	un millón	one million
2,000,000	dos millones	two million

Los meses del año
The months of the year

enero	January
febrero	February
marzo	March
abril	April
mayo	May
junio	June
julio	July
agosto	August
septiembre	September
octubre	October
noviembre	November
diciembre	December

Los días de la semana
The days of the week

lunes	Monday
martes	Tuesday
miércoles	Wednesday
jueves	Thursday
viernes	Friday
sábado	Saturday
domingo	Sunday

Tablas

**TABLAS DE CONVERSIÓN POR UNIDADES
SÍMBOLOS Y PREFIJOS EN UNIDADES *SI*
(SISTEMA INTERNACIONAL)**

UNIDADES DE BASE

Cantidad	Unidad	Símbolo
Longitud	Metro	m
Masa	Kilogramo	kg
Tiempo	Segundo	s
Corriente eléctrica	Amperios	A
Temperatura termodinámica	Kelvin	K
Cantidad de sustancia	Mol	mol
Intensidad luminosa	Candela	cd

UNIDADES SI SUPLEMENTARIAS

Cantidad	Unidad	Símbolo
Ángulo plano	Radián	rad
Ángulo sólido	Estereorradián	sr

PREFIJOS SI

Factor de multiplicacion	Prefijo	Símbolo
$1\ 000\ 000\ 000\ 000\ 000\ 000 = 10^{18}$	exa	E
$1\ 000\ 000\ 000\ 000\ 000 = 10^{15}$	peta	P
$1\ 000\ 000\ 000\ 000 = 10^{12}$	tera	T
$1\ 000\ 000\ 000 = 10^{9}$	giga	G
$1\ 000\ 000 = 10^{6}$	mega	M
$1\ 000 = 10^{3}$	kilo	k
$100 = 10^{2}$	hecto	h
$10 = 10^{1}$	deka	da
$0.1 = 10^{-1}$	deci	d
$0.01 = 10^{-2}$	centi	c
$0.001 = 10^{-3}$	milli	m
$0.000\ 001 = 10^{-6}$	micro	$\propto$
$0.000\ 000\ 001 = 10^{-9}$	nano	n
$0.000\ 000\ 000\ 001 = 10^{-12}$	pico	p
$0.000\ 000\ 000\ 000\ 001 = 10^{-15}$	femto	f
$0.000\ 000\ 000\ 000\ 000\ 001 = 10^{-18}$	atto	a

UNIDAD SI DERIVADA CON NOMBRES ESPECIALES			
Cantidad	Unidad	Símbolo	Fórmula
Frecuencia (de un fenómena periódico)	hertz	Hz	$1/s$
Fuerza	newton	N	$kg \cdot m/s^2$
Presión, esfuerzo	pascal	Pa	N/m^2
Energía, trabajo, cantidad de calor	joule	J	$N \cdot m$
Potencia eléctrica, flujo radiante	vatio	W	J/s
Cantidad de electricidad, carga eléctrica	culombio	C	$A \cdot s$
Potencia eléctrica, diferencia de potencial, feuerza eléctromotriz	voltio	V	W/A
Capacidad eléctrica	faradio	F	C/V
Resistencia eléctrica	ohm	Ω	V/A
Conductancia	siemens	S	A/V
Flujo magnético	weber	Wb	$V \cdot s$
Densidad del flujo magnético	tesla	T	Wb/m^2
Inductancia	henrio	H	Wb/A
Flujo luminoso	Lumen	lm	$cd \cdot sr$
Iluminancia	lux	lx	lm/m^2
Actividad (de radionúclidos)	becquerel	Bq	$1/s$
Dosis absorbida	gray	Gy	J/kg

Tablas

FACTORES DE CONVERSIÓN

Para convertir	a	Multiplicar por
LARGO		
1 milla (normativa de E.U.)	km	1.609 344
1 yarda = 1 yd	m	0.9144
1 pie = 1ft	m	0.3048
	mm	304.8
1 pulgada = 1 in	mm	25.4
ÁREA		
1 milla^2 (normative de E.U.)	km^2	2.589 998
1 acre (agrimensura de E.U.)	ha	0.404 6873
	m^2	4046.873
1 yd^2	m^2	0.836 1274
1 ft^2	m^2	0.092 903 04
1 in^2	mm^2	645.16
VOLUMEN, MÓDULO DE SECCIÓN		
l acre ft	m^3	1233.489
1 yd^3	m^3	0.764 5549
100 tablón ft	m^3	0.235 9737
1 ft^3	m^3	0.028 316 85
	L(dm^3)	28.3168
1 in^3	mm^3	16 387.06
	mL (cm^3)	16.3871
1 barril (42 galones de E.U.)	m^3	0.158 9873
CAPACIDAD (FLUIDO)		
1 galón (líquido E.U.)* 1 gal	L**	3.785 412
1 cuarto (líquido E.U.) = 1qt	mL	946.3529
1 pinta (líquido E.U.) = 1 pt	mL	473.1765
1 onza fluida (E.U.) = 1 fl oz	mL	29.5735
1 gal (líquido E.U.)	m^3	0.003 785 412
*1 galón (Reino Unido) aprox. 1.2 gal (E.U.)	**1 litro aprox. 0.001 cúbico meter	
SEGUNDO MOMENTO DEL ÁREA		
1 in^4	mm^4	416 231 4
	m^4	416 231 4 10^{-7}
ANGULO PLANO		
1° (grado)	rad	0.017 453 29
	mrad	17.453 29
1' (minuto)	urad	290.8882
1" (segundo)	urad	4.848 137

VELOCIDAD		
1 ft/s	m/s	0.3048
1 milla/h	km/h	1.609 344
	m/s	0.447 04
TASA DE VOLUMEN DEL FLUJO		
1 ft^3/s	m^3/s	0.028 316 85
1 ft^3/min	L/s	0.471 9474
1 gal/min	L/s	0.063 0902
1 gal/min	m^3/min	0.0038
1 gal/h	mL/s	1.051 50
1 millón gal/d = 1 million gal/d	L/s	43.8126
1 acre ft/s	m^3/s	1233.49
INTERVALO DE TEMPERATURA		
1° F	°C or K	0.555 556 $^5/_9°C = ^5/_9K$
TEMPERATURA EQUIVALENTE ($t_{oC} = T_K - 273.15$)		
t_{oF}	t_{oc}	$t_{oF} = ^9/_5 t_{oC} + 32$
MASA		
1 tonelada (corta ***) = 1 ton	tonelada métrica	0.907 185
	kg	907.1847
1 libra = 1 lb	kg	0.453 5924
1 onza = 1oz	g	28.349 52
***1 tonelada larga, (2,240 lb)	kg	1016.047
MASA POR UNIDAD DE ÁREA		
1 lb/ft^2	kg/m^2	4.882 428
1 oz/yd^2	g/m^2	33.905 75
1 oz/ft^2	g/m^2	305.1517
DENSIDAD (MASA POR UNIDAD DE VOLUMEN)		
1 lb/ft^3	kg/m^3	16.01846
1 lb/yd^3	kg/m^3	0.593 2764
1 ton/yd^3	t/m^3	1.186 553
FUERZA		
1 tonf (tonelada–fuerza)	kN	8.896 44
1 kip (1,000 lbf)	kN	4.448 22
1 lbf (libra–fuerza)	N	4.448 22
MOMENTO DE FUERZA, TORSION		
1 lbf·ft	N·m	1.355 818
1 lbf·in	N·m	0.112 9848
1 tonf·ft	kN·m	2.711 64
1 kip·ft	kN·m	1.355 82

Tablas

FUERZA POR UNIDAD DE LONGITUD		
1 lbf/ft	N/m	14.5939
1 tonf/ft	kN/m	29.1878
1 lbf/in	N/m	175.1268

PRESIÓN, ESFUERZO, MÓDULO DE ELASTICIDAD (FUERZA POR UNIDAD DE ÁREA) (1 Pa = 1 N/m²)		
1 tonf/in²	MPa	13.7895
1 tonf/ft²	kPa	95.7605
1 kip/in²	MPa	6.894 757
1 lbf/in²	kPa	6.894 757
1 lbf/ft²	Pa	47.8803
Atmósfera	kPa	101.3250
1 pulgada de mercurio	kPa	3.376 85
1 pie (columna de agua a 32°F)	kPa	2.988 98

TRABAJO, ENERGÍA, CALOR (1J = 1N·m = 1W·s)		
1 kWh (550 ft·lbf/s)	MJ	3.6
1 Btu (Int. Table)	kJ	1.055 056
	J	1055.056
1 ft·lbf	J	1.355 818

COEFFICIENT DE TRANSFERENCIA DE CALOR		
1 Btu/(ft²·h·°F)	W/(m²·K)	5.678 263

CONDUCTIVIDAD TERMICA		
1 Btu/(ft·h·°F)	W/(m·K)	1.730 735

ILUMINANCIA		
1 lm/ft² (pie candela)	lx (lux)	10.763 91

LUMINANCIA		
1 cd/ft²	cd/m²	10.7639
1 pie lambert	cd/m²	3.426 259
1 lambert	kcd/m²	3.183 099

General

Herramientas y Equipamiento

Llave Ajustable
Adjustable Wrench

Llave
Wrench

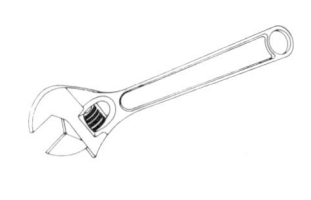

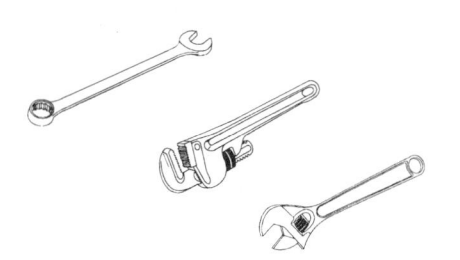

Cadena
Chain

Abrazadera
Clamp

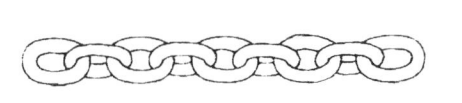

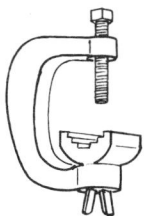

Extinguidor/Extintor de Incendio
Fire Extinguisher

Chicharra
Socket Wrench

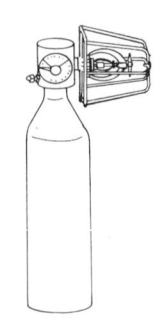

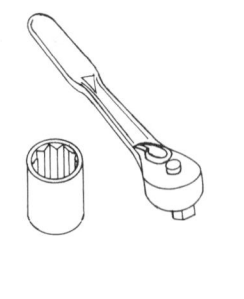

General: Herramientas y Equipamiento

Cinta Métrica
  Tape

Abrazadera
  Bench Vise

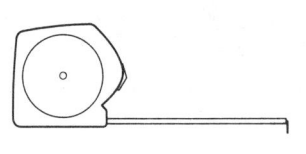

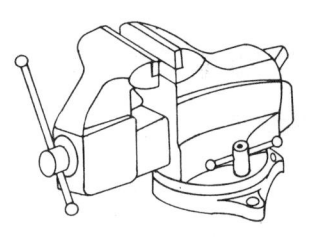

Grúa Hidraúlica
  Crane

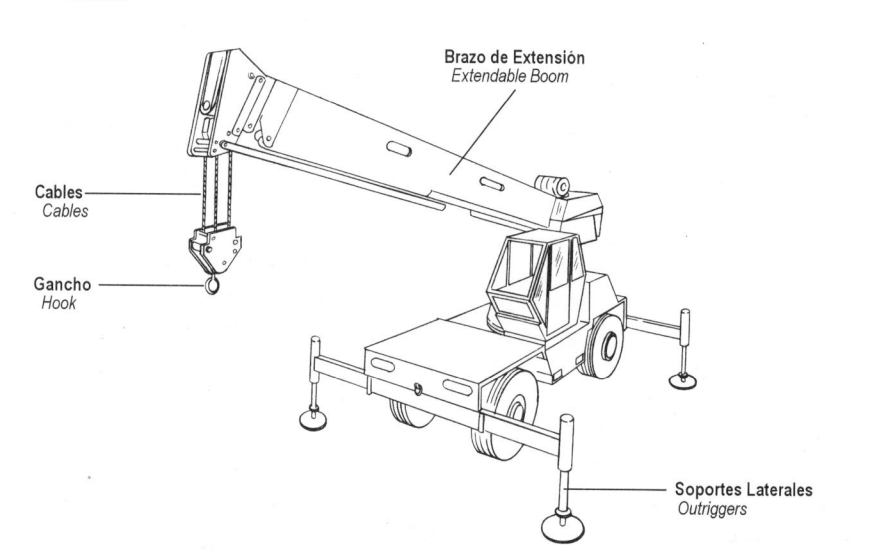

Brazo de Extensión
Extendable Boom

Cables
Cables

Gancho
Hook

Soportes Laterales
Outriggers

Escalera/Escala
  Ladder

Preparación de Terreno

Herramientas y Equipamiento

Retroexcavadora
Backhoe-Crawler Type

Retroexcavadora/Cargador con Ruedas
Backhoe/Loader-Wheel Type

Tractor Oruga
Tractor-Crawler Type

Tractor Cargador con Ruedas
Tractor Loader-Wheel Type

Tractor Cargador con Ruedas, pequeño
Tractor Loader-Wheel Type, small

Camion de Volteo
Dump Truck

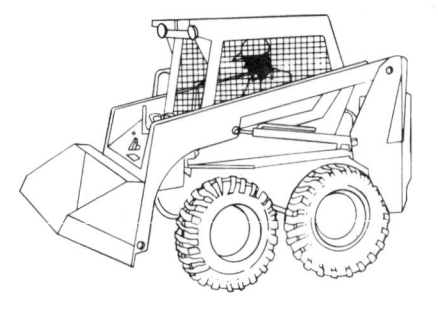

Preparación de Terreno: Herramientas y Equipamiento

Niveladora
Grader

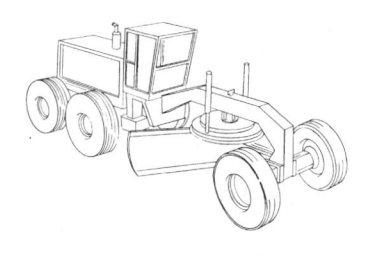

Camion de Excavaciones
Gradall

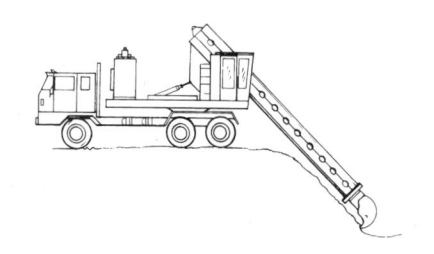

Aplanadora
Roller

Excavadora de Zanjas
Trencher

Compactadora
Compactor Roller

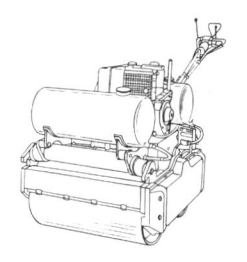

Compactadora Manual
Compactor-Vibrator Plate

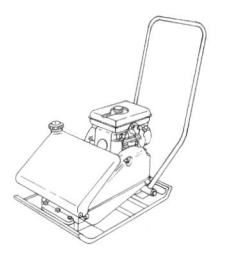

Preparación de Terreno: Sistemas y Piezas

Apuntalamiento de Zanja
Trench Shoring

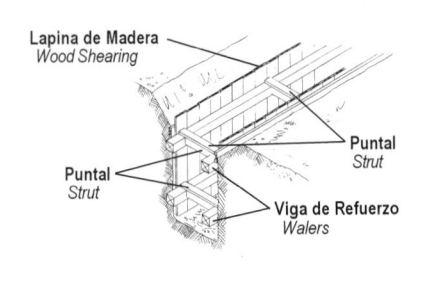

Lapina de Madera
Wood Shearing

Puntal
Strut

Puntal
Strut

Viga de Refuerzo
Walers

Sistema Séptico
Septic Systems

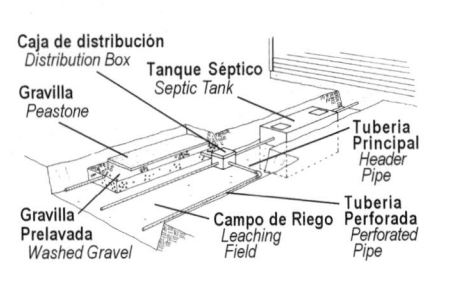

Caja de distribución
Distribution Box

Gravilla
Peastone

Tanque Séptico
Septic Tank

Tuberia Principal
Header Pipe

Gravilla Prelavada
Washed Gravel

Campo de Riego
Leaching Field

Tuberia Perforada
Perforated Pipe

Pavimento
Paving

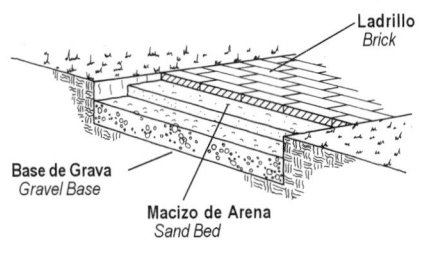

Ladrillo
Brick

Base de Grava
Gravel Base

Macizo de Arena
Sand Bed

Cerca de Malla Metálica, Industrial
Chain Link Fence, Industrial

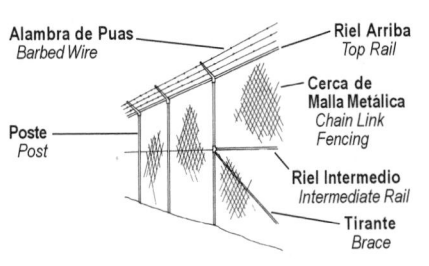

Alambra de Puas
Barbed Wire

Poste
Post

Riel Arriba
Top Rail

Cerca de Malla Metálica
Chain Link Fencing

Riel Intermedio
Intermediate Rail

Tirante
Brace

Sistema de Hidrante
Fire Hydrant System

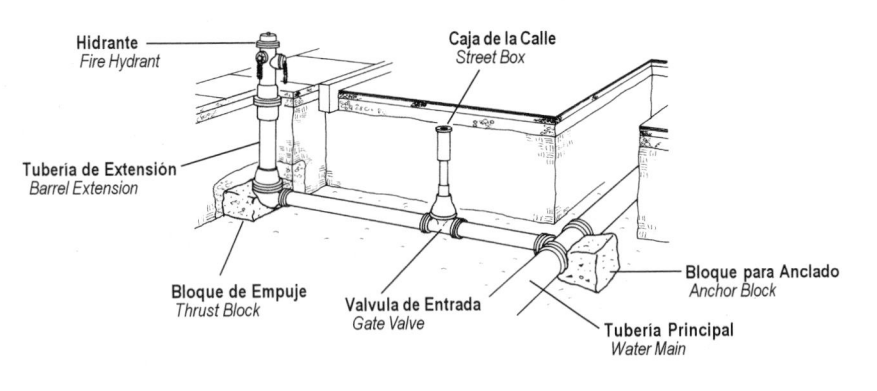

Hidrante
Fire Hydrant

Caja de la Calle
Street Box

Tuberia de Extensión
Barrel Extension

Bloque de Empuje
Thrust Block

Valvula de Entrada
Gate Valve

Bloque para Anclado
Anchor Block

Tuberia Principal
Water Main

Hormigón

Herramientas y Equipamiento

Cuchara Toro
Bull Float

Cuchara Metalica
Magnesium Float

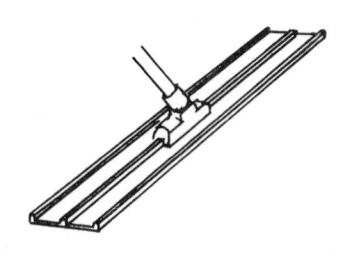

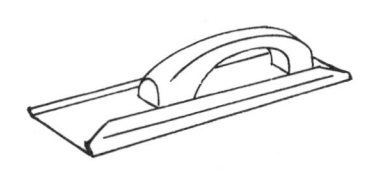

Cuchara de Goma
Rubber Float

Martillo para Texturizado
Bush Hammer

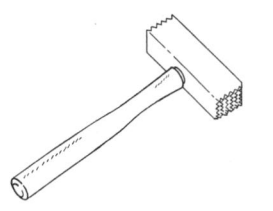

Cepillo de Acabado
Finishing Broom

Palustre Eléctrico
Power Trowel

Hormigón: Herramientas y Equipamiento

Vibrador
Vibrator

Sierra para Hormigón/Concreto
Concrete Saw

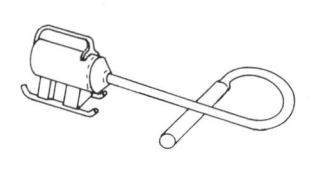

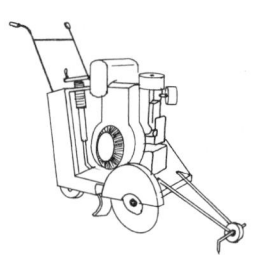

Bomba para Hormigón/ Concreto
Concrete Pump

Paleta de Acero
Steel Trowel

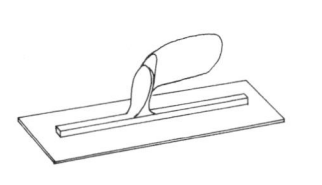

Hormigón: Sistemas y Piezas

Apuntalador Ajustable Horizontal/
Puntal Horizontal Ajustable
Adjustable Horizontal Shore

Puntal Compuesto de Acero y Madera
Composite Metal and Wood Shore

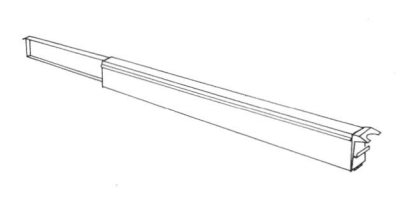

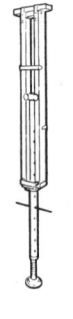

Hormigón: Sistemas y Piezas

Losa de Concreto
Concrete Flat-Plate

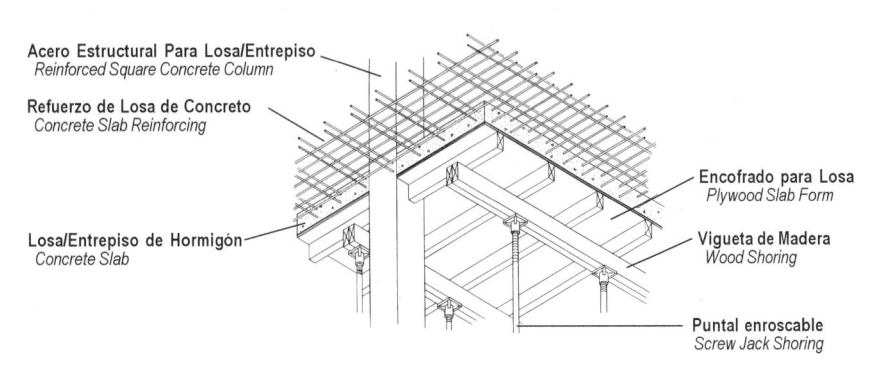

Acero Estructural Para Losa/Entrepiso
Reinforced Square Concrete Column

Refuerzo de Losa de Concreto
Concrete Slab Reinforcing

Losa/Entrepiso de Hormigón
Concrete Slab

Encofrado para Losa
Plywood Slab Form

Vigueta de Madera
Wood Shoring

Puntal enroscable
Screw Jack Shoring

Zapata/Fundación Directa
Spread Footings

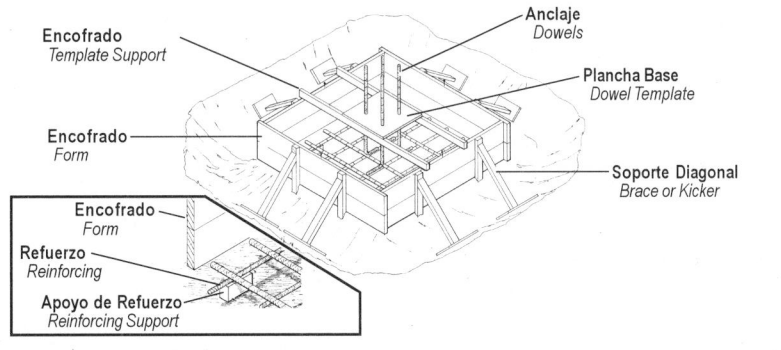

Anclaje
Dowels

Encofrado
Template Support

Plancha Base
Dowel Template

Encofrado
Form

Soporte Diagonal
Brace or Kicker

Encofrado
Form

Refuerzo
Reinforcing

Apoyo de Refuerzo
Reinforcing Support

Apuntalador de Acero/Puntal de Acero
Steel Shore

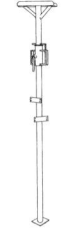

Estructura de Andamios
Structural Scaffolding

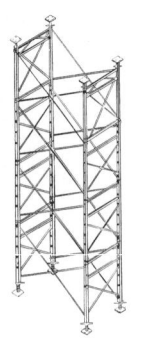

137

Mamposteria

Herramientas y Equipamiento

Mezcladora para Hormigón/Concreto
  Mixer

Llana de Albañil y Cepillo Automático
  Mason's Trowel and Jointer

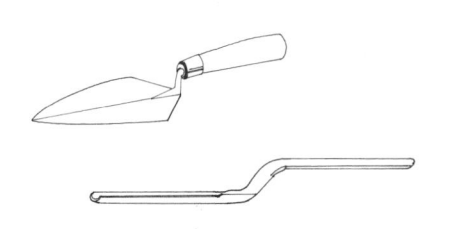

Sistemas y Piezas

Pared de Bloques de
Hormigón/Concreto
  Concrete Block Wall

Chimenea de Ladrillo
  Brick Chimney

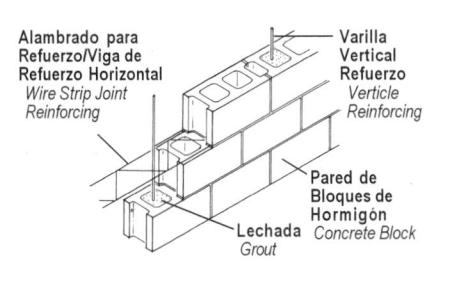

- Alambrado para Refuerzo/Viga de Refuerzo Horizontal
  Wire Strip Joint Reinforcing
- Varilla Vertical Refuerzo
  Verticle Reinforcing
- Pared de Bloques de Hormigón
  Concrete Block
- Lechada
  Grout

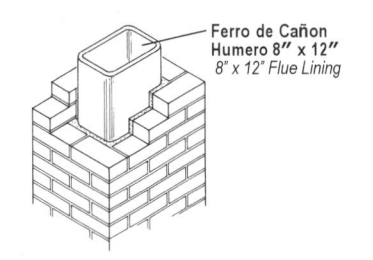

- Ferro de Cañon Humero 8" x 12"
  8" x 12" Flue Lining

Muro con Recubrimiento
de Bloque de Ladrillo
  Brick Veneer Wall System

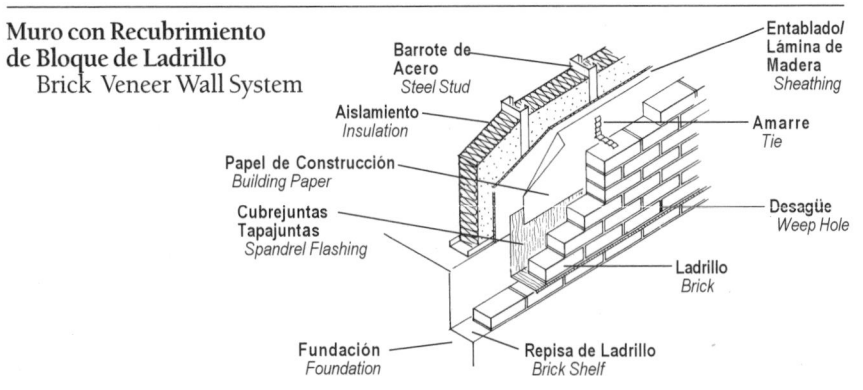

- Barrote de Acero
  Steel Stud
- Aislamiento
  Insulation
- Papel de Construcción
  Building Paper
- Cubrejuntas Tapajuntas
  Spandrel Flashing
- Fundación
  Foundation
- Repisa de Ladrillo
  Brick Shelf
- Entablado/ Lámina de Madera
  Sheathing
- Amarre
  Tie
- Desagüe
  Weep Hole
- Ladrillo
  Brick

Acero Estructural

Sistemas y Piezas

Cubierta Metálica Sobre Vigas
Steel Roof Deck on Joists

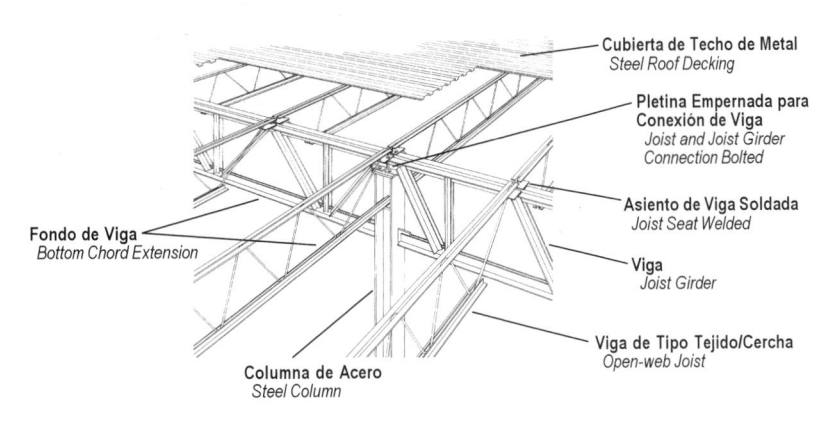

Cubierta de Techo de Metal
Steel Roof Decking

Pletina Empernada para Conexión de Viga
Joist and Joist Girder Connection Bolted

Asiento de Viga Soldada
Joist Seat Welded

Viga
Joist Girder

Viga de Tipo Tejido/Cercha
Open-web Joist

Fondo de Viga
Bottom Chord Extension

Columna de Acero
Steel Column

Cubierta y Vigas en Muralles de Soporte
Deck and Joists on Bearing Walls

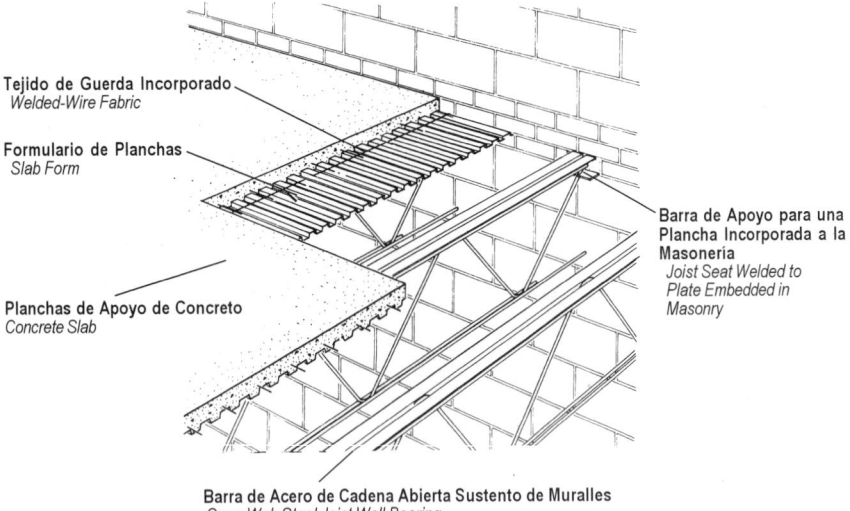

Tejido de Guerda Incorporado
Welded-Wire Fabric

Formulario de Planchas
Slab Form

Barra de Apoyo para una Plancha Incorporada a la Masoneria
Joist Seat Welded to Plate Embedded in Masonry

Planchas de Apoyo de Concreto
Concrete Slab

Barra de Acero de Cadena Abierta Sustento de Muralles
Open Web Steel Joist Wall Bearing

Carpintería

Herramientas y Equipamiento

Extensión Electrica
 Electrical Cord

Mangas de Aire
 Air Hose

Compresor de Aire
 Air Compressor

Tira Líneas de Cal
 Chalk Line

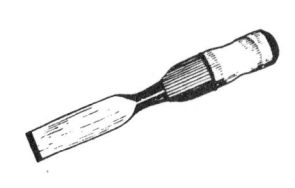

Cincel
 Chisel

Pata de Cabra
 Crow Bar

Carpintería: Herramientas y Equipamiento

Taladro
Drill

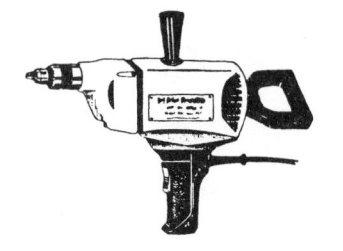

Palanca, Plana
Flat Bar

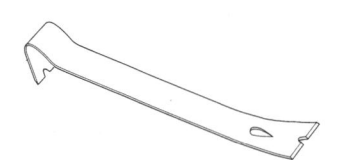

Martillo
Hammer

Pistola para Clavos/Clavadora Automático
Nail Gun

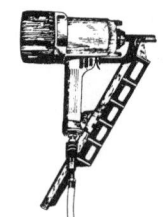

Saca Clavos
Nail Puller

Escuadra
Speed Square

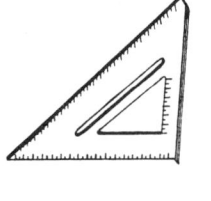

Carpintería: Herramientas y Equipamiento

Cinta para Medir/Cinta Métrica
  Tape Measure

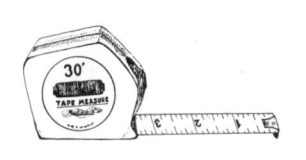

Cinturón para Herramientas
  Tool Pouch

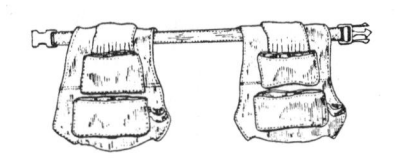

Cuchilla/Navaja
  Utility Knife

Roto Sierra/Sierra Eléctrica
  Chain Saw

Serrucho
  Hand Saw

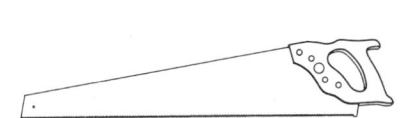

Sierra Reciprocadora
  Reciprocating Saw

Carpintería: Herramientas y Equipamiento

Sierra Circular de Mano
Worm-drive Saw

Fresadora/Ranuradora
Router

Lijadora
Sander

Caladora Eléctrica
Saber Saw

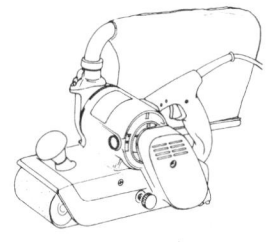

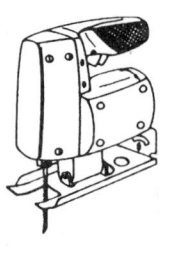

Carpintería: Sistemas y Piezas

Nomenclatura Para Estructuras de Madera
Wood Framing Nomenclature

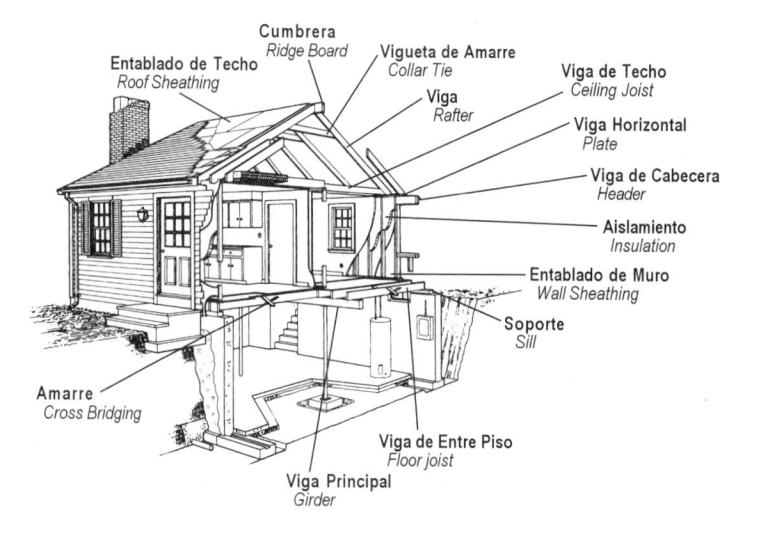

Cumbrera
Ridge Board

Entablado de Techo
Roof Sheathing

Vigueta de Amarre
Collar Tie

Viga de Techo
Ceiling Joist

Viga
Rafter

Viga Horizontal
Plate

Viga de Cabecera
Header

Aislamiento
Insulation

Entablado de Muro
Wall Sheathing

Soporte
Sill

Amarre
Cross Bridging

Viga de Entre Piso
Floor joist

Viga Principal
Girder

Carpintería: Sistemas y Piezas

Cubierta de Madera
Wood Deck

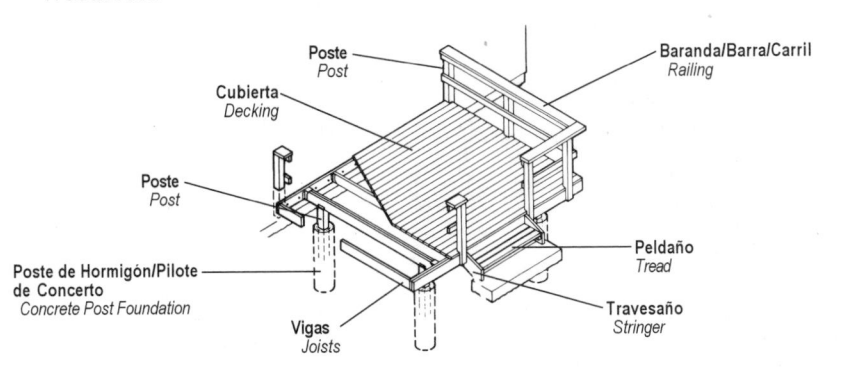

Poste
Post

Cubierta
Decking

Poste
Post

Poste de Hormigón/Pilote de Concerto
Concrete Post Foundation

Vigas
Joists

Baranda/Barra/Carril
Railing

Peldaño
Tread

Travesaño
Stringer

Gabinetes de Cocina
Kitchen Cabinets

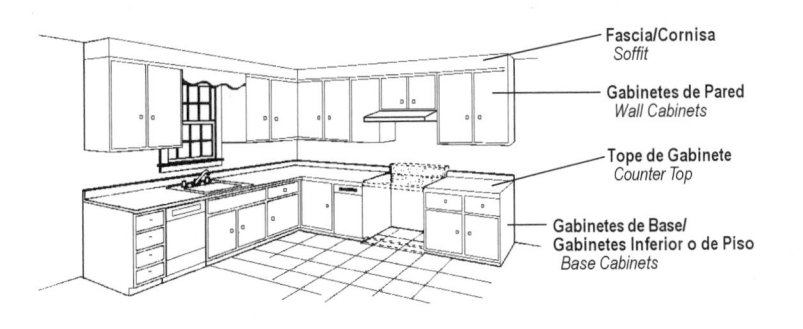

Fascia/Cornisa
Soffit

Gabinetes de Pared
Wall Cabinets

Tope de Gabinete
Counter Top

Gabinetes de Base/
Gabinetes Inferior o de Piso
Base Cabinets

Escalera
Stairs

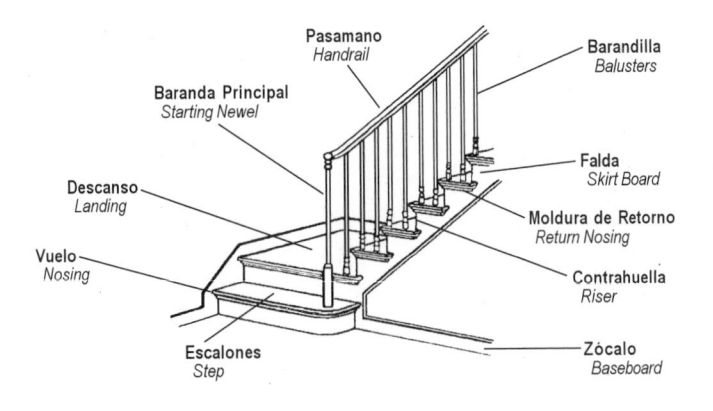

Pasamano
Handrail

Baranda Principal
Starting Newel

Descanso
Landing

Vuelo
Nosing

Escalones
Step

Barandilla
Balusters

Falda
Skirt Board

Moldura de Retorno
Return Nosing

Contrahuella
Riser

Zócalo
Baseboard

Carpintería: Sistemas y Piezas

Estructura de la Pared
Wall Framing

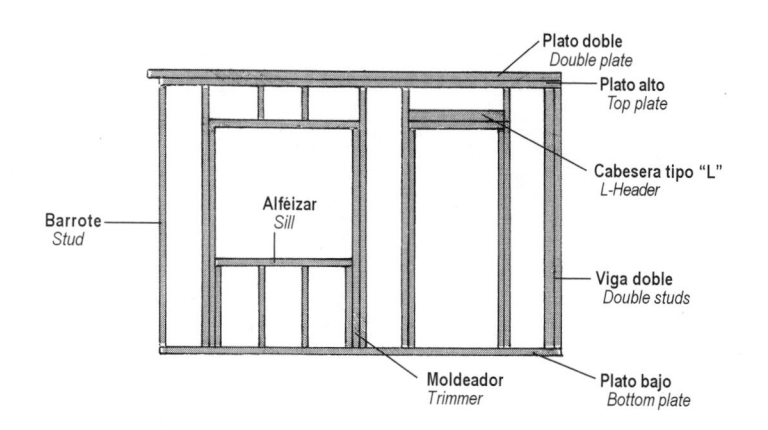

Plato doble
Double plate

Plato alto
Top plate

Cabesera tipo "L"
L-Header

Alféizar
Sill

Barrote
Stud

Viga doble
Double studs

Moldeador
Trimmer

Plato bajo
Bottom plate

Ventana de Celosía de Aluminio
Jalousie Window

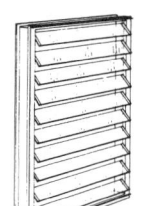

Ventana Batiente
Casement Window

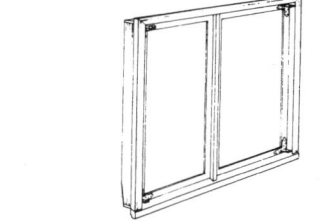

Ventana Colgante Doble de Madera
Double Hung Window

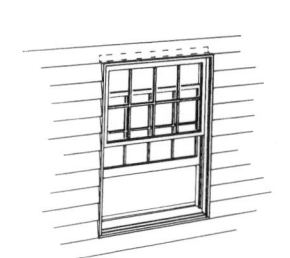

Claraboya/Tragaluz
Skylight

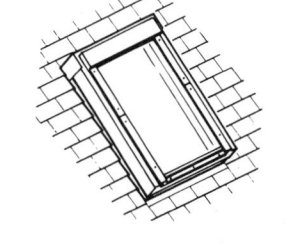

Carpintería: Sistemas y Piezas

Ventana Corrediza de Madera
Sliding Window

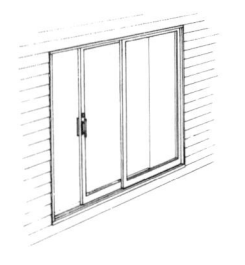

Puerta
Door

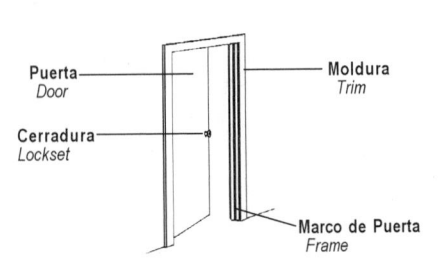

Puerta — Door

Cerradura — Lockset

Moldura — Trim

Marco de Puerta — Frame

Puerta Corredizas, Deslizante de Dobla Hoja
Sliding Door

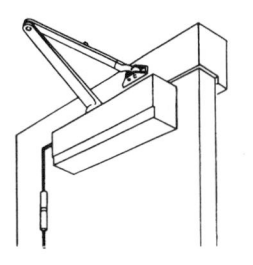

Brazo de Puerta
Door Closer

Cerraduras
Locksets

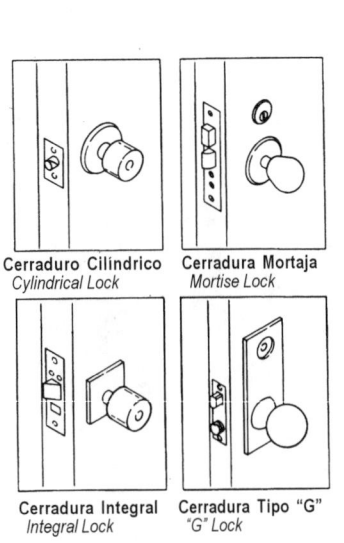

Cerraduro Cilindrico
Cylindrical Lock

Cerradura Mortaja
Mortise Lock

Cerradura Integral
Integral Lock

Cerradura Tipo "G"
"G" Lock

Carpintería: Sistemas y Piezas

Acero de Bajo Calibre
Light Gauge Steel

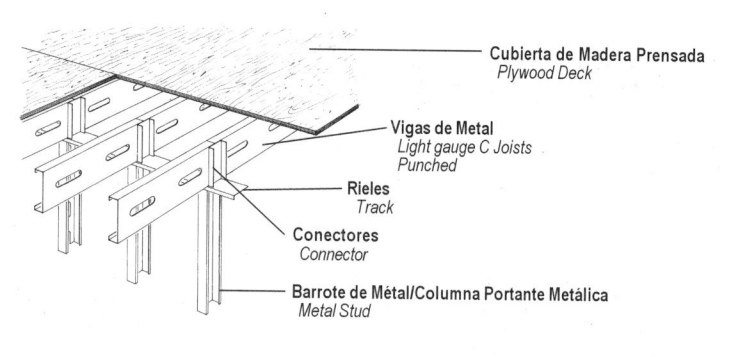

Cubierta de Madera Prensada
Plywood Deck

Vigas de Metal
Light gauge C Joists
Punched

Rieles
Track

Conectores
Connector

Barrote de Metal/Columna Portante Metálica
Metal Stud

Covertura de Vinil
Vinyl Siding

Estructura de Metal
Metal Framing

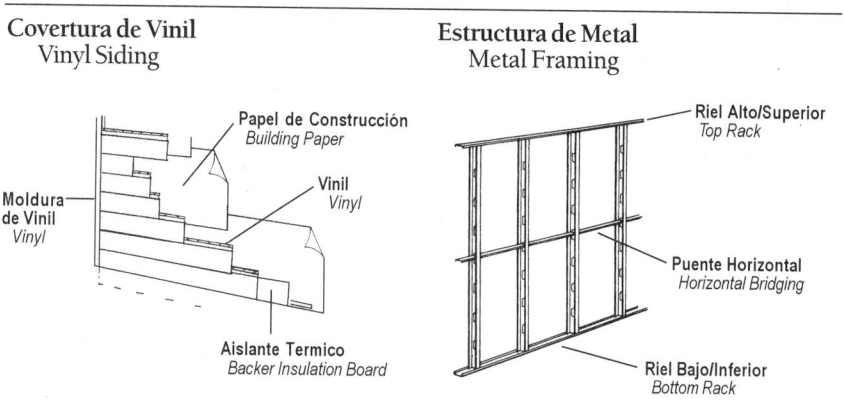

Papel de Construcción
Building Paper

Vinil
Vinyl

Moldura
de Vinil
Vinyl

Aislante Termico
Backer Insulation Board

Riel Alto/Superior
Top Rack

Puente Horizontal
Horizontal Bridging

Riel Bajo/Inferior
Bottom Rack

Viga de Madera Compuesta
Composite Wood Joists

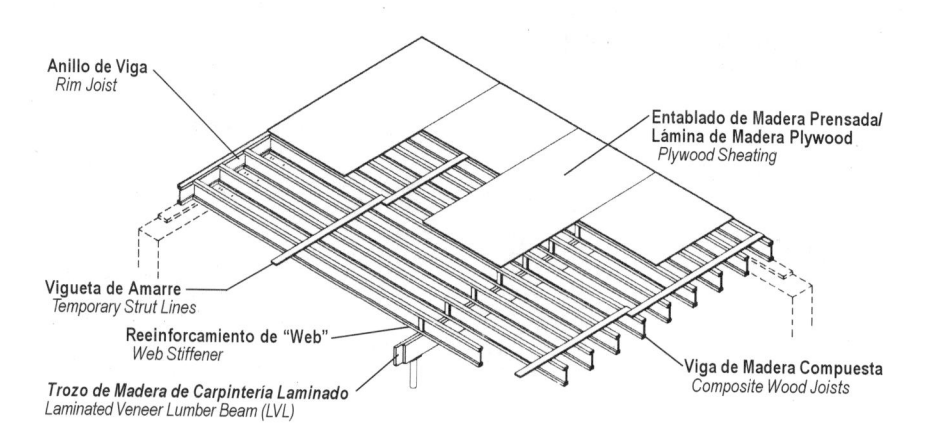

Anillo de Viga
Rim Joist

Entablado de Madera Prensada/
Lámina de Madera Plywood
Plywood Sheating

Vigueta de Amarre
Temporary Strut Lines

Reeinforcamiento de "Web"
Web Stiffener

Trozo de Madera de Carpinteria Laminado
Laminated Veneer Lumber Beam (LVL)

Viga de Madera Compuesta
Composite Wood Joists

Techumbre

Sistemas y Piezas

Teja de Arcilla
Clay Tile

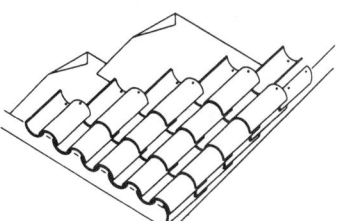

Tejas de Asfalto
Asphalt Shingles

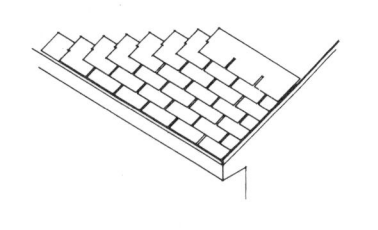

Tejas de Madera
Wood Shingles

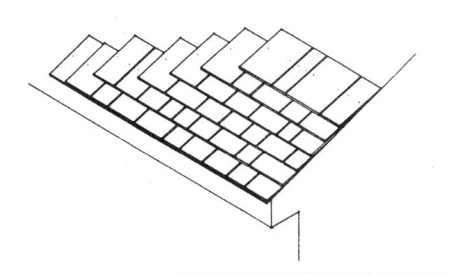

Lámina Separada de Techumbre
Single Ply Roofing

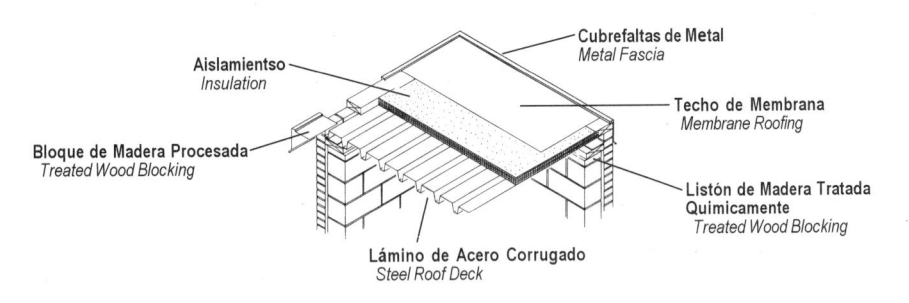

Cubrefaltas de Metal
Metal Fascia

Aislamientso
Insulation

Techo de Membrana
Membrane Roofing

Bloque de Madera Procesada
Treated Wood Blocking

Listón de Madera Tratada
Quimicamente
Treated Wood Blocking

Lámino de Acero Corrugado
Steel Roof Deck

Techumbre: Sistemas y Piezas

Sistema de Techo
Roofing System

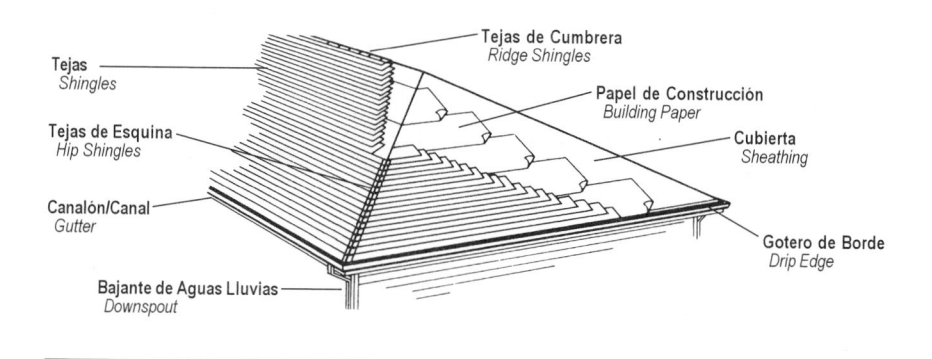

Tejas de Cumbrera
Ridge Shingles

Tejas
Shingles

Papel de Construcción
Building Paper

Tejas de Esquina
Hip Shingles

Cubierta
Sheathing

Canalón/Canal
Gutter

Gotero de Borde
Drip Edge

Bajante de Aguas Lluvias
Downspout

Molduras Exterior
Exterior Trim

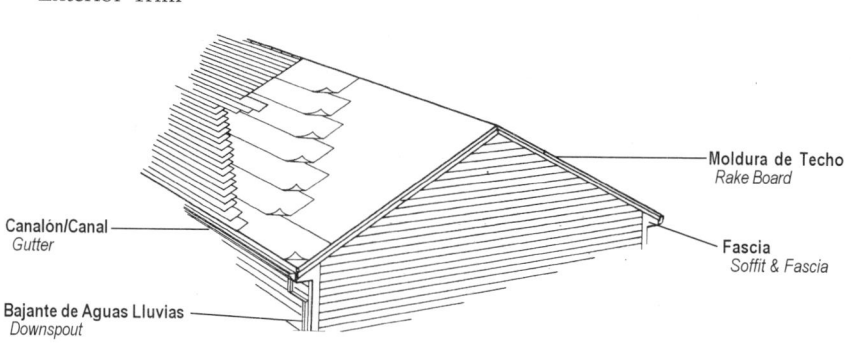

Moldura de Techo
Rake Board

Canalón/Canal
Gutter

Fascia
Soffit & Fascia

Bajante de Aguas Lluvias
Downspout

Acabados

Herramientas y Equipamiento

Andamio Con Ruedas
  Rolling Scaffold

Herramienta de Esquina
  Corner Tool

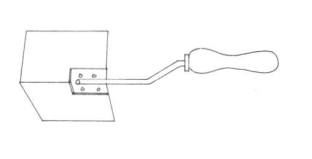

Espátula
  Finishing Knife

Brocha
  Paint Brush

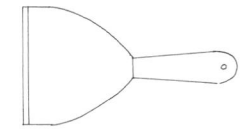

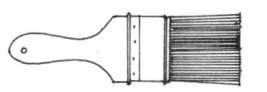

Llana de Tabla de Yeso
  Drywall Trowel

Rodilla de Pintar
  Roller Frame

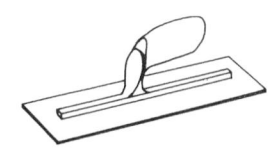

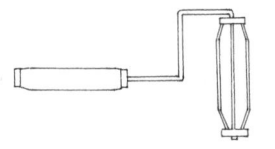

Acabados: Sistemas y Piezas

Panel de Yeso/Tablero de Yeso
Gypsum Plasterboard

Sistema de Cieloraso/Cielo Falsa de Suspensión Visible
Suspended Ceiling System

Barrotes de Madera
Wood Studs

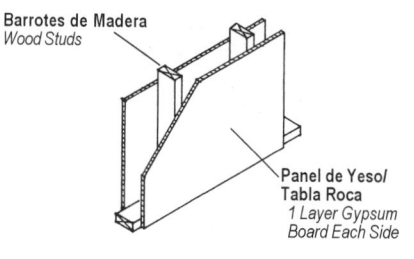

Panel de Yeso/Tabla Roca
1 Layer Gypsum Board Each Side

Sistema de Suspensión
Suspension System

Canales de Carga
Carrier Channels

Colgantes
Hangers

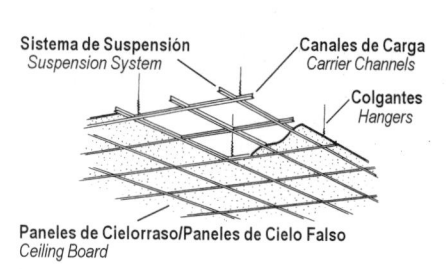

Paneles de Cielorraso/Paneles de Cielo Falso
Ceiling Board

Instalaciones Mecánicas

Herramientas y Equipamiento

Llave
  Box Wrench

Soporte para Tuberías
  Pipe Hanger

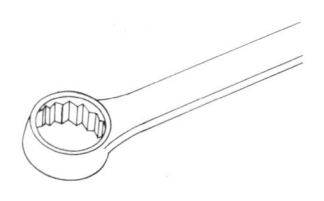

Llave Tirso/Llave Stilson
  Pipe Wrench

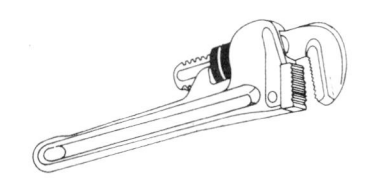

Sistemas y Piezas

Bañera/Tina
  Bathtub

Lavamanos/Lavabo
  Sink

Instalaciones Mecánicas: Sistemas y Piezas

Pocera/Inodoro/Sanitario
Toilet

Drenaje de Piso
Heelproof Floor Drain

Drenaje de Ducha
Shower Drain

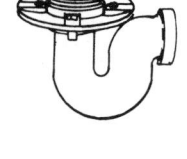

T para Tuberia de Acabado Simple
Tee-Plain End Pipe

Codo de Hierro de 45°
45° Elbow-malleable Iron

Válvula
Valve

Soporte de Viga Lateral
Side Beam Bracket

Soporte de Acero Mediano-Soldado
Medium Welded Steel Bracket

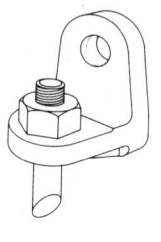

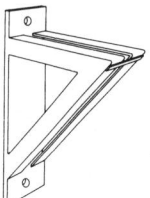

Abrazadera Tipo "C"
C-Clamp

Abrazadera para Vigas Tipo "I"
I-Beam Clamp

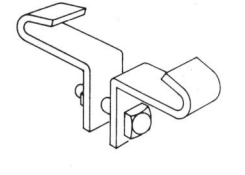

Extensión para Tuberias
Extension Pipe or Riser Clamp

Abrazadera de Anillo Separado
Split Ring Pipe Clamp

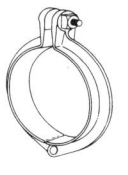

Instalaciones Mecánicas: Sistemas y Piezas

Abrazadera para Tubería de Metal
Alloy Steel Pipe Clamp

Abrazadera para Tubería Mediana
Medium Pipe Clamp

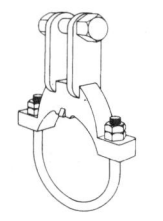

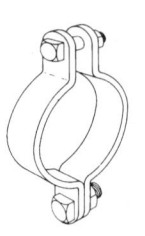

Suporte de Tuberias
Pipe Supports

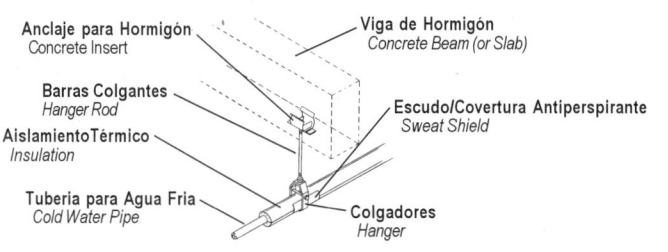

Anclaje para Hormigón
Concrete Insert

Viga de Hormigón
Concrete Beam (or Slab)

Barras Colgantes
Hanger Rod

AislamientoTérmico
Insulation

Escudo/Covertura Antiperspirante
Sweat Shield

Tuberia para Agua Fria
Cold Water Pipe

Colgadores
Hanger

Sistema de Calefacción
Heating System

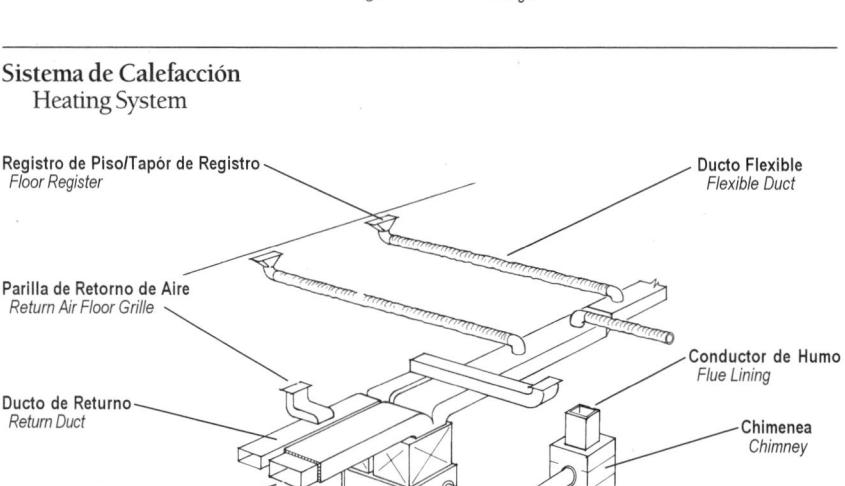

Registro de Piso/Tapór de Registro
Floor Register

Ducto Flexible
Flexible Duct

Parilla de Retorno de Aire
Return Air Floor Grille

Conductor de Humo
Flue Lining

Ducto de Returno
Return Duct

Chimenea
Chimney

Conducto Suplidor Insulado
Insulated Supply Duct

Regulador de Corriente de Aire
Draft Adjuster

Caldera de Aceite
Oil Fired Furnace

Tuberia para Humo
Smoke Pipe

Instalaciones Mecánicas: Sistemas y Piezas

Sistema de Conducto
Ductwork

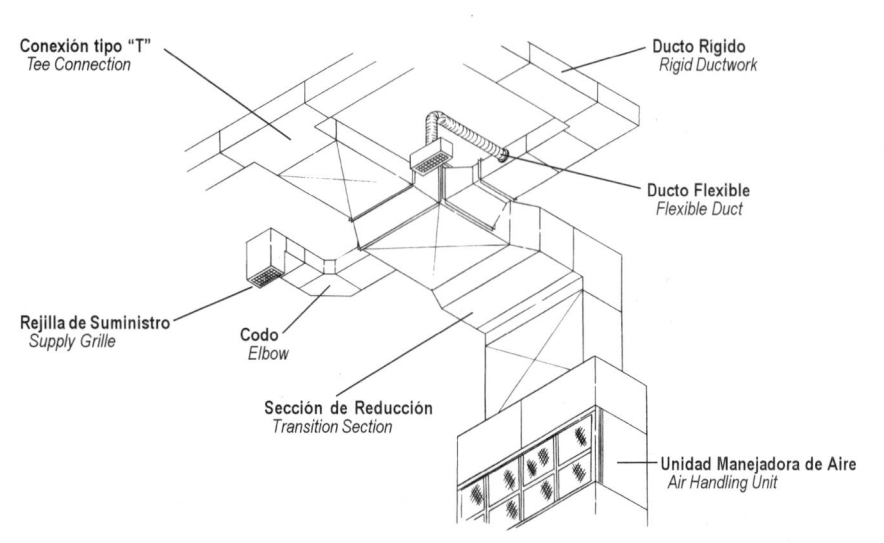

Conexión tipo "T"
Tee Connection

Ducto Rigido
Rigid Ductwork

Ducto Flexible
Flexible Duct

Rejilla de Suministro
Supply Grille

Codo
Elbow

Sección de Reducción
Transition Section

Unidad Manejadora de Aire
Air Handling Unit

Electricidad

Herramientas y Equipamiento

Dobla Tubos Manual
(para Tubo Metálico)
  Hand Bender

Dobla Tubos Para PVC
  "Hot Box" PVC Bender

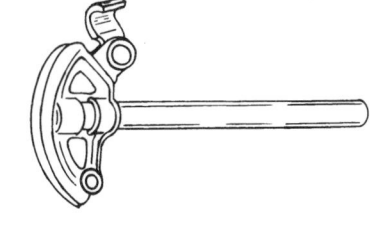

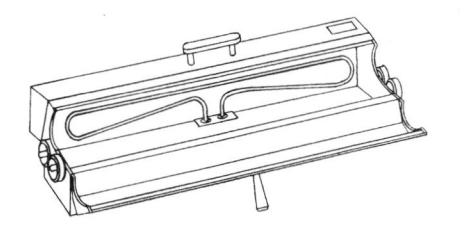

Herramienta de Compresión Manual
  Compression Hand Tool

Destornillador
  Screwdriver

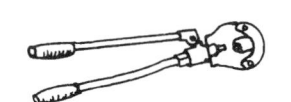

Electricidad: Sistemas y Piezas

Servicio Electrico
Electrical Service

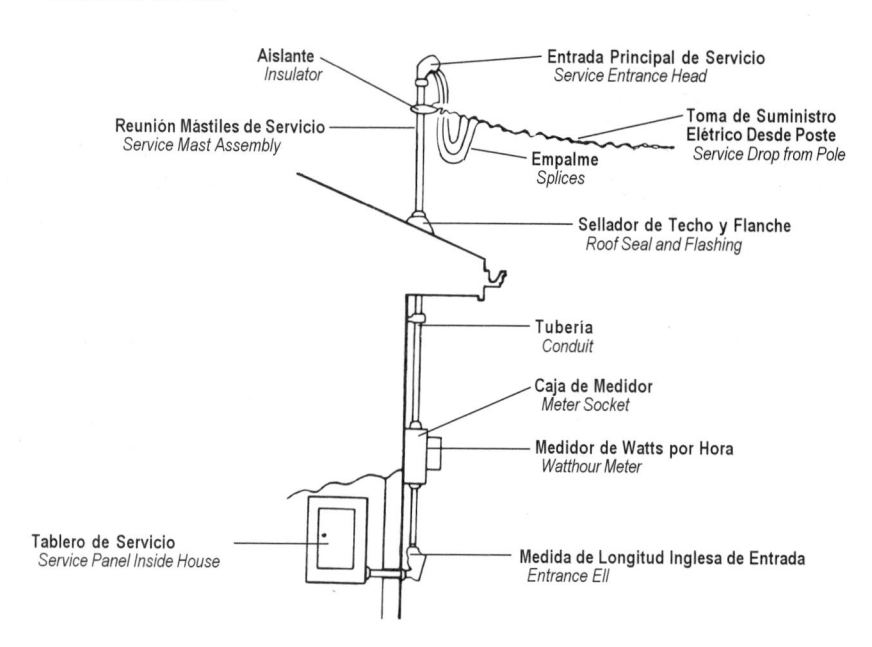

Aislante
Insulator

Reunión Màstiles de Servicio
Service Mast Assembly

Entrada Principal de Servicio
Service Entrance Head

Toma de Suministro
Elétrico Desde Poste
Service Drop from Pole

Empalme
Splices

Sellador de Techo y Flanche
Roof Seal and Flashing

Tuberia
Conduit

Caja de Medidor
Meter Socket

Medidor de Watts por Hora
Watthour Meter

Tablero de Servicio
Service Panel Inside House

Medida de Longitud Inglesa de Entrada
Entrance Ell

Interruptor/Switch
Electrical Switch

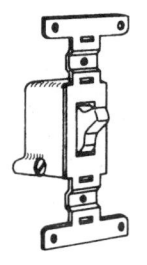

Tama Corriente Doble
Duplex Receptacle

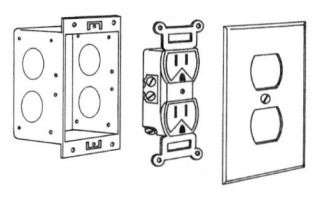

Electricidad: Sistemas y Piezas

Conector Adaptable de PVC
PVC Jacket Connector

Conector de Aluminio Aislado Tipo SER
SER, Insulated, Aluminum

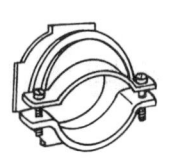

Reforzado Para 600 Voltios
600 Volt, Armored

Conector de Cable Reforzado Para 5 KV
5 KV Armored

Soporte de Cable
Cable Support

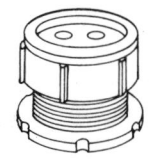

Topa/Caja de Acometida
Service Entrance Cap

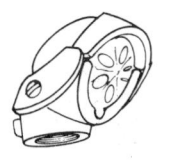

Electricidad: Sistemas y Piezas

Conector Con Tornillos para Tuberia EMT
EMT Set Screw Connector

Conector para Tuberia EMT
EMT Connector

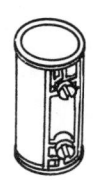

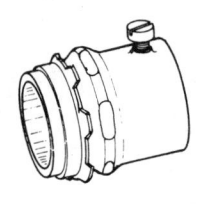

Conector para Tuberia EMT y Tuberia Conduit
EMT to Conduit Adapter

Adaptador de Tuberia EMT a Tuberia Greenfield
EMT to Greenfield Adapter

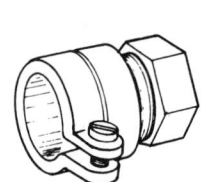

Tuberia de Aluminio "Conduit"
Aluminum Conduit

Codo de Aluminio
Aluminum Elbow